QuickBASIC
Advanced Techniques

Peter G. Aitken

PROGRAMMING
S E R I E S

CORPORATION
LEADING COMPUTER KNOWLEDGE

QuickBASIC®
Advanced Techniques

© 1989 by Que® Corporation

Library of Congress Catalog No.: 89-50352

ISBN 0-88022-431-2

93 92 91 90 89   8 7 6 5 4 3 2 1

Interpretation of the printing code: the rightmost double-digit number is the year of the book's printing; the rightmost single-digit number, the number of the book's printing. For example, a printing code of 89-1 shows that the first printing of the book occurred in 1989.

QuickBASIC Advanced Techniques is based on Version 4.5 of QuickBASIC.

DEDICATION

To my children,
Benjamin and Clair

Publishing Manager

Allen L. Wyatt, Sr.

Product Development Specialist

Bill Nolan

Project Coordinator

Gregory Croy

Editing

Brown Editorial Service

Editorial Assistant

Ann K. Taylor

Technical Editor

Gordon N. Arbuthnot

Indexer

Sherry Massey

Illustrations

Susan Moore

Cover Design

Dan Armstrong

Production

April Anderson
Jennifer Matthews
Diana Moore
Jon Ogle
Joe Ramon
Dennis Sheehan
Peter Tocco

Composed in Garamond and OCRB
by Que Corporation and Precision Printing

ABOUT THE AUTHOR ▼

Peter G. Aitken

Peter G. Aitken is an assistant professor at Duke University Medical Center in Durham, North Carolina. A widely published author, he has beta-tested numerous commercial software packages and has served as a microcomputer consultant to government and industry. Mr. Aitken has written and marketed DigScope, a scientific software package.

CONTENT OVERVIEW

TABLE OF CONTENTS ▼

3   Debugging Techniques 83

II Programming Topics

▼ *ACKNOWLEDGMENTS*

I would like to acknowledge the assistance of all the people at Que who helped this book on its path from concept to completion, especially Allen Wyatt, Greg Croy, Bill Nolan, Gordon Arbuthnot, and Lynn Brown.

TRADEMARK ACKNOWLEDGMENTS

Que Corporation has made every reasonable effort to supply trademark information about company names, products, and services mentioned in this book. Trademarks indicated below were derived from various sources. Que Corporation cannot attest to the accuracy of this information.

Codeview is a trademark and Microsoft, Microsoft QuickBASIC, and MS-DOS are registered trademarks of Microsoft Corporation.

Hercules Graphics Card is a trademark of Hercules Computer Technology.

IBM is a registered trademark of International Business Machines Corporation.

Lotus is a registered trademark of Lotus Development Corporation.

Macintosh is a registered trademark of Apple Computer, Inc.

Turbo Assembler, Turbo C, and Turbo Debugger are registered trademarks of Borland International, Inc.

Introduction

The programming language known as BASIC (Beginners' All-purpose Symbolic Instruction Code) does not have a particularly good reputation among many experienced programmers. And, as it was originally implemented on IBM Personal Computers, BASIC deserved every bit of its bad reputation. It was an interpreted language, which caused programs to execute slowly. Each line of source code required a line number, and it was impossible to use explanatory labels to identify sections of code. Editing facilities were prehistoric. There was, at best, only rudimentary support for structured and modular programming—two important concepts that I deal with later in the book. These and other shortcomings made BASIC unsuitable for all but the simplest programming tasks. Programmers trying to write, debug, and maintain large, complex programs using BASIC either gave up in frustration or tore out a lot of hair on their way to a finished product.

Well, things have changed—a lot! Over the past few years, several software publishers have brought out versions of BASIC that solve the problems inherent in the early releases. Led by Microsoft QuickBASIC (QB), these products have evolved to the point where BASIC is a full-featured, powerful language suitable for the most demanding programming tasks. Among QB's advanced features are the following:

❏ Programmer-defined variable structures

❏ Support for structured programming with functions and subprograms

1

❏ A sophisticated, "smart" editor that simplifies many aspects of programming

❏ An on-line help system that provides context-sensitive information not only about QB itself but also about the variables and procedures in your program

❏ Facilities for modular programming

❏ Mixed-language support, allowing the QB programs to use procedures written in C, assembler, and other languages

❏ An integrated debugger plus support for stand-alone debugging programs

If you have bought this book, you most likely already own QB and are using it to write programs. Perhaps you are a relative newcomer, just getting your feet wet in the sea of programming. Or you may be a professional consultant, using QB to create complex applications for your customers. Of course, individual programs perform widely different tasks; the PC is used in fields as diverse as investment analysis, oil exploration, medical diagnostics, and baseball scouting. Yet, there is a core of fundamental tasks that most programs share, such as keyboard input, screen management, and data manipulation. In this book I show you how QB programs can maximize control over many of these important functions, including the following:

❏ Use of a mouse

❏ Pull-down menus

❏ Pop-up screen windows

❏ Automatic video hardware detection

❏ Access to operating system functions

❏ Data sorting and searching

This is not intended for use by novices. You should have at least some familiarity with the elements of BASIC as implemented in QB version 4.0 or 4.5: program structure, statement syntax, variables and arrays, expressions, operators, and functions. You should also know how to use the QB environment to load, edit, compile, and run programs. I will be covering some of the advanced features of BASIC and the QB environment, but you should refer to the QB documentation or an introductory QB book if you need to brush up on the basics (pun intended).

The goal of this book is twofold. I want to provide "how-to" information on some of the advanced programming tasks that can be accomplished with QB. On the other hand, I want to provide useful subroutines that can be incorporated directly into your programs.

These two goals conflict in at least one way. Some of the routines presented should, from the standpoint of speed and size, be written in assembly language. This is a book about BASIC, however, so I have written all routines in BASIC except for one case, where assembler's speed was essential. Of course, the speed advantage of assembler will be less and less of a factor as computers get faster and faster.

The programs in this book were developed on the following system:

- ❏ AT "clone" running at 8 megahertz, 0 wait states
- ❏ 2 megabytes of memory
- ❏ 44-megabyte hard disk
- ❏ VGA color monitor

I mention the hardware for two reasons. First, there may be places in the text where timings are mentioned, and knowing the hardware involved gives you a point of reference. Second, whereas this system may seem ordinary to some, to others it might appear as some sort of a "dream system." Believe me, I understand. I spent several years programming on a floppy-disk PC with a monochrome monitor. More powerful hardware can certainly ease the task of program development. Yet, remember this: The quality of your programs has nothing to do with your hardware and everything to do with you. Hard work, knowledge, and creativity are infinitely more important than the number of megahertz and megabytes.

Before you get started, I need to explain the typographic conventions used in this book. *Italics* are used for new terms when they are first introduced and also to indicate variables. Program elements are `monospaced`. **Boldface** type is used to indicate user entry. For example, to start QuickBASIC and load a quick library, you enter

QB /L *libname*

where *libname* is a placeholder for the name of the desired quick library.

Good programming!

Part I

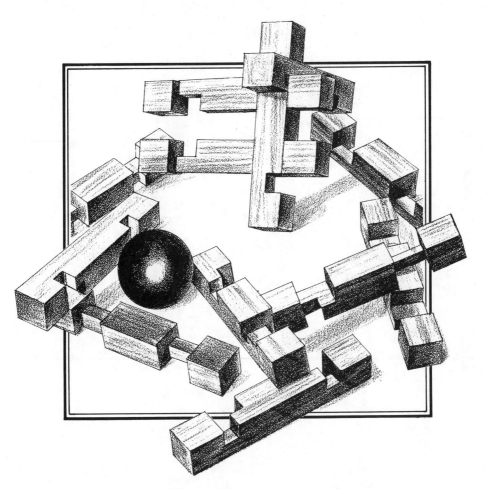

Using QuickBASIC

Compiler/Linker Use

Your productivity as a programmer will increase in direct proportion to your familiarity with the programming tools being used. This refers not only to the language you are using, but also to the specific implementation of the language. You need to know the details of BASIC, of course—how to display text on the screen, dimension an array, compare two numbers, and so on. You also have to know the details of QuickBASIC (QB)—how to start a new program, copy text, create a library. The better you know QB, the easier and faster your programming will be.

Knowing QB means more than knowing "how to"; it also means knowing what can be done. If you do not remember how QB performs a certain task, you can always look it up. If you do not even know that QB *can* perform a certain task, you may just assume that it cannot be done and end up compromising your program. Let me give a couple of examples.

Imagine that you are writing a program and would like to present graphical information on one area of the screen without overwriting text in other areas. If you know the ins and outs of QB's VIEW statement, you can go right ahead and write the necessary code. If you do not know the details of the VIEW statement but do know that QB has the capability to define graphics viewports, you can look up the necessary information. If, however, you are not even aware that QB supports viewports, you may just abandon the clever screen display you had been planning.

7

The same concept holds for the QB programming environment itself. You can write, compile, and run programs without using many of the QB environment's features. Yet, knowing and using these features can greatly increase the ease and speed of programming. Did you know, for example, that Alt-F1 can be used to move backward through the last 20 help screens that you looked at? Many QB programmers are not aware of this feature because it has no equivalent in the QB menu system. This feature can be very helpful if you have been browsing through QB's help system in search of certain information and need to go back a screen or two.

Most of this book deals with the BASIC language itself. This chapter and part of the next chapter, however, deal with certain aspects of the program development process. I am not attempting to provide a complete tutorial; rather, I concentrate on more advanced topics. Many of QB's features are mentioned only in passing or not at all. This chapter's goals are the following:

❑ To describe how to use some of the advanced features of the QB programming environment.

❑ To explain "stand-alone" program development and describe its advantages and disadvantages when compared to the QB environment.

As mentioned in the Introduction, I am assuming that readers of this book have at least a passing familiarity with QB. You should know how to start writing a new program and how to load an existing program from disk, edit it, and run it. If you have gotten that far with QB, you already have some inkling of its power and sophistication. Yet, the function of some of the menu commands may not be clear to you, and you may not even be aware that there are important QB commands that cannot be accessed using the menus. Take a look now at some of QB's advanced commands, starting with the menu system.

Understanding the QuickBASIC Menu System

The QB menu system enables you to access most of the program's functions, using either the keyboard or a mouse. You need to know your way around these menus to take full advantage of QB's power. Many of the more advanced features can be accessed via menus. Remember, the "easier" menu functions are mentioned only briefly here. See your QB manual if you need more information on them.

You need to be using QB's extended, or full, menus to access some of its advanced features. As shown in figure 1.1, there is a Full Menus command on the Options menu. If a bullet is displayed next to the command, Full Menus is toggled on. If no bullet is displayed, select the Full Menus command to activate it.

Fig. 1.1. *To obtain access to the full QuickBASIC menu system, toggle* Full Menus *on.*

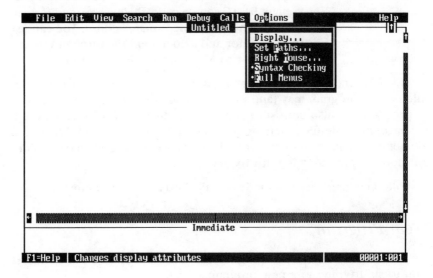

File Menu

The commands on the File menu are used to load, save, and name disk files. To understand the File menu commands fully, you need to know about the three types of files that the QB editor can work with. This can be somewhat confusing and is discussed in greater detail in Chapter 2. In brief, however, here it is.

Module   A disk file that contains BASIC source code. A QB program consists of at least one module (known as the *main module*), and it may contain one or more additional modules and/or other file types. The QB "smart" editor automatically checks syntax and adjusts formatting in modules.

Include file   A text file that is imported into a module using the
                     $INCLUDE metacommand. The import occurs when
                     the module is compiled, so you do not see the
                     contents of an include file when you edit the module
                     that imports it. Include files can be edited separately;
                     they contain BASIC source code, although restric-
                     tions exist on statements allowed in an include file.
                     Syntax and formatting are checked by the QB editor.

Document file   Any text file. Because these files do not normally
                     contain BASIC source code, their syntax and format-
                     ting are ignored by the ''smart'' editor. You can use
                     the QB editor and a document file for your grocery
                     list, a letter to Mom, or anything you like.

It is important to realize that in QB, a ''program'' is not a particular
file type. A program may (and most do) consist of a single module file.
A program can also consist of multiple modules and include files. QB
manages multiple-file programs quite nicely, by means of .MAK files. You
do not need to know the details of this yet; I cover it in depth in discussions
of modular programming in Chapter 2.

Following are brief summaries of all the File menu commands.

New Program

This command clears any program currently loaded in QB and enables
you to start typing in a new program.

Open Program...

This command loads an existing module (program) file from disk. If
the program that you specify consists of more than one module, all of
the modules are loaded.

Print...

Use this command to produce a printout of all or part of the currently
loaded program.

Exit

This command quits QB and returns to DOS.

DOS Shell

Select this command to return temporarily to the DOS prompt while you retain QB (and any program files) in memory. While the DOS prompt is displayed, you can run other programs and perform DOS functions, such as formatting a diskette. Typing **EXIT** at the prompt returns you to QB, exactly as you left it.

Actions you can do while in the DOS shell depend on the amount of memory your computer has and on the size of the program you want to run. Because QB remains in memory, the amount of memory available for other programs is significantly decreased. If you try to run a program that is too big for the available memory, you get an error message.

Save

This command saves the file in the active window to disk.

Save As...

This command has two uses. First, it enables you to change the name of a file before saving. If you load a file from disk, modify it, and then use the Save or Save All command, the file will be saved with its original name, overwriting the earlier version of the file on the disk. There may be times when you want to keep both the original and new versions of a file. Save As... prompts you for a new file name and leaves the original version of the file, under the original name, unchanged on disk.

The second use of the Save As... command is to change the format that a file is saved in. By default, QB saves program files in a special binary format that allows for faster loading and saving than ASCII format files. However, files in this format can only be edited using the QB editor. Save As... enables you to save program files in ASCII format, which you can then edit using another text editor, incorporate into word processing documents, and so on. Note that ASCII is the default format for saving document and include files; in fact, these files cannot be saved in binary format.

Merge...

The Merge... command loads a file from disk and inserts it in the current file (the one in the active View window) at the line the cursor is on. If the file being merged is a module file, it must have been saved to disk in ASCII format (using the Save As... command). The merged file remains unchanged on disk.

The last four File menu commands are used when you want to edit more than one file at once. The QB editor has the ability to work with more than one file at a time, a feature that I will discuss in more detail in discussions about modular programming.

Create File...

This command is used when you begin editing a new file that will be part of the program in memory. When you create a new file, you must specify its name and whether it is a module, include, or document file. If you create a file when there are no other modules loaded in QB, the new file is considered to be the main module of the program.

Load File...

This command loads a file from disk into memory. You must specify the file name and whether it is a module, include, or document file. Other files that are currently loaded into QB are not affected by the Load File... command. This is in contrast to the Open Program... command, which erases any files currently loaded into QB before you load the new file.

Unload File...

This command is the reverse of the Load File... command—it removes a single file from QB's memory while not affecting any other files currently loaded into QB. After this command unloads a file, the file still exists on disk.

Save All

Use this command to save all currently loaded files to disk. When you are working with multiple files, the Save command saves only the file that is displayed in the active View window. Use Save All to save all loaded files to disk.

Edit Menu

The commands on the Edit menu are fairly straightforward, having to do primarily with moving, copying, and deleting blocks of text. The New SUB... and New FUNCTION... commands begin a new procedure (the term *procedure* is used to refer to both subprograms, defined with the SUB...END SUB statements, and functions, defined with FUNCTION...END FUNCTION). I will discuss this in more detail in Chapter 2, which covers structured and modular programming.

View Menu

The View menu commands are used to select which program components are displayed in QB's View window. The View window is normally the largest window on the QB screen and is the only window in which source code can be edited. (I will discuss QB's other windows momentarily.) You can view only one program component at a time (actually, you can view two components using the split screen option; I will get to that in a minute, too). Separate files (that is, separate modules) are, of course, separate components. Procedures within a module are also considered to be separate components—separate from each other and separate from module-level code in that module. This will be clearer if you look at an example.

The program in listing 1.1, DEMO1.BAS, consists of module-level code plus two procedures named product and quotient. In the listing, DEMO1.BAS appears in its entirety—you see the module-level code and the procedure-level code. You could display the program in this way by using the Save As... command (on the File menu) to save the program in text format, then using the DOS TYPE command to display the file on the screen. If, on the other hand, you load the file into QB, the View window will display only the module-level code, as shown in figure 1.2.

The two procedures have, in fact, been loaded; but because they are separate components, they are not visible. By using the first two commands on the View menu, SUBs... and Next SUB, you can view any program component that is currently loaded into QB.

SUBs...

When you select the SUBs command, QB displays a listing of all loaded program components. Each module name is displayed in uppercase letters. The names of any procedures in each module are displayed indented under

Listing 1.1. *DEMO1.BAS*

```
DECLARE FUNCTION product% (X%, Y%)
DECLARE FUNCTION quotient! (X%, Y%)

DEFINT A-Z

CLS
INPUT "Enter two integers A and B "; A, B
PRINT "The product of A and B is ", product(A, B)
PRINT "The quotient of A and B is ", quotient(A, B)

END
FUNCTION product (X, Y)
    product = X * Y
END FUNCTION

FUNCTION quotient! (X, Y)
    quotient = X / Y
END FUNCTION
```

Fig. 1.2. *When DEMO1.BAS is initially loaded into QuickBASIC, the View window displays only the module-level code.*

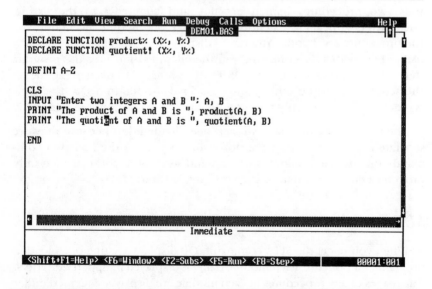

the module name. Select the component `quotient` by highlighting its name. Next, select whether `quotient` is to be edited in the active window or edited in a split window. If you choose the active window, the selected program component is displayed in the View window as shown in figure 1.3, and you can proceed with editing. If you select the split window, the View window is split horizontally into upper and lower windows. The newly selected program component is displayed in the lower window, and the original contents of the View window are displayed in the upper window. Figure 1.4 shows how the screen will look after the SUBs command is used to display the function `quotient` in a split window.

Fig. 1.3. *To display and edit procedure-level code in the View window, use the View menu to select the procedure to edit in the active window.*

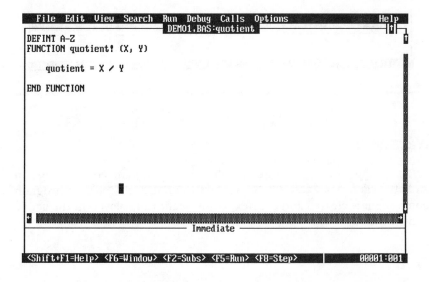

Only one of the split windows can be active at any time (the active window is where editing takes place). Use F6 and Ctrl-F6 to cycle up or down through QB's screen windows, making each "active" in turn (the cycle will include the Immediate window as well as the View windows). Pressing Ctrl-F10 toggles the active window between partial-screen and full-screen display. The active window can also be expanded or shrunk a line at a time with Alt-Plus and Alt-Minus (Alt with the + or − key on the numeric keypad; use Shift-Alt-Plus or Shift-Alt-Minus on the alphanumeric keypad).

Fig. 1.4. You can display two program components at once with QuickBASIC's split windows.

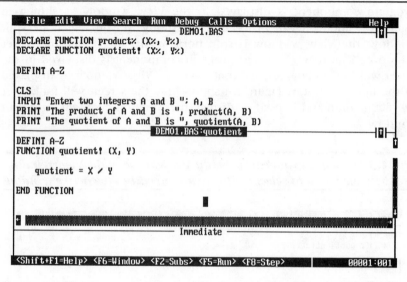

Next SUB

This command cycles through all loaded program components, in alphabetical order. Each time you select Next SUB, the current program component is cleared and the next component is displayed in the active view window.

Split

The Split command helps you move between split-screen and full-screen mode. If you are working in full-screen mode, Split divides the View window horizontally into two windows. Initially, the new window displays the same program component that is displayed in the original window. By scrolling the windows independently, you can view different parts of a single program component. Or, with the SUBs... or Next SUB command, you can display a different program component in one of the windows.

Next Statement

The `Next Statement` command positions the cursor on the next program statement to be executed. This is most useful when a program has been paused during execution for debugging purposes. I cover this in more detail in discussions on debugging in Chapter 3.

Output Screen

The `Output Screen` command switches your screen display from the QB environment to the output screen created by your program. After you view your program's output, pressing any key returns you to the QB screen.

Include File

When the cursor is on a program line that contains an `$INCLUDE` metacommand, the `Include File` command loads the referenced file into the active View window for editing. The result is the same as if you had loaded the file with the `Load File` command on the File menu.

Included Lines

The `Included Lines` command is a toggle. When the toggle is on, as indicated by an adjacent bullet, files referenced in `$INCLUDE` statements are displayed in high-intensity text as part of the file that references them. No editing is possible when you use this mode.

Search Menu

The commands on the Search menu are used to search for and optionally change text in your program. You should become familiar with all of the search commands, because they can save you a great deal of work. See the QB documentation for more information.

Run Menu

The Run menu commands are used to compile and execute programs and to create libraries. The `Restart` and `Continue` commands are used primarily when you debug a program and will be discussed in Chapter 3. The `Make Library...` command is used to create a quick library and is discussed in Chapter 2. The other Run menu commands are summarized here.

Start

The Start command compiles the currently loaded program and begins execution at the beginning of the program.

Modify COMMAND$...

The Modify COMMAND$... command is useful only with programs that use QB's COMMAND$ function. When a program is started from the DOS prompt, the COMMAND$ function returns any parameter(s) entered after the program name on the command line. Because there is no "command line" for programs run from within the QB environment, Modify COMMAND$... is provided so that you can specify a command line to be passed to the program.

Make EXE File...

When you run a BASIC program from within the QB environment, the executable code produced by the compiler and linker is kept in memory. When you exit QB, the executable code is lost and must be regenerated the next time you run the program from within QB. When a program is in its final form, however, you will probably want to create a stand-alone version that can be executed from the DOS command line, that is, without first invoking QB. Such a stand-alone program is called an *executable file* and has the extension .EXE. To create one from your program, use the Make EXE File... command.

To create .EXE files, QB must have access to two programs supplied as part of the QB package: the command-line BASIC compiler (BC.EXE) and the Microsoft Overlay Linker (LINK.EXE). These files must be in the current directory or in another directory you specify with the PATH environment variable. (See your DOS reference manual for an explanation of PATH.)

One other file, a QB library, must also be available. The two libraries provided with QB are BRUN45.LIB and BCOM45.LIB. Both of these libraries perform essentially the same function, but in different ways. An option that you set in the Make EXE File dialog box, which is shown in figure 1.5, determines which library to use in creating the .EXE files.

Fig. 1.5. *Specify compiler options in the* Make EXE File *dialog box when QuickBASIC compiles your program to an executable file.*

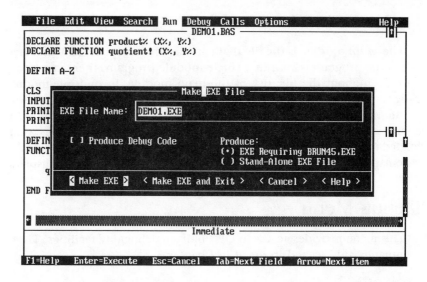

If you select `EXE Requiring BRUN45.EXE`, your program will be linked with BRUN45.LIB. This option results in smaller .EXE files; however, the run-time module BRUN45.EXE (also supplied with QB) must be present when your program runs. If you select `Stand-Alone EXE File`, your program will be linked with BCOM45.EXE. The resulting .EXE file is larger but does not need BRUN45.EXE in order to run.

The other option that must be specified in the `Make EXE File` dialog box is whether debug code should be produced. If the `Produce Debug Code` option is toggled on, the resulting .EXE file is larger and will run more slowly than if debug code had not been produced. You must turn debug code on if you want your program to do the following during execution:

❏ Check all arithmetic operations for overflow and underflow.

❏ Ensure that array subscripts are within the bounds specified in the array's `DIM` statement.

❏ Report line locations (numbers or labels) where run-time errors occur.

❏ Check each `RETURN` statement for a preceding `GOSUB`.

❏ Halt execution in response to Ctrl-Break at any point in program execution.

Set Main Module...

The *main module* is the file that contains the first statement executed when the program is run. In a single-module program, there can be no confusion about the identity of the main module. In multiple-module programs, QB usually does a good job of keeping track of which module is the main module (it is the first one listed in the SUBs dialog box). In some cases, however, you will need to explicitly tell QB which of several loaded modules is the main module. To do so, use the Set Main Module... command and indicate the main module in the dialog box that QB displays.

Debug Menu

This menu provides access to QB's built-in debugging facilities. These commands are covered in detail in Chapter 3.

Calls Menu

The Calls menu displays a list of all the procedure calls that were made as your program executed up to the current point. The procedures are listed in reverse order, that is, the most recently called procedure is at the top of the list. The Calls menu is primarily a debugging tool and will be covered in detail in Chapter 3.

Options Menu

The Options menu controls certain aspects of the QB environment. Any changes made on this menu take effect immediately. They are also saved to disk and remain in effect the next time you start QB.

Display...

With the Display... command you specify the foreground and background colors used to display normal text, the current statement, and breakpoint lines. You can also set the tab width (number of spaces), and whether or not scroll bars are displayed at the edges of the View windows. Scroll bars are useful only if you have a mouse.

Set Paths...

The Set Paths... command tells QB where to look for certain types of files. If you do not specify a path, QB looks for files in the current directory (the directory from which QB was started). You can specify a distinct path for each of four categories of files, as shown in the Set Paths... dialog box (see fig. 1.6).

Fig. 1.6. *The* Set Paths... *command on the Options menu tells QuickBASIC where to look for certain files.*

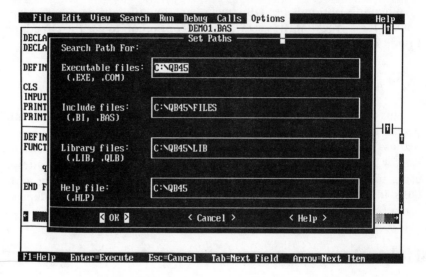

The syntax for the path specifications is the same as for the DOS PATH command. QB does not check the syntax, but simply accepts whatever you enter. If QB is not able to find one or more files that are in directories specified with the Set Paths command, check your entries for errors.

Be aware that the Include Files path is used only when QB needs a file in response to an $INCLUDE metacommand. The Open Program... command (on the File menu) always looks for .BAS files in the current directory.

Right Mouse...

This command selects the actions that QB takes in response to clicking the mouse button on the right. The two choices are to activate context-sensitive help (the same as pressing F1) or to execute the program up to the line containing the cursor. If you are using a mouse, you can select the former option while initially writing a program and the latter while debugging it.

Syntax Checking

When this option is on, QB checks each line of your program as you enter it for correct BASIC syntax. Turn this option off to use the QB editor to edit a non-BASIC file.

Full Menus

This command toggles the QB menu display between the "full" menu display and an "easy" display that omits some of the advanced menu commands. The easy menus are supposed to make the environment easier to use for beginners. Unless you get confused very easily, however, I advise using full menus at all times. The sooner you start experimenting with QB's advanced menu commands, the sooner you will become adept at using them.

Help Menu

The Help menu provides access to QB's extensive on-line, context-sensitive help system. Refer to the QB documentation for details.

Shortcut Keys

You just had a tour of the more advanced aspects of QB's menu system. In addition to being available on menus, many of the menu commands can be accessed via "shortcut keys." For example, the `Next SUB` command can be selected directly by pressing Shift-F2 (hold down the Shift key and press function key F2). In most cases, using a shortcut key is faster than selecting a command from a menu. The corresponding shortcut key is displayed next to each menu command that has one.

There are also some QB commands that cannot be accessed via the menu system but only by a shortcut key. These shortcut keys are more difficult to learn because you are not reminded of them every time you use a menu. Table 1.1 summarizes the QuickBASIC shortcut keys.

Table 1.1. *QuickBASIC Shortcut Keys without a Corresponding Menu Command*

Key	Action
Alt-F1	Pages backwards through previously viewed help screens, up to a maximum of 20.
Ctrl-F2	Displays the previous procedure in the active view window.
F6	Makes the next window active.
Shift-F6	Makes the previous window active.
F7	Executes the program up to the line containing the cursor.
F8	Executes the next program statement, tracing through any procedure that is called.
Shift-F8	Steps back through the last 20 program statements that were recorded by the History On or Trace On commands.
F10	Executes the next program statement, tracing around any procedure that is called.
Shift-F10	Steps forward through the last 20 program statements that were recorded by the History On or Trace On commands.
Ctrl-F10	Toggles the active window between full-screen and partial-screen display.

Stand-Alone Program Development

Most QB programmers will find themselves using the QB programming environment exclusively. And why not? Its "smart" editor, help system, and other features make it an extremely powerful and convenient tool. Yet, there is another way to write and compile QB programs that does not use the QB environment at all. First, however, you need to understand the steps between a program as written by a programmer and a program that can be executed by a computer (if you know this already, you can skip ahead).

Steps in Program Development

The BASIC statements and functions that you combine to create a program are known as source code. Your computer cannot understand these English-like statements; they must be translated into binary code called *machine language* before they can be executed. This translation is called *compilation* and, as you might expect, is performed by a program called a *compiler*. The output of the compiler is machine-language instructions known as *object code*. If the object code is saved in a disk file, the file will have an extension of.OBJ.

The third step is known as *linking*. A program called (of course) a *linker* combines the object code created by the compiler with other information, such as library routines your program calls, and produces an executable file. This file, which is the actual program that the computer loads and runs, has an extension of .EXE. The three steps of program development are illustrated in figure 1.7.

Fig. 1.7. *The three major steps in program development.*

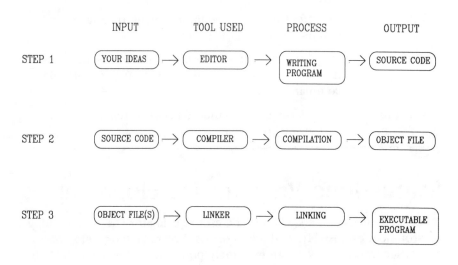

Within the QuickBASIC Environment

When you are using the QB programming environment, the second and third steps are completely transparent. Selecting the Run command invokes the QB compiler, which compiles your source code and puts the resulting object code in memory rather than in a disk file. The linker is also invoked, producing an executable program file, which is also placed in memory instead of on disk. Finally, QB "steps aside" while your program runs. When the program is finished, pressing any key returns you to QB.

Sounds like a pretty good system, right? You can compile, link, and run a program with a single keystroke, then return to the editor to make modifications and correct mistakes with another keystroke. This feature is an important component of QB's power and popularity.

Outside the QuickBASIC Environment

Yet another way to develop programs had been in use for many years before integrated programming environments like QB came along. It is still used by many experienced programmers. I call this method "stand-alone program development" because it uses separate, or stand-alone, programs for the editing, compiling, and linking steps. Stand-alone development has both advantages and disadvantages compared to the QB environment. To a great extent, the method you use will depend on your own personal preferences.

If you own QB, you already have two of the three programs needed for stand-alone development: the QB disks contain a stand-alone compiler, BC.EXE, and a stand-alone linker, LINK.EXE. The one additional program you will need is an editor. Any text editor can be used, including EDLIN, the line editor that is provided with DOS. EDLIN is extremely limited, however, and you will be much better off with one of the many specialized programming editors or word processors that can create unformatted files. Some of these editors have very sophisticated abilities that greatly simplify the task of writing programs.

Disadvantages of Stand-Alone Program Development

One disadvantage of stand-alone program development is the need for a separate text editor. Whereas almost any text editor will do, I believe that it is worthwhile to get one that is specialized for programming. If you do a lot of programming, the cost of a good editor will quickly be repaid in time savings.

Another disadvantage is that stand-alone program development denies you the special features of the QB environment, such as source code formatting, syntax checking, and automatic generation of DECLARE statements.

The final disadvantage is that the write/compile/test cycle is slower than in the QB environment. The reason is that the QB environment keeps everything it needs—editor, source code, compiler, and so on—in memory at the same time. In contrast, working in stand-alone mode requires that programs and files be swapped back and forth to disk, which is a slower process than accessing memory. As you will see later in this chapter, there are methods for significantly speeding up the stand-alone development cycle. Nevertheless, the QB environment always maintains some speed advantage.

Advantages of Stand-Alone Program Development

Given the disadvantages of stand-alone program development, why would anyone use it in preference to the QB environment? As you will soon see, there are significant advantages to the stand-alone method that often outweigh the disadvantages.

Editor

Whereas the editor in the QB environment is powerful and easy to use, you may simply prefer the style and commands of a separate programming editor. Using a separate editor is particularly advantageous if you write programs in more than one language, because a separate editor enables you to use the same programming editor at all times.

Suppose that, in addition to QB, you use C and assembly language. No matter which version of assembly language you prefer, you have to use a stand-alone editor because there are no integrated assembly language environments available. Perhaps you also use Borland's Turbo C, which does have an integrated environment. The Turbo C editor, however, uses a completely different set of commands than the QB editor. By using stand-alone development and a single program editor, you can avoid the problems inherent in trying to learn and remember two or three different editors.

Program Size

Another advantage is the ability to deal with large programs. The QB environment is itself a large program, leaving a limited amount of memory that must be shared by source, object, and executable code. By using stand-alone development, you will be able to deal with much larger programs. The program size limitations of the QB environment are more pronounced if your computer has less than 640K of memory.

Libraries

Libraries of compiled object code can be used in the QB environment as well as in stand-alone program development. The type of library used in stand-alone program development offers significantly more flexibility than the type of library used in the QB environment. Library use is covered in more detail later in this chapter and in Chapter 2.

Debugging

The QB environment contains some fundamental debugging capabilities, covered in Chapter 3. For more powerful debugging abilities, however, turn to a stand-alone debugger such as Microsoft's CodeView, which I also cover in Chapter 3. To be able to debug a BASIC program with one of these debuggers, you will have to compile it with the command-line compiler.

Options

There are a number of compilation options available only when you use the command-line compiler. These include the ability to do the following:

❏ Create listing files for use during debugging

❏ Store arrays in row order

❏ Increase dynamic array size beyond 64k

❏ Create smaller .EXE files if your program does not use the communications ports or will always run on a computer with a math coprocessor

Clearly there are times—particularly if you are developing a large, complex application—when you will have to use stand-alone development instead of the QB environment. Take a look now at how the command-line compiler and linker are used.

BC.EXE, the Command-Line Compiler

The command-line compiler takes a single BASIC source file at a time and translates it into object code (.OBJ file). The compiler is started from the DOS prompt by typing **BC**. Information can be passed to the compiler in two ways: on the command line or in response to compiler prompts.

Passing Information on the Command Line

When you enter information on the command line, the syntax is

BC *sourcefile, objectfile, listfile options;*

The *sourcefile* specifies the BASIC source code file to be compiled and is the only required command-line entry. If you omit the file name extension, .BAS is assumed. A *sourcefile* can include drive and/or path information.

The *objectfile* specifies the destination for the object code. If *objectfile* is not specified, the compiler writes the object code to a file with the same name as *sourcefile* and attaches the .OBJ extension.

The *listfile* specifies the destination for the compiler listing file. The default is NUL.LST, meaning that no listing file is created. A list file contains your source code along with the relative address of each line plus any error messages generated during compilation. List files can be used during debugging.

The *options* parameter is a list of one or more compiler option switches, discussed in the next section.

If you enter a compiler command line that specifies only *sourcefile*, the compiler will prompt you for *objectfile* and *listfile*. If you terminate the command line with a semicolon, these prompts are suppressed, and the compiler uses the defaults.

Responding to Prompts

If you enter only BC at the DOS prompt, the compiler prompts you for the necessary information, as follows:

```
Source Filename [.BAS]:
Object Filename [basename.OBJ]:
Source Listing [NUL.LST]:
```

You must enter a source file name. To accept the defaults for the object file name and source listing, simply press Enter on those lines.

Compiler Options

The command-line compiler has a number of options you can activate with switches included on the command line when you invoke the compiler. Each switch consists of a sequence of one or more characters preceded by a forward slash (/) or a dash (-). Option switches can appear in any order on the command line. If you are responding to compiler prompts rather than entering all information on the command line, you can include the option switches at the end of any prompt. Thus, the following two compiler invocations are equivalent:

```
A> bc sortdata /O/X;
```

```
A> bc
Source Filename [.BAS]: sortdata /O/X
Object Filename [basename.OBJ]:
Source Listing [NUL.LST]:
```

The compiler option switches and their effects are

/A	Specifies that the *listfile* will contain not only lines of source code and their relative address but also the disassembled object code (that is, assembly language) for each line of BASIC source code. This option has an effect only when you have specified (either on the BC command line or in response to BC prompts) that a *listfile* should be produced.
/AH	Allows dynamic arrays to occupy all available memory (normally, they are limited to 64K per array). This option applies only to dynamic arrays of numbers, fixed-length strings, and records. Static arrays and variable-length string arrays remain limited to 64K.
/C:n	Sets the size, in bytes, of the receive buffer for each asynchronous communications port (also called the *serial port* or *RS-232 port*). The default buffer size is 256 bytes per port.
/D	Produces the same effect as the Produce Debug Code toggle (Run menu, Make EXE File... command) within the QB

environment. It directs the compiler to generate debugging code for run-time error checking and enables program termination with Ctrl-Break.

/E   Tells the compiler that the program contains **ON ERROR** with **RESUME** *linenumber* statements.

/MBF   Creates a program that uses the Microsoft Binary Format (MBF) and can therefore exchange data with programs compiled with old versions of QB. MBF was used by early versions of QB to store floating-point numbers on disk. More recent versions of QB use the widely accepted IEEE format.

/O   Creates programs that link with BCOM45.LIB and therefore do not require BRUN45.EXE at execution time. Programs compiled with the /O option are larger but run slightly faster than programs compiled without it. The compiler default is to produce programs that link with the BRUN45.LIB library and therefore require the BRUN45.EXE module at run-time.

/R   Allocates memory storage for arrays in row-major order rather than the default column-major order. To illustrate, consider an integer array dimensioned as follows:

```
DIM X%(10,10)
```

With column-major order, array elements would be arranged in physical memory as follows:

```
X%(0,0)
X%(1,0)
X%(2,0)
   .
   .
   .
X%(10,0)
X%(0,1)
X%(1,1)
   .
   .
X%(9,10)
X%(10,10)
```

Specifying the /R option would result in the following arrangement:

```
X%(0,0)
X%(0,1)
X%(0,2)
     .
     .
     .
X%(0,10)
X%(1,0)
X%(1,1)
     .
     .
     .
X%(10,9)
X%(10,10)
```

Use the /R option if you are linking your BASIC program with routines written in another language that uses row-major order for array storage.

/S Causes the compiler to write string literals (quoted strings) to the object file instead of to the symbol table. Use this option if a program that contains a lot of string literals causes an Out of memory error message during compilation.

/V Enables event trapping for the following:

Item trapped	BASIC statement
Communications ports	ON COM
Function keys	ON KEY
Light pen	ON PEN
Music buffer	ON PLAY
Joystick	ON STRIG
Timer	ON TIMER

When trapping is enabled, the program checks before the execution of each statement to see whether any of the specified events has occurred.

/W Enables event trapping for the same events as /V, except that event checking occurs at each program line number or label rather than at every program statement. Compared with /V, the /W option results in a somewhat smaller, faster program. The response to trapped events, however, may not be as quick, particularly if your program has long sections of code with no line numbers or labels.

/X   Tells the compiler that the program contains ON ERROR
          statements with RESUME, RESUME NEXT, or RESUME 0.

/ZD   Tells the compiler to include line-number information in
          the object file. These line numbers correspond to the lines
          of the source code. Use this option if you plan to debug
          your program using the Microsoft Symbolic Debugger
          (SYMDEB).

/ZI   Results in a object file that contains debugging information
          used by the Microsoft CodeView debugger.

The Compilation Process

Once you have entered all the necessary information, the BC.EXE
compiler loads the source file and begins compiling it. This process may
take only a second or two for short programs and can take several minutes
for long ones. Compilation speed is also influenced by the speed of your
computer and disk. As it works, the compiler prints information on the
screen about any errors it encounters. Using the short program in listing
1.2 for an example, look closely at the code to see that there are several
intentional errors. When the compiler tries to process the program, it
produces error messages as shown in Figure 1.8.

*Fig. 1.8. The output of the command line compiler when it tries to
compile the program in Listing 1.2.*

```
C>bc demo1err;
Microsoft (R) QuickBASIC Compiler Version 4.50
(C) Copyright Microsoft Corporation 1982-1988.
All rights reserved.
Simultaneously published in the U.S. and Canada.
   0030    0006    INPUT "Enter two integers A and B : A, B
                                                        ^ Syntax error
   0039    0006    FUCTION product (X, Y)
                        ^ Equal sign missing
                          ^ Syntax error
   0087    0010    product = X * Y
                    ^ Variable required
   0087    0010    END FUNCTION
                    ^ END SUB/FUNCTION without SUB/FUNCTION
   0092    0010    quotient = X ! Y
                               ^ Invalid character
                                 ^ Syntax error

43917 Bytes Available
43042 Bytes Free

    0 Warning Error(s)
    7 Severe  Error(s)

C>
```

Listing 1.2. DEMO1ERR.BAS

```
DECLARE FUNCTION product% (X%, Y%)
DECLARE FUNCTION quotient! (X%, Y%)

DEFINT A-Z

CLS
INPUT "Enter two integers A and B ; A, B
PRINT "The product of A and B is ", product(A, B)
PRINT "The quotient of A and B is ", quotient(A, B)

END

FUCTION product% (X, Y)
    product = X * Y
END FUNCTION

FUNCTION quotient! (X, Y)
    quotient = X | Y
END FUNCTION
```

The compiler prints each line of source code that contains an error. Below each line are one or more messages describing the error that was detected plus a caret (^) pointing to the place in the line of source code where the compiler thinks the error is located. The two numbers at the start of each line are the code and data offsets of the corresponding statement. This information is of no real use at this point and can be ignored.

Having error messages displayed on the screen is of limited usefulness, because they are no longer available when you return to your editor to correct the problem. One alternative is to direct the messages to your printer, providing a printed error list that you can refer to. You could also direct the error messages to a disk file and refer to them from within your editor. Both of these alternatives are executed using the DOS command-line redirection facility:

```
BC demo1err; > PRN          (for printer output)
BC demo1err; > errors.txt   (for output to a file)
```

If you have examined DEMO1ERR.BAS carefully, you are aware that there are only three errors in the program. Yet, the compiler reported seven errors. This is because certain errors can cause multiple error messages. For example, the misspelling of the word FUNCTION in the definition of product caused four of the seven error messages. Once the three errors are corrected, the program will compile without errors.

LINK.EXE, the Command-Line Linker

As mentioned earlier, the object code produced by the compiler must be combined with other information to produce the final executable program. this is the function of the linker.

Invoking the Linker from the Command Line

You must pass information to the linker to tell it which file(s) to link. As with the compiler, you have more than one way to pass this information.

Information is passed to the linker on the command line with the following syntax:

LINK *objectfile(s), exefile, mapfile, libraries options;*

The *objectfile(s)* is the only required command-line parameter; it specifies the object file(s) that are to be linked. Your *objectfile(s)* may contain disk and/or path information. If a file extension is not given, .OBJ is assumed. If more than one object file name is given, they can be separated with either spaces or plus signs (+).

The *exefile* specifies the name for the executable file being created. The default is the name of the first object file listed in *objectfile(s)*, with an .EXE extension.

The *mapfile* specifies the name of the map file to be created. The default is NUL.MAP, meaning that no map file is created. A map file, sometimes useful during debugging, lists the relative addresses and the sizes of all the program's segments and public symbols. Entering PRN for *mapfile* sends the map file to the printer.

The *libraries* parameter gives the names of one or more libraries that contain procedures used by your program. All QB programs must be linked with either BRUN45.LIB or, if the /O compiler option is used, BCOM45.LIB. You need not name these libraries in the LINK command line because the compiler places the default library name in the object file itself. If BRUN45.LIB or BCOM45.LIB is not located in the current directory, however, you must specify its name, preceded by disk and/or path information, as input to the linker.

If you are linking with libraries other than the default, give their name(s) without any extension; the .LIB extension is assumed. If more than one library is listed, separate each name with a plus sign.

The *options* parameter is one or more of the linker options, discussed later.

If you enter a linker command line that specifies only *objectfile(s)*, the linker prompts you to enter *exefile* and *mapfile*. To suppress these prompts and accept the defaults, terminate the linker command line with a semicolon.

Invoking the Linker in Response to Prompts

You can start the linker by entering only **LINK** at the DOS prompt, in which case you are prompted to enter the necessary information:

```
Object Modules [.OBJ]:
Run File [basename.EXE]:
List File [NUL.MAP]:
Libraries [.LIB]:
```

Only the object module(s) name is required. To accept the default for any of the other items, press Enter on that line.

Invoking the Linker in a Response File

The Microsoft linker can also accept information from a disk file called a response file. This is done with an entry in the format

LINK *@filename*

at the DOS prompt, where *filename* is the response file.

A *response file* is a short text file that contains the same information that you would enter on the LINK command line or in response to prompts. Items that would be separated with commas when entered on the command line or that would be entered in response to different prompts must be on separate lines in the response file. Using a response file can save a lot of keystrokes when you repeatedly execute a link session with a lot of object files, libraries, and/or options.

Linker Options

All linker options begin with a forward slash (/). The dash character is not acceptable. Link options can be abbreviated or spelled out in full. The following list gives the abbreviation for each option followed by the full option name in brackets on the right.

/B   [/BATCH] If the linker cannot find an object or library file that it needs, it will normally prompt the user for a new path name. The /B option suppresses these prompts; the linker continues without using the missing file. The program will probably not link correctly, because of unresolved external references. This option is used primarily when you are using a batch file to link more than one program. Specifying /B means that the entire batch process will not be halted by one missing file.

/CO   [/CODEVIEW] Directs the linker to prepare an executable file containing the information needed by the Microsoft CodeView debugger. The /CO linker option has an effect only with object files that were compiled using the /ZI compiler option.

/E   [/EXEPACK] Directs the linker to remove repeated sequences of bytes from the .EXE file and to optimize the load-time relocation table. Depending on the specifics of your program, the /E option may result in smaller and faster programs.

/HE   [/HELP] Displays a list of all linker options on the screen.

/I   [/INFORMATION] Displays a progress report during the linking process. This report includes the current phase of linking and the names of the object files being linked.

/LI   [/LINENUMBERS] Creates a map file that also contains the source code's line numbers and their associated addresses. This option works only when you have also specified the /M linker option.

/M   [/MAP] Directs the linker to produce a map file. The file will have the same name as the first object file specified in *objectfile(s)*, with the extension .MAP. A map file can also be produced by specifying its name on the linker command line or in response to the List File prompt.

/PAU   [/PAUSE] Causes the linker to pause during the link session, just before the .EXE file is written to disk, and prompt the user. You can then insert a new diskette to hold the .EXE file. This option is useful primarily if you are using a system that has floppy disk drives only.

/Q   [/QUICKLIBRARY] Directs the linker to create a Quick Library from the specified object file(s). When using this option you must specify BQLB.LIB, which contains Quick Library support routines, in the linker library list.

A number of additional linker options exist that I do not mention here. Some of them are almost never used in linking BASIC programs. Others perform actions that are performed automatically by the BASIC compiler.

Using a RAM Disk To Speed Up Program Development

When you are using stand-alone program development, each edit/compile/link/test requires the following steps:

1. Load your editor from disk.

2. Load your source code file from disk and edit it.

3. Save the source code to disk and exit your editor.

4. Load your compiler from disk.

5. The compiler loads the source code from disk, compiles it, and saves the object file to disk.

6. Load your linker from disk.

7. The linker loads the object file(s) and any necessary library modules from disk, then links them.

8. The resulting executable file is saved to disk.

9. The executable file is loaded from disk, and the program runs.

10. If the program needs further work, return to step 1.

Have you noticed that this sequence involves many disk reads and writes? If you are programming on a floppy disk system, you probably are spending more time watching your disk activity lights flash on and off than actually writing your program. Even with a fast hard disk, speed suffers in comparison to the memory-based system used by the QB environment. This is because accessing data stored in RAM is always faster than accessing data on disk.

You can significantly speed up the program development cycle by minimizing disk accesses and maximizing memory accesses. To do this, create a *RAM disk* (also called a *virtual drive*). A RAM disk is nothing more than a section of memory that has been configured so that it appears to DOS and your programs as a disk. The VDISK utility, supplied with most versions of MS-DOS, is one example of a RAM disk program. For example, on a computer with two floppy drives (A: and B:), a RAM disk would be set up as drive C:. When reading from or writing to a RAM disk, programs work as though they are interacting with a physical disk. The process occurs much faster, however, because data is being transferred to and from memory rather than to and from an actual disk.

Disadvantages of RAM Disks

RAM disks have two disadvantages. The first is that data in a RAM disk is lost when the computer is turned off, so it is necessary to copy new or modified files from a RAM disk to a physical disk before you end a work session. This step does not apply, of course, to programs such as editors and compilers that are copied from a physical disk to the RAM disk but are not modified during a work session.

The second disadvantage is that a RAM disk occupies memory. If your system has a good amount of extended or expanded memory, you can set up a RAM disk there, not impinging on the 640K of DOS memory. If, however, you are limited to 640K or less, a RAM disk takes up some of the memory that might otherwise be used by your editor or compiler. In this case, the performance advantage provided by the RAM disk may well be offset by the decrease in memory available to your programs.

Selecting Files To Place on a RAM Disk

If you decide to use a RAM disk in your programming, you will need to determine which of your program development files to place there—unless, of course, you have enough memory to create a RAM disk large enough to hold everything! You will gain the most speed advantage by using a RAM disk for those files that are read from and/or written to disk most often.

The primary candidates for a RAM disk are those files that are both read and written during the program development cycle. First, think of the object files for your programs. The object file is written to disk by the compiler and then read by the linker. It has no other use and need not be saved, so it is an excellent candidate for a RAM disk.

The executable program file is written to disk by the linker and then read from disk when you load it for testing. You will, of course, eventually want a copy of the .EXE file on a physical disk, once the program is finished and all the bugs are out. During development and testing, however, there is no reason not to use a RAM disk for the .EXE file. If it should be lost due to a power failure or other problem, you can always recompile and link, as long as the source code is intact.

Listing and map files are written by the compiler or linker, then read when you look at their contents during debugging.

The source code file is read and written by the editor, then read again by the compiler. It might seem like a good choice for a RAM disk. The volatile nature of a RAM disk makes this a risky idea, however. If the data on the RAM disk is lost, you will lose all editing changes made since the beginning of the work session. It is better to play it safe and keep your source code on a physical disk.

Secondary candidates for a RAM disk are those files read during the program development cycle. This category includes your program development tools—editor, compiler, and linker—as well as library (.LIB) files. Because the original copies remain on the physical disk, there is no danger in putting them on a RAM disk. This does not apply, of course, to libraries that you are modifying—only to those being linked, unchanged, with your program.

Using the RAM Disk

When you use a RAM disk, the details of the edit/compile/link cycle will vary depending on the details of the RAM disk setup you are using. Of course, you must copy the desired files onto the RAM disk. Copying your editor, compiler, and linker onto the RAM disk, however, is not enough. You also need to ensure that DOS runs the programs from the RAM disk and not from their original location on the physical disk. This can be done in three ways. (In these and the following examples, assume that the RAM disk has been set up as drive E:.)

1. Specify the RAM disk drive letter when you invoke the program. For example,

   E:BC *progname*;
   E:LINK *progname*,,*libname*;

2. Make the RAM disk the default drive by entering its drive letter at the DOS prompt.

3. Include the RAM drive in the PATH environment variable *before* the disk/directory that contains the physical copy of the program. Thus, if BC.EXE and LINK.EXE are located on hard disk C:, directory \QB45, your PATH environment variable, would read:

```
PATH = E:\;C:\QB45 .....
```

See your DOS reference manual for an explanation of the PATH variable and how to set it. This method works only if C:\QB45 is not the current directory at the time BC or LINK is invoked because DOS always looks for executable programs in the current directory before searching the disks and directories specified by PATH.

If you are using a RAM disk for object, listing, and executable files, you must tell the compiler and linker where to find input files and where to put output files. Consider a situation in which you are running your compiler and linker from your hard disk and using the RAM disk for the temporary files just mentioned. Your command lines would be as follows:

```
BC progname, e:\, e:\;
LINK e:\progname, e:\, e:\;
```

The compiler would read *progname*.BAS from the default directory, compile it, and write *progname*.OBJ and *progname*.LST to the RAM disk. The linker would read *progname*.OBJ from the RAM disk and write both *progname*.EXE and *progname*.MAP to the RAM disk.

Use of Batch Files

The use of batch files can simplify the stand-alone edit/compile/link cycle. This is true regardless of whether you are using a RAM disk or are working entirely from a hard disk or floppies.

A *batch file*, which has a .BAT extension, is an ASCII text file that contains DOS commands. Executing a batch file has the same effect as if you had actually entered those commands at the DOS prompt. A batch file can be created with a text editor or directly from the DOS command line. More general information about batch files can be found in your DOS documentation.

Look at a sample of batch file commands. You are using a program editor named EDIT to write a program named DATABASE.BAS. The program is compiled with several compiler options and then linked with a user-supplied library. Each development cycle requires the following entries at the DOS prompt:

edit database.bas	(to edit the source file)
bc database /O/V;	(to compile)
link database,,external.lib;	(to link)
database	(to run and test the program)

By putting these commands in a batch file named C.BAT, you can execute the entire sequence by entering the single letter C at the DOS prompt. When you are finished editing and exit the editor, the compiler is invoked; when compilation is finished, the linker is invoked, and so on.

Perhaps you have noticed a flaw in this approach. If your program contains one or more errors, the compiler reports the error(s) but does not create an object file. If the linker cannot find DATABASE.OBJ, it will not operate. What is more likely to happen, however, is that the linker will find the last version of DATABASE.OBJ and will proceed with linking, producing an outdated version of DATABASE.EXE. When you test the program, you will wonder what happened to all the changes you just made!

One solution to this problem is to create two batch files: C.BAT, containing the edit and compiler commands; and L.BAT, containing the link and execute commands. You would execute L.BAT only after seeing that compilation was successful.

A more elegant solution is to use the batch file IF command in conjunction with the DOS errorlevel parameter to conditionally control batch file operation. Many programs, including BC.EXE, set the value of errorlevel upon program termination depending on whether an error occurred during program execution. If a compilation error occurred, BC sets errorlevel to 1; if no error occurred, it is set to 0.

You can change the original batch file to read

```
edit database.bas
bc database /O/V;
IF ERRORLEVEL 1 GOTO nogood
link database,,external.lib;
database
nogood:
```

With this batch file, `database` is linked and executed only if the compilation was error-free.

Summary

This chapter has provided an introduction to the advanced features of the QB programming environment. You may not use all of these features regularly, and in fact there may be some that you never use. By being aware of what's available, however, you will be able to take maximum advantage of the QB environment as suits your programming preferences and style.

The chapter also took a look at the "stand-alone" method of program development. This method has both advantages and disadvantages when compared to the QB environment, and your choice will depend largely on personal preferences. Because there are programming tasks that can be accomplished only when you use stand-alone development, you should have at least some familiarity with it.

2

Structured and Modular Programming

If you are relatively new to computer programming, you may never have heard of the terms *structured programming* and *modular programming*. On the other hand, if you have been programming for a while and have read some books and magazines in the field, you have almost certainly heard them. In either case, it is worth your while to develop a clear understanding of these concepts. Without such an understanding, your development as a programmer will be severely limited for all but the simplest programming projects. In this chapter I will explain the following:

❑ Concepts of structured programming and modular programming, and the relationship between them

❑ Tools available in QuickBASIC for structured programming and modular programming

❑ Ways to use code written in other programming languages in your QuickBASIC programs

This last topic may not seem related to the subject of the chapter; but, as you will soon see, it is.

Defining the Terms

Let me dive right in and start with a couple of definitions.

Structured programming is the principle of program design in which individual program functions are written as functionally independent sections of code.

Modular programming is the method of program development in which a program's code is maintained in two or more separate files.

These definitions may not make a great deal of sense to you right now, but they will be clearer soon. The important thing to realize at this point is that structured programming and modular programming are independent, although related, concepts. You can write a fully structured program without using modular programming at all. Conversely, you could theoretically write a modular program that was totally unstructured. In practice, however, the two methods are usually used in conjunction.

Structured Programming

This discussion covers the advantages and methods of structured programming in QuickBASIC (QB), then explores procedures, which are the main tool for structuring your code.

Advantages

❑ Structured programs are easier to write. Structured programming breaks complex programming tasks into a number of smaller, simpler tasks whose code and variables are isolated from the rest of the program. By tackling these smaller tasks individually, you will make progress much faster than if you tried to tackle the entire program at once.

❑ Structured programs are easier to debug. In a structured program, most of the code and data are isolated in discrete procedures. This makes tracking down problems much simpler. You know, for example, that a problem with your program's data entry screen will be found in the data entry procedure.

❑ Structured programs are easier to maintain. Because a structured program's various parts are isolated from each other, you can usually modify one part of the program without worrying whether the changes will cause problems in another part.

Structured Programming in QuickBASIC

QuickBASIC supports two types of elements that are used in structured programming: subprograms and functions. These two elements, referred to collectively as *procedures*, are very similar to each other. In fact, they differ in only one significant way. I will provide details soon, but it will be helpful to look at an example first.

Listing 2.1 shows a simple demonstration program that was written with no regard for the principles of structured programming. This program accepts a line of text from the keyboard and then takes two actions:

1. If the string contains lowercase letters, they are converted to uppercase. Other characters are not changed.

2. The new string is displayed in the center of the screen, surrounded by a double-lined box.

Listing 2.1. *Unstructured Demonstration Program*

```
' Program accepts a line of text, converts lowercase letters
' to uppercase, and displays the new string in a box, centered
' on the screen

DEFINT A-Z

CLS
LOCATE 5, 1
LINE INPUT "Enter some text: ", TEXT$

' NEWTEXT$ will hold the converted string

NEWTEXT$ = ""

' Loop once for each character in the input.

FOR I = 1 TO LEN(TEXT$)

' Extract the Ith character.

    TEMP$ = MID$(TEXT$, I, 1)
```

Listing 2.1 *continues*

Listing 2.1 continued

```
' If it is a lowercase letter, convert it to uppercase.

    IF ASC(TEMP$) > 96 AND ASC(TEMP$) < 123 THEN
        TEMP$ = CHR$(ASC(TEMP$) - 32)
    END IF

' Tack the character onto the end of NEWTEXT$.

    NEWTEXT$ = NEWTEXT$ + TEMP$

NEXT I

' Establish screen coordinates of top left corner or the box.

BOXROW = 12
BOXCOL = (80 - LEN(NEWTEXT$)) \ 2

' Draw the box.

LOCATE BOXROW, BOXCOL - 1
PRINT CHR$(201)
LOCATE BOXROW + 1, BOXCOL - 1
PRINT CHR$(186)
LOCATE BOXROW + 2, BOXCOL - 1
PRINT CHR$(200)
LOCATE BOXROW, BOXCOL + LEN(NEWTEXT$) + 2: PRINT CHR$(187)
LOCATE BOXROW + 1, BOXCOL + LEN(NEWTEXT$) + 2
PRINT CHR$(186)
LOCATE BOXROW + 2, BOXCOL + LEN(NEWTEXT$) + 2
PRINT CHR$(188)
LOCATE BOXROW, BOXCOL
PRINT STRING$(LEN(NEWTEXT$) + 2, CHR$(205))
LOCATE BOXROW + 2, BOXCOL
PRINT STRING$(LEN(NEWTEXT$) + 2, CHR$(205))

' Print the text.

LOCATE BOXROW + 1, BOXCOL + 1
PRINT NEWTEXT$

END
```

This program may seem fine to you, and in fact it works perfectly well, producing output as shown in figure 2.1. If, however, the programmer had applied structured programming principles to this project, the program would appear as shown in listing 2.2. For the sake of brevity, I have omitted comments from this listing. Compare listing 2.2 with listing 2.1, noting that the code is essentially identical but is arranged differently.

Fig. 2.1. *The output of the demonstration program.*

```
Enter some text: QuickBasic Advanced Techniques




                                    QUICKBASIC ADVANCED TECHNIQUES

       C>
```

Listing 2.2. *Structured Demonstration Program*

```
DECLARE SUB PrintInBox (TEXT$)
DECLARE FUNCTION AllCaps$ (TEXT$)

DEFINT A-Z

CLS
LOCATE 5, 1
LINE INPUT "Enter some text: ", TEXT$

TempString$ = AllCaps$(Text$)
CALL PrintInBox(TempString$)

END



FUNCTION AllCaps$ (TEXT$)

NEWTEXT$ = ""

FOR I = 1 TO LEN(TEXT$)
```

Listing 2.2 continues

Listing 2.2 continued

```
    TEMP$ = MID$(TEXT$, I, 1)

    IF ASC(TEMP$) > 96 AND ASC(TEMP$) < 123 THEN
        TEMP$ = CHR$(ASC(TEMP$) - 32)
    END IF

    NEWTEXT$ = NEWTEXT$ + TEMP$

NEXT I

AllCaps$ = NEWTEXT$

END FUNCTION


SUB PrintInBox (TEXT$)

BOXROW = 12
BOXCOL = (80 - LEN(TEXT$)) \ 2

LOCATE BOXROW, BOXCOL - 1
PRINT CHR$(201)
LOCATE BOXROW + 1, BOXCOL - 1
PRINT CHR$(186)
LOCATE BOXROW + 2, BOXCOL - 1
PRINT CHR$(200)
LOCATE BOXROW, BOXCOL + LEN(TEXT$) + 2
PRINT CHR$(187)
LOCATE BOXROW + 1, BOXCOL + LEN(TEXT$) + 2
PRINT CHR$(186)
LOCATE BOXROW + 2, BOXCOL + LEN(TEXT$) + 2
PRINT CHR$(188)
LOCATE BOXROW, BOXCOL
PRINT STRING$(LEN(TEXT$) + 2, CHR$(205))
LOCATE BOXROW + 2, BOXCOL
PRINT STRING$(LEN(TEXT$) + 2, CHR$(205))

LOCATE BOXROW + 1, BOXCOL + 1
PRINT TEXT$

END SUB
```

The main body of the program—the part up to the END statement—is now only eight lines long. The majority of the program statements—those that do most of the actual work of the program—have been segregated into two separate sections, or procedures, following the END statement. Here are the specifics.

❏ The program statements that convert letters in the input string from lower- to uppercase have been put in a function named AllCaps$.

❏ The program statements that draw the box and print the converted string have been put in a subprogram named PrintInBox.

❏ Program execution is directed to these procedures using the function name on the right side of an equal sign and including the subprogram name in a CALL statement.

In a nutshell, this is what structured programming is all about—dividing your source code into discrete sections, or procedures, that perform specific tasks, then calling those procedures from the main program as needed. Do not worry right now about the details of functions, subprograms, and call statements.

QuickBASIC Procedures: Subprograms and Functions

As mentioned earlier, QB supports two types of procedures: subprograms and functions. These two types of procedures are alike in almost every respect. The major difference is that a function returns a value to the calling program, whereas a subprogram does not.

This difference will be clearer if you look again at the sample function and subprogram in listing 2.2. AllCaps$ is a function—it returns a value to the calling program; this value is assigned to the variable TempString$, as follows:

```
TempString$ = AllCaps$(TEXT$)
```

In contrast, PrintInBox is a subprogram. It performs a task—in this case, screen display—but does not return a value. It is invoked with a CALL statement:

```
CALL PrintInBox(TempString$)
```

A user-defined function can be invoked using its name anywhere an intrinsic QB function or a variable name could be used. For example, the previous two statements could be combined as:

```
CALL PrintInBox(AllCaps$(TEXT$))
```

Later in the chapter I detail how to invoke user-defined procedures. Note here that both subprograms and functions can modify the arguments passed to them by the calling program (something also covered later in the chapter). In this sense, both types of procedures can "return" one or more values to the calling program. Only a function, however, returns a value in its name.

Defining a Procedure

A subprogram is defined using the following syntax:

```
SUB subname [parameterlist] [STATIC]
    [STATIC variablelist]
    .

    .
    statements
    .

    .
END SUB
```

The syntax for defining a function is almost identical:

```
FUNCTION funcname [parameterlist] [STATIC]
    [STATIC variablelist]
    .

    .
    statements
    .

    .
END FUNCTION
```

Here are brief descriptions of the components of a procedure definition:

❑ The *subname* or *funcname* is the name that identifies the procedure.

❑ The *parameterlist* is an optional list of one or more variables. This list indicates the number and type of the arguments that are passed to the procedure by the calling program.

❑ STATIC is an optional keyword that applies to local variables (those used in the procedure). In the absence of the STATIC keyword, local variables default to automatic.

❑ The *statements* are the BASIC statements that make up the body of the procedure.

❑ END SUB or END FUNCTION marks the end of the procedure definition.

Now for the details which, unless specified otherwise, are the same for functions and subprograms.

funcname

The name given to a function can be up to 40 characters long. Naming rules are the same as for regular BASIC variables. And like regular variables, function names have a data type associated with them. This is the type of the value that the function returns. It is specified just as for regular variables: by appending a type suffix (**%**, **#**, **$**, and so on) to *funcname*, with a **DEF***type* statement, or by letting the *funcname* default to single precision. The *funcname* must be unique—the name cannot used by a variable or another procedure in the same program. It is an excellent idea to make the *funcname* reflect the task performed by the function.

subname

The rules for naming a subprogram are the same as those for naming a function, except that no return data type declaration is needed.

parameterlist

Some procedures take no arguments, in which case there is no parentheses or *parameterlist* in the procedure definition. If a procedure does take arguments, the number and data type of these arguments must be indicated in the procedure definition parameter list. The following section explains the distinction between an argument and a parameter.

A *parameter* is a variable that appears in a procedure definition. An *argument* is a value (a variable, expression, or constant) that is passed to the procedure when it is called. Within the procedure, the value of each argument is available in the corresponding parameter. This example will illustrate.

```
       .
       .
     . X = 100
     CALL SubProg (X, 12/4, "Smith")
       .
       .
```

```
SUB SubProg (A, B, C$)
.
.
.
END SUB
```

X (a variable), 12/4 (an expression), and "Smith" (a constant) are arguments. A, B, and C$ are parameters. Within SubProg, the variables A, B, and C$ have (at least initially) the values 100, 3, and "Smith", respectively.

Now that you know the distinction between an argument and a parameter, you are ready to examine the syntax of *parameterlist*.

If *parameterlist* contains more than one parameter, each must be separated from its neighbors by a comma. Each parameter can be any valid variable name (except for fixed-length strings) or an array name followed by empty parentheses. Take a look at some examples and their meanings. In these examples, assume that the default variable type is SINGLE, that is, there are no DEF*type* statements.

- ☐ SUB ProcName (X)

  ProcName accepts one single precision argument.

- ☐ SUB ProcName (X$,Y%)

  ProcName accepts one string argument and one integer argument.

- ☐ SUB ProcName (X AS DOUBLE, Y AS INTEGER)

  ProcName accepts one double precision argument and one integer argument.

- ☐ SUB ProcName (Array(), Info() AS STRING)

  ProcName accepts a single precision array and a string array as arguments.

STATIC

To understand the STATIC keyword, you must first understand the difference between global and local variables.

Variables used in a procedure are called *local* variables. A local variable has no connection with other variables of the same name that may exist in the main program or in other procedures. Look at the program in listing 2.3.

Listing 2.3. *Demonstrating Local Variables*

```
VALUE = 1
PRINT "Before calling SubProg, VALUE = ";VALUE
CALL SubProg
PRINT "After returning from SubProg, VALUE = ";VALUE
END

SUB SubProg
     PRINT "Within SubProg, VALUE = ";VALUE
END SUB
```

The output of this program is

```
Before calling SubProg, VALUE = 1
Within SubProg, VALUE = 0
After returning from SubProg, VALUE = 1
```

The variable VALUE defined in SubProg is local to that procedure. This is in contrast to the variable VALUE defined in the main program, which is a global variable. A global variable is defined throughout the main program at the module level, that is, outside any procedures.

All local variables are *automatic* by default, meaning that they are initialized to 0 (for numeric variables) or to the null string (for string variables) each time the procedure is called. The value of an automatic local variable is not "remembered" between calls to the procedure. A static local variable, on the other hand, keeps its value between calls to the procedure. Including the STATIC keyword on the first line of the procedure definition makes all of the procedure's variables STATIC. You can make some of a procedure's variables static while leaving the others automatic by listing the variables in a STATIC statement within the body of the procedure. Listing 2.4 shows an example of this.

Listing 2.4. *Demonstrating Automatic and Static Local Variables*

```
FOR I = 1 to 5
     CALL SUB1
     CALL SUB2
     CALL SUB3
NEXT I
```

Listing 2.4 continues

Listing 2.4 continued

```
SUB SUB1
    I = I + 1
    J = J + 1
    PRINT "SUB1: ";I,J
END SUB


SUB SUB2
    STATIC I
    I = I + 1
    J = J + 1
    PRINT "SUB2: ";I,J
END SUB


SUB SUB3 STATIC
    I = I + 1
    J = J + 1
    PRINT "SUB3: ";I,J
END SUB
```

The output of this program is

```
SUB1:  1       1
SUB2:  1       1
SUB3:  1       1
SUB1:  1       1
SUB2:  2       1
SUB3:  2       2
SUB1:  1       1
SUB2:  3       1
SUB3:  3       3
SUB1:  1       1
SUB2:  4       1
SUB3:  4       4
SUB1:  1       1
SUB2:  5       1
SUB3:  5       5
```

Note how SUB3 "remembers" the value of both I and J between calls, SUB2 remembers I but not J, and SUB1 remembers neither.

To make an array static, list it in a STATIC statement with an empty set of parentheses (and an AS *type* specification if the array is not of the default data type). The array must be dimensioned after the STATIC statement but before being used. For example:

```
SUB CalcArray
    STATIC Array() AS DOUBLE
    DIM ARRAY(10,10) AS DOUBLE
    .
    .
    .
END SUB
```

I will have more to say about global and local variables later in the chapter.

Statements in Procedures

With a few exceptions, all valid BASIC statements and expressions are allowed within a procedure definition. This includes CALLs to other procedures (including itself—see ''Recursion'' later in this chapter). The exceptions are

❏ definitions of other procedures: DEF FN ... END DEF, FUNCTION ... END FUNCTION, or SUB ... END SUB

❏ COMMON

❏ DECLARE

❏ DIM SHARED

❏ OPTION BASE

❏ TYPE ... END TYPE

There is no limit on the number of statements in a procedure, although good programming practice encourages relatively short procedures. If you have a complex function to program, break it up into several small procedures.

Returning a Value from a Function

A function returns a value by assigning the value to the function name. For example,

```
FUNCTION Larger(X, Y)

    IF X > Y THEN
        Larger = X
```

```
    ELSE
        Larger = Y
    END IF

END FUNCTION
```

If the function does not assign a value to the function name, the function will return either 0 or a null string, depending on its data type.

Exiting a Procedure

Procedure execution terminates and control passes back to the calling program when the END SUB or END FUNCTION statement at the end of the procedure definition is reached. There can be only one END SUB or END FUNCTION statement in a procedure definition, and it must be at the end of the definition.

You can also exit from a procedure by executing an EXIT SUB or EXIT FUNCTION statement anywhere in the body of the procedure. For example,

```
FUNCTION Larger(X, Y)

    IF X = Y THEN
        PRINT "X and Y are equal"
        EXIT FUNCTION
    END IF

    IF X > Y THEN
        Larger = X
    ELSE
        Larger = Y
    END IF

END FUNCTION
```

There is no limit to the number of EXIT... statements in a procedure.

Declaring a Procedure

In addition to defining each procedure, you should also declare each procedure with the DECLARE statement. The syntax is

DECLARE SUB *subname* [*parameterlist*]

or

DECLARE FUNCTION *funcname* [*parameterlist*]

The *subname*, *funcname*, and *parameterlist* are the same as the name and parameter list in the first line of the procedure definition. Note the difference here between a definition and a declaration: A procedure definition contains the lines of code that are executed when the procedure is called. A procedure declaration is a single line that serves only to inform the compiler about the procedure's name and parameters.

One reason for declaring procedures is to resolve forward and external references. A *forward reference* occurs when a call to a procedure is located in the source code before the procedure definition. An *external reference* occurs when a program calls a procedure located in another file or in a library. Procedure declarations permit the compiler to deal with these situations. In effect, the DECLARE statement tells the compiler "Do not worry—this procedure is defined somewhere else."

The second reason for declaring procedures is to permit type checking of arguments. Type checking means that each time the procedure is called, the arguments in the CALL statement are checked against the *parameterlist* in the DECLARE statement to see if they are the right number and data type. This is a valuable programming aid, because passing the wrong number and/or type of arguments to a procedure can cause program bugs that are extremely hard to track down.

When you are working in the QuickBASIC editor, DECLARE statements are automatically generated for procedures that are defined in that file. The DECLARE statements are generated each time you save the file and are placed at the beginning of the file. For external procedures, you will have to insert the procedure declarations yourself.

When you use a stand-alone editor, all procedure declarations are your responsibility. The QB manual states that when you are using BC and LINK for stand-alone program development, there are some conditions under which a procedure need not be declared. Ignore this! While technically accurate, it is a bad idea to declare some procedures and not others. The list of DECLARE statements at the start of a program serves as documentation of the procedures that the program calls. Omitting one or two declarations, even if the compiler allows it, can be confusing.

Calling Procedures

Because functions return a value whereas subprograms do not, the method of calling them differs.

Calling a Function

A function is called by using its name (along with arguments, if any) anywhere that a variable name or an intrinsic QB function could be used. Here are some examples.

```
Array(12) = Func(A, B)
PRINT "The answer is ";Func(A, B)
X# = LOG(Func(A, B))
NUM = Func(A, B) / Func(C, D)
```

Calling a Subprogram

You can call a subprogram using the `CALL` statement followed by the subprogram's name and arguments, if any, in parentheses:

```
CALL SubProg1            (no arguments)
CALL SubProg2 (A, B)
```

You can also call a subprogram using its name alone on a line without the `CALL` keyword. If you use this method, omit the parentheses around the arguments.

```
SubProg1
SubProg2 A, B
```

Passing Arguments

When an argument is passed to a procedure, its data type must agree with the type of the corresponding parameter in the procedure's definition. The source of the argument, however, is completely flexible. Thus, a procedure that takes a string argument can be called with any of the following arguments:

- ❑ String variable
- ❑ String literal
- ❑ String constant
- ❑ An element of a string array
- ❑ String element of a user-defined record

The same flexibility is available for numeric arguments. The following are some examples. In these examples I include the procedure's declaration but not its definition.

Passing Variables and Literals

```
DECLARE SUB SubFunc (A as INTEGER, B as SINGLE, C$, D$)
.

.
City$ = "Chicago"
Z% = 5
CALL SubFunc(Z%, 3, City$, "Illinois")
.

.
```

Passing Array Elements and Constants

```
DECLARE SUB SubFunc (A AS INTEGER, B AS SINGLE, C$, D$)

CONST COUNTRY = "United States", RATE = 0.12
DIM Cities(100) AS STRING, CustNum(100) AS INTEGER
.

.
CALL SubFunc(CustNum(55), RATE, Cities(55), COUNTRY)
.

.
```

Passing Record Elements

```
DECLARE SUB SubFunc(A AS INTEGER, B AS STRING)

TYPE CustRecord
     Number AS INTEGER
     Address AS STRING
     City AS STRING
END TYPE

DIM Customer AS CustRecord
.

.
CALL SubFunc(Customer.Number, Customer.City)
.

.
```

Passing an Entire Array

```
DECLARE SUB SubFunc(A() AS INTEGER)
   .
   .
DIM X(100) AS INTEGER
   .
   .
CALL SubFunc(X())
   .
   .
```

Passing an Entire Record

```
DECLARE SUB SubFunc(A AS CustRecord)
TYPE CustRecord
    Number AS INTEGER
    Address AS STRING
    City AS STRING
END TYPE

DIM Customer AS CustRecord
   .
   .
CALL SubFunc(Customer)
   .
   .
```

Passing Arguments by Value or by Reference

QuickBASIC always passes an argument to a procedure in the form of an address. The corresponding parameter in the procedure is given the same address, so by reading the value of the parameter, the procedure can obtain the value of the argument.

There are two ways in which a QB program can pass arguments to a procedure. First, the program can make a copy of the argument and pass the address of the copy to the procedure. The procedure can obtain the value of the argument but, because it does not know the address of the original argument, cannot modify it. This is known as *passing by value*, although the term is not really correct, because the argument's value is not actually passed.

In the second method, the program can pass the address of the argument itself to the procedure. Knowing the argument's address, not only can the procedure read the argument's value, but also change it. This is known as *passing by reference*.

Literals, constants, and expressions are always passed by value. QuickBASIC's default is for variables to be passed by reference, but you can specify a variable argument to be passed by value. This should be done if you want to ensure that the procedure cannot modify the argument.

To make QB pass a variable argument by value instead of by reference, enclose the variable name in parentheses in the CALL statement. This causes QB to treat the variable as an expression, which is always passed by value. Thus, in the following call:

```
CALL SubProg(Amount, (Percentage))
```

Amount is passed by reference, and *Percentage* is passed by value.

Shared Variables

QuickBASIC's default arrangement, as discussed earlier, is for the local variables within each procedure to be distinct from both global variables (those defined within the module but outside any procedure) and from local variables defined in other procedures. This segregation of variables is, in fact, a major factor in the power of procedures.

At times, however, one or more of your procedures will need access to module-level variables without passing them as arguments. For example, a database program might keep its data in an array of records. The procedures in the program manipulate the data in various ways: sort, search, print, and so on. Clearly, most or all of the program's procedures need access to the main data array. This could be done by passing the array as an argument to each of the procedures that needs access to it. It is better, however, to use the SHARED statement to make the array accessible within those procedures. An array or any other module-level variable can be shared with selected procedures or with all procedures.

Sharing Variables with Selected Procedures

To make a module-level variable accessible within a specific procedure, include the variable name in a SHARED statement within the procedure definition. If the variable's data type was initially assigned with an AS clause, the SHARED statement must also include an AS clause. When you list an array in a SHARED statement, use the array name followed by empty parentheses. For example,

```
    .
    .
    .
DIM DataArray(1000) AS INTEGER
    .
    .
    .
SUB SubProc
SHARED DataArray() AS INTEGER
    .
    .
    .
END SUB
```

Sharing Variables with All Procedures in a Module

To make a module-level variable accessible within all procedures in the same module, include the SHARED keyword in a COMMON, DIM, or REDIM statement. These statements must be in the module-level code. For example,

```
DIM SHARED DataArray(1000)
COMMON SHARED Count%, Total, CityName$
REDIM SHARED NameArray$(100)
```

It is also possible to share variables among modules. I show how this is done in this chapter's section, "Modular Programming."

Recursive Procedures

QuickBASIC procedures can be *recursive*, meaning that they can call themselves (or call other procedures that then call the first procedure). Some types of data manipulation lend themselves to recursion. An example involves writing a program that takes a string as input and counts the frequency with which each of the lowercase letters appears in the string. One approach might be termed *linear*: Identify the letters one by one until you reach the end of the string. This is shown schematically in figure 2.2. This approach is perfectly valid.

The recursive approach would look at the problem in a different way. The letter count for any string is equal to

(the first character) + (the rest of the string)

Because (the rest of the string) is also a string, this formula can be applied to it as well. By repeatedly (recursively) applying the formula until (the rest of the string) is null, you can obtain the desired answer. This approach is schematized in figure 2.3; the code is shown in listing 2.5.

Fig. 2.2. *A nonrecursive algorithm for counting letters in a string.*

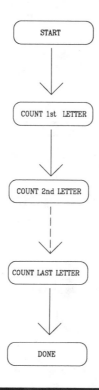

Exercise care when you use recursive programming. An ever-present danger is that you will get caught in an *infinite recursion*, in which the procedure calls itself over and over again until your computer crashes. Any recursive paradigm must have a foolproof "escape clause" that will terminate the recursion at a reasonable level under any circumstance.

Adjusting Stack Size

The *stack* is an area of memory used by QB for temporary storage. Procedures in particular make heavy use of the stack, because the stack is used to store arguments, automatic variables, and return addresses. Recursion really eats up stack space, because each new call to the procedure requires a new block of storage on the stack. Each time the program returns from a procedure, the stack space used by the procedure call is freed. The danger is that recursion will go deep enough to use up the entire stack, resulting in an Out of stack space run-time error.

Fig. 2.3. *A recursive paradigm for counting letters in a string.*

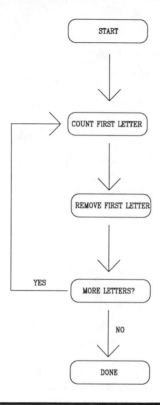

Listing 2.5. *Using a Recursive Programming Paradigm*

```
DECLARE SUB CountLetters (X$)

' Program to demonstrate recursion in a QuickBASIC procedure

' COUNT(I) will hold the count for the Ith letter

DIM COUNT(26) AS INTEGER

DO
    CLS
    LINE INPUT "Enter some text (a blank to exit): "; TEXT$
    IF TEXT$ = "" THEN END
```

```
            CALL CountLetters(TEXT$)
            PRINT
            PRINT "Lowercase letter count:"
            PRINT

            FOR I = 1 TO 26 STEP 2
                PRINT CHR$(I + 96); ": "; COUNT(I), CHR$(I + 97); ": ";
                    COUNT(I + 1)
            NEXT I

            PRINT
            PRINT "Press any key to continue ..."
            WHILE INKEY$ = "": WEND

LOOP

END


SUB CountLetters (X$)

SHARED COUNT() AS INTEGER

' See whether the first character of X$ is a lowercase letter.
' If so, make an index that is 1 for "a", 2 for "b", and so on.
' Then increment the indexed element of COUNT

IF ASC(X$) > 96 AND ASC(X$) < 123 THEN
    INDEX% = ASC(X$) - 96
    COUNT(INDEX%) = COUNT(INDEX%) + 1
END IF

' Remove the first letter from X$

X$ = RIGHT$(X$, LEN(X$) - 1)

' If there is anything left, call CountLetters again

IF LEN(X$) > 0 THEN
    CALL CountLetters(X$)
END IF

END SUB          ' end of CountLetters
```

Such an error can also occur in a program without recursion but with many deeply nested procedures that use lots of automatic variables.

QB's default stack size is approximately 1200 bytes, sufficient for most situations. You can increase the stack size with the CLEAR statement:

CLEAR ,,*bytes*

where *bytes* is the new stack size. In addition to setting the stack size, CLEAR also does the following:

- ❏ Clears all variables to 0 or the null string
- ❏ Closes all files
- ❏ Clears the stack
- ❏ Clears all COMMON variables

It is best, therefore, to use the CLEAR statement at the beginning of a program where the above actions will not have any harmful effects. You can estimate the amount of stack space that a recursive procedure will need by calling the FRE(-2) function, which returns the number of bytes of unused stack space. Here is the procedure to follow:

1. Within the body of the recursive procedure, convert the line that contains the recursive call into a comment so that the procedure will be called only once.

2. Call the FRE(-2) function just before the call to the procedure and again at the end of the procedure. The difference between the two values is the amount of stack space used by a single call to the procedure.

3. Determine the maximum number of times the procedure will be called and multiply this by the amount of stack space used by a single call. This is the total stack size required.

If you apply this procedure to the program in Listing 2.5, you will see that the procedure CountLetters uses 16 bytes of stack space with each call. If you further estimate that the maximum string length that will be entered is 100 characters (the procedure is called once per character), then the stack size needed is 16*100 or 1600 bytes. You should, therefore, execute CLEAR ,,1600 at the start of the program.

Keeping Recursion Shallow

After all this trouble, you can of course expect that some user will enter a string 200 characters long, crash the program, and then come to you to complain! To make recursive programs really bulletproof, insert a statement that checks the parameter(s) passed to the recursive procedure on the first call to ensure that recursion will not go too deep. Again using the letter counting program for an example, insert the following right after the SHARED statement in the procedure CountLetters:

```
IF LEN(X$) > 100 THEN
     PRINT "String too long"
     EXIT SUB
END IF
```

The *GOTO* Statement

A lot of the bad press that BASIC has received centers on the GOTO statement. It is quite true that early BASIC programs used GOTO with great abandon. Much of this use was unavoidable, however, because early implementations of BASIC lacked the tools for structured programming.

Why not use GOTO? When program execution is transferred to another section of code with GOTO (or one of its variants such as ON...GOTO), no record is kept of where execution came from. The path that execution takes through the program is unstructured, weaving here and there willy-nilly. The result of relying on GOTO for program flow control is all too often a mess, known for obvious reasons as "spaghetti code."

In a structured program, the flow of execution is controlled with loops (such as FOR...NEXT), selection statements (such as IF...THEN...ELSE), and procedure calls. During execution, the program always knows where it has been. Execution is essentially linear, top down, beginning to end, with any side trips (in such forms as procedure calls) always returning to the point of departure. Spaghetti is reserved for dinner.

If the truth be told, there are programming situations in which a GOTO statement can be used without harm. There are no programming tasks that cannot be solved *without* GOTO, however, so it seems best to avoid it altogether.

Guidelines for Structured Programming

To master structured programming, you must of course be familiar with its tools: functions, subprograms, and so on. Equally important, you must learn to "think structured" when working on a program. To a great extent, this is a skill that comes with practice and experience. Here are some tips that may help.

❑ "Think structured" from the very first moment that you start to plan a program. Conceive your program from the ground up as a collection of independent procedures.

❑ Make procedure-level code perform the real work of the program. The module-level code should serve primarily, if not solely, to direct program execution among the various procedures.

❑ Use local variables as much as possible. Do not use the SHARED attribute as a replacement for arguments. Use it only when necessary.

❑ Keep your procedures easy to understand and relatively short. Break a complex task into several small procedures rather than cramming it into one whopper.

❑ Use program comments ("remarks") liberally. The code you write today may be clear to you tomorrow, but next month it may seem like Greek.

❑ Do not use GOTO—never, no how, no way.

I strongly urge you to put in the effort necessary to become proficient at structured programming. Once you do, I predict that you will be amazed at how much easier complex programming tasks are.

Modular Programming

As defined at the beginning of this chapter, the modular programming technique keeps a program's code in two or more separate disk files. As you will see, *code* can mean either source code or object code.

The primary advantage of modular programming is that it enables you to use tested and debugged sections of code in more than one program without having to re-enter the program statements. As you become more experienced as a programmer, you will find that you have developed BASIC code for various tasks that are common to many programs: data entry, screen display, and so on. If you have been writing structured programs, most or all of this code will be in the form of QB procedures.

Modular Programming with QuickBASIC Modules

Recall that in QB, a *module* is a disk file that contains executable BASIC statements. Statements within a module, but outside any procedure, are referred to as *module-level code*. Statements within a procedure are referred to as *procedure-level code*.

The module that contains the first program statement to be executed is the *main module*. The main module may or may not contain procedure-level code, but it always contains at least some module-level code. This is because program execution cannot start inside a procedure.

The QB environment enables you to load one or more *secondary modules* in addition to the main module. This is done with the Load Files... command on the Files menu. (If you are starting a secondary module from scratch, use the Create File... command.) A secondary module may contain only procedure-level code, only module-level code, or a combination of both.

Secondary Modules That Contain Module-Level Code

A QB program can pass execution from the main module to module-level code in a secondary module with the CHAIN statement. CHAIN is, in effect, a GOTO statement that has a different module as its destination. CHAIN is a holdover from the days of interpreted BASIC and has no place in modern structured programming. The same statements made about GOTO earlier in this chapter also apply to CHAIN; do not use CHAIN—never, no how, no way.

Secondary Modules That Contain Only Procedure-Level Code

You treat modules differently when they contain only procedures. Procedures in a secondary module are accessed in the same way as procedures located in the main module. Structured programming, therefore, is not compromised. By keeping frequently used procedures in a separate procedures-only module, you can easily use them in all of your programs.

Two special considerations apply when you keep procedures in a separate module. The main module must contain DECLARE statements for these procedures, but the DECLARE statements automatically generated by QB are placed in the same module as the procedure—that is, in the secondary module. One solution is to use QB's editing facilities to cut the automatically generated DECLARE statement(s) from the secondary module and paste them into the main module. Another solution is to place the DECLARE statements in a separate file and then use the $INCLUDE metacommand to read them into the main module at compile time.

The second consideration involves data visibility. Variables defined in one module are not normally available in other modules. The SHARED keyword does not work, because it only shares variables within a module. To share one or more variables across modules, you must use the COMMON statement. The syntax of COMMON is

COMMON [SHARED][/*blockname*/] *variablelist*

A COMMON statement must appear at the module-level in each of the program modules that needs access to the variables.

SHARED   By including the SHARED keyword, the variables that have been declared COMMON are available to all of the procedures in the module that contains the COMMON statement. Without the SHARED keyword, the COMMON variables are available only to the module-level code.

/*blockname*/   Including a *blockname* in the COMMON statement puts the common variables in a ''named'' common block. Without *blockname*, the variables are in a ''blank'' common block. The *blockname* can be between 1 and 40 characters long. Using named blocks, common variables can be shared selectively. With unnamed blocks, there is no alternative but to share common variables *en masse*.

variablelist The variables that are to be shared between modules. Note that the variable names need not be identical in each module's COMMON statement. The only necessity is that the order and data type of the variables match.

Listings 2.6 and 2.7 show some examples of using these modules.

To separate a program into two modules, one containing the module-level code and one containing the procedures, follow these steps:

1. Save the entire program under its original name.

2. Delete all the module-level code (but not the DECLARE statements). Insert comments to the effect that this is a procedure-only module.

3. Insert COMMON SHARED statement(s) as needed.

4. Use Save As to save the module under a new name.

5. Select New Program to clear memory.

6. Use Open Program to load the original program.

Listing 2.6. *Using an Unnamed* COMMON *Block To Share Variables between Modules*

```
' main module, module-level code

COMMON X%, Y%

X% = 100
Y% = 200
.
END


=================================================================

' secondary module containing procedures

COMMON SHARED A%, B%
.
.
END


SUB Proc1

PRINT A%         ' output is 100, value of X% in main module

END SUB


SUB Proc2

PRINT B%         ' output is 200, value of Y% in main module

END SUB
```

Listing 2.7. *Using Named* COMMON *Blocks To Share Variables Selectively among Procedures*

```
' main module

COMMON /Block1/ A, B
COMMON /Block2/ C, D
 .
 .
 .
END


================================================================


' secondary module containing procedures

COMMON /Block1/ W, X
COMMON /Block2/ Y, Z
 .
 .
 .
END


SUB Proc1

SHARED W, X
 .
' in this procedure, the variables W and X have the values
' assigned to A and B in the main module
 .
END SUB


SUB Proc2

SHARED Y, Z
 .
' in this procedure, the variables Y and Z have the values
' assigned to C and D in the main module
 .
 .
END SUB
```

7. Press **F2** to access the SUBs... dialog box, then use the Delete command to delete all of the procedures, one at a time.

8. Return to the View window and add any needed COMMON statement(s) to the program.

9. Save the program, which now consists only of module-level code.

The .MAK File

When you save a multiple-module program (with the Save All command), QB automatically creates a special file that contains the names of all of the program's modules. This file has the name of the program's main module with the extension .MAK. The .MAK file is simply a text file listing the names of the program's modules, with the main module listed first.

When you load the main module of the program (using Open Program... on the Files menu), QB uses the .MAK file to locate and load the secondary modules. If the .MAK file is not available, use the Load File command to load each secondary module. If you delete a module from a multiple-module program, the .MAK file is updated when you next save the program.

Creating an .EXE File

When you are working with multiple modules in the QB environment, the steps for creating an executable (.EXE) file are no different than if you were working with a single module. When the .EXE file is created, QB includes the code for all of the procedures contained in the currently loaded modules, not just those procedures used by the program. This results in a larger .EXE file. If there are only a few small, unused procedures, the size difference will probably be negligible. Otherwise, you should delete the unused procedures before you create the .EXE file. Do *not* save the module from which you deleted the procedures, or they will be gone forever! You want to retain the complete version of the module on disk.

Modular Programming with Libraries

A library is like a secondary module in that it contains a portion of your program's code separate from the main module. Unlike a module, however, the code in a library has already been compiled. It is *object code*, stored in a special library format. Libraries can contain only procedures.

QB uses two types of libraries: quick libraries for use in the QB environment, and stand-alone libraries for use with the command-line compiler and linker.

Quick Libraries

A *quick library* is a collection of procedure in object code format that can be loaded into QB. Once loaded, the quick library procedures can be called by any program running in the QB environment.

Loading a Quick Library

A quick library must be loaded into QB when you start QB from the DOS command prompt—you cannot load a quick library once QB has started, and you cannot load more than one quick library at a time. To start QB and load a quick library, enter

```
QB /L libraryname
```

at the DOS prompt. The *libraryname* can be the name of a quick library that you have created, or QB.QLB, a quick library supplied with QB. QB.QLB contains support for the CALL INTERRUPT and CALL ABSOLUTE statements. If QB is started with /L but no library name, QB.QLB is loaded.

Creating a Quick Library

To create a new quick library, select the Make Library... command from the Run menu. A dialog box opens, as shown in figure 2.4. You must specify the library name (QB will supply the .QLB extension if you do not specify one) and whether debug code is to be included in the library. Including debug code results in a larger library with slower-executing procedures. The error-detecting capabilities of this code are minimal. Procedures should be thoroughly debugged before including them in a library, so you will rarely if ever use the debug code option.

When a new quick library is created, it includes everything that is currently loaded into QB—and I mean *everything*! All of the procedures in all of the modules are compiled and put in the quick library, as is all of the module-level code. If a quick library is loaded, its contents go into the new quick library as well.

What is this about module-level code going into the new quick library? Didn't I say above that libraries can contain only procedures? Strictly speaking, this is not true. Module-level code is included when a quick

Fig. 2.4. *The* Make Library... *dialog box.*

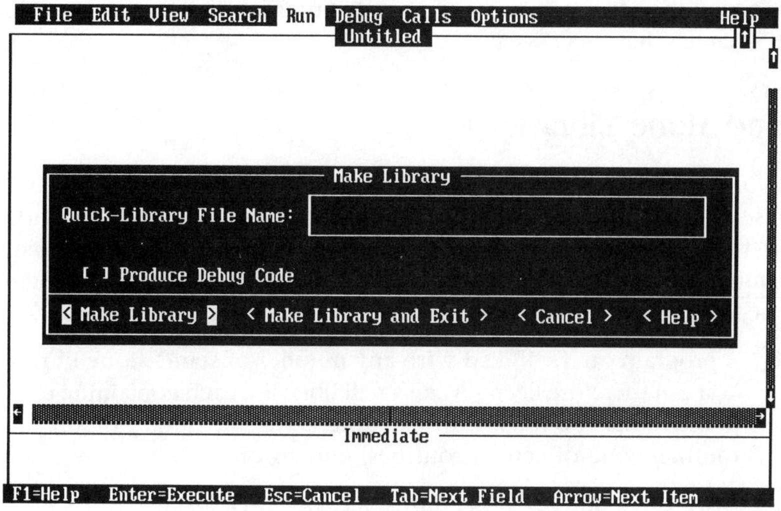

```
 File  Edit  View  Search  Run Debug  Calls  Options                    Help
                              Untitled

           ┌──────────────────── Make Library ────────────────────┐
           │ Quick-Library File Name:  ┌──────────────────────────┐│
           │                           └──────────────────────────┘│
           │    [ ] Produce Debug Code                              │
           │◄ Make Library ►   < Make Library and Exit >   < Cancel >   < Help >│
           └────────────────────────────────────────────────────────┘


                              ── Immediate ──

 F1=Help   Enter=Execute   Esc=Cancel   Tab=Next Field   Arrow=Next Item
```

library is created. The catch, however, is that a program cannot access module-level code in a quick library, so it might as well not be there.

It is wise to do some housecleaning before you create a quick library. First, delete all module-level code from the QB environment. Next, delete any procedures that you do not want in the quick library. Failure to do so will result in a quick library file that is larger than necessary.

Limitations of Quick Libraries

Because you can load only one quick library at a time, each one has to be completely self-contained, consisting of all of the procedures needed by your program. It is also difficult to determine exactly which procedures are in a particular quick library. There is no way to do so from within the QB environment. You must use the utility program QLBDUMP.BAS, supplied with QB, to check a quick library's contents.

If you need to delete a procedure from a quick library, you cannot do so directly. You must load the associated module(s) into QB, delete the procedure's source code, then create a new quick library. For this reason, modifying a procedure in a quick library is very inconvenient.

Finally, when you create a .EXE file and a quick library is loaded, code for all of the library's procedures is included in the .EXE file even if few or none of the procedures are used by the program. This means your .EXE file is larger than necessary.

Stand-Alone Libraries

Libraries can be used in stand-alone program development as well. These libraries, which have the .LIB extension, are like quick libraries in that they contain procedures in compiled, object-code form that is combined with your program when the executable file is created. Stand-alone libraries are, however, significantly more flexible than quick libraries.

❏ A program can be linked with any number of stand-alone libraries. You can therefore keep several small libraries, each containing related procedures. You might, for example, have one library of keyboard routines, one of screen routines, and so on.

❏ Only those library procedures actually used by the program are included in the executable file.

❏ The "librarian" (LIB.EXE), provided with QB, makes the task of maintaining libraries a snap.

When QB creates a quick library, a stand-alone library containing the same procedures is automatically created as well. It has the same name as the quick library, with a .LIB extension. Using a stand-alone library is as simple as linking it with the object code created when your program was compiled. Additional information on creating and maintaining libraries outside the QB environment is given in Appendix A.

Mixed-Language Programming

Mixed-language programming is just what it sounds like—developing a program using two or more languages. You might wonder how this is possible—are not different languages incompatible with each other? Well, yes and no.

At the source-code level, different languages are indeed incompatible. If you include lines of C or Pascal code in a BASIC program, the compiler will not understand them and will report an error. The same is true if you include a few lines of BASIC code in a C or Pascal program.

Once the source code has been compiled to object code, however, things are different. No matter what the language of the original source code, any compiler for the PC must produce object code that can be executed by the PC's processor. Upon compilation, differences between programming languages disappear and, for all practical purposes, all object code is equivalent. There are some minor differences, but they are easily dealt with, as you will see momentarily. At link time, therefore, object code from different languages can be combined to create a single executable program.

Reasons for Mixed-Language Programming

There are several reasons to use mixed-language programming.

❏ You may already have complicated routines written in another language. Rather than recode these routines in BASIC, you can save a lot of time by simply linking the existing object code into your BASIC program.

❏ Certain portions of your program may benefit from maximum possible execution speed. While assembly language is more difficult to use than BASIC and other high-level languages, it has a definite speed advantage.

❏ Specific programming tasks may be easier to accomplish in another language. The C language, for example, with its flexible use of pointers, simplifies certain operations that are difficult to code in BASIC.

Interfacing Your BASIC Program with a Non-BASIC Procedure

There are two steps to take so that your QB program can use a procedure written in another language.

1. Use the DECLARE statement to define the protocol used by your QB program to pass parameters to the procedure.

2. Use a CALL or CALLS statement to invoke the procedure.

I will discuss these in turn.

Declaring Non-BASIC Procedures

Using the DECLARE statement for a non-BASIC procedure is slightly more involved than using it for a BASIC procedure. The syntax for declaring a non-BASIC procedure is

> DECLARE FUNCTION *procname* [CDECL][ALIAS *"aliasname"*]
> [*parameterlist*]

or

> DECLARE SUB *procname* [CDECL][ALIAS *"aliasname"*]
> [*parameterlist*]

FUNCTION declares the external procedure to be a function, which returns a value, whereas SUB declares it to be a subprogram, which does not return a value. Otherwise, the syntax for declaring non-BASIC functions and subroutines is identical.

procname	The name that the BASIC program will use in a CALL or CALLS statement to invoke the external procedure. The *procname* can be up to 40 characters long. If *procname* is a function, a type-declaration suffix character can be used to specify the data type of the value returned by the function.
CDECL	Indicates that the declared procedure uses the C language convention for passing parameters, which is different from the BASIC convention. The calling program and the called procedure must agree on the order in which parameters are passed. BASIC programs pass—and BASIC procedures expect—parameters in the same order as listed in the procedure call. Consider the following CALL in a BASIC program:

CALL MonthlyPayment (a, b, c, d)

The BASIC program passes the parameters in left-to-right order so that after the call parameter d is the top parameter on the stack, parameter c is right below it (that is, at the next lower memory address), and so on. If *MonthlyPayment* is a BASIC procedure, it expects to find the parameters in this order, and everything is fine.

The C language, on the other hand, passes parameters in right-to-left order, so C procedures expect to find them on the stack in that order. If MonthlyPayment is a C procedure and is passed parameters in BASIC order, it may well tell you that the payments on that new Ferrari are only $12 a month, leading to an unwise purchase! By including the CDECL keyword in a procedure definition, you instruct the program to pass parameters in the right-to-left order expected by C procedures.

Pascal and Fortran procedures accept arguments in the same order as BASIC, so no special treatment is necessary. In procedures written in assembly language, the order in which parameters are received is explicitly coded in the procedure—there is no default order.

ALIAS

The ALIAS keyword signals that the external function exists (as an object file or in a library) under the name *aliasname* and not under *procname*. ALIAS is used when an external procedure has a name that conflicts with a BASIC keyword or with the name of a BASIC procedure already in your program. For example, you may have a BASIC procedure named PrintData and a Pascal procedure also named PrintData. Use the ALIAS keyword in the declaration of the Pascal procedure as follows:

DECLARE SUB TypeData ALIAS "PrintData" ...

You can then use CALL PrintData to invoke the BASIC procedure and CALL TypeData to invoke the Pascal procedure.

parameterlist

A list of one or more parameters to be passed to the procedure. If more than one parameter is listed, use commas to separate them. Each parameter entry has the following syntax:

[BYVAL | SEG] *variable* [AS TYPE]

Here *variable* and AS TYPE are used exactly as described earlier in this chapter for declarations of BASIC procedures. BYVAL specifies that the indicated parameter is to be passed by value rather than by reference. SEG specifies that the parameter is to be passed by far reference. This means that the procedure is passed the parameter's segment as well as its offset. The called procedure must make proper use of the far reference. SEG cannot, obviously, be used with BYVAL. Note that the BYVAL keyword results in true passing by value (the argument's value is placed on the stack), not the pseudo "passing by value" that results when an argument is enclosed in its own set of parentheses.

Calling a Non-BASIC Procedure

Calling non-BASIC procedures is similar to calling BASIC procedures.

Calling a Non-BASIC Function

A non-BASIC function—that is, a procedure that returns a value—is called in the same manner as a BASIC function. Simply use the procedure's name anywhere that a BASIC variable or intrinsic function could be used.

Calling a Non-BASIC Subprogram

A non-BASIC subprogram can also be called in the same manner as a BASIC subprogram, by using CALL with the argument list in parentheses or using the subprogram's name by itself with no parentheses around the argument list:

```
CALL CProcedure (X, Y)
CProcedure X, Y
```

A third way to call a non-BASIC subprogram is with the CALLS statement. CALLS works the same way as CALL but passes all arguments by far reference. In other words, using CALLS is the same as using CALL with the SEG keyword applied to each argument.

```
CALL CProcedure (SEG X, SEG Y)
```

is the same as

```
CALLS CProcedure (X, Y)
```

Appendix A demonstrates the step-by-step procedures to use an assembly language procedure in a QB program.

Summary

This chapter explored the concepts of structured and modular programming and explained the importance of applying these concepts to your programming projects. The chapter also looked at the tools available in QB for writing structured and modular programs. It is difficult to over-emphasize the importance of this material, and I encourage you to master these programming techniques. If you do, you will be quickly and amply rewarded with savings in time and effort, particularly if you tackle large, complex programming projects.

The chapter have also looked at the techniques for mixed-language programming, that is, using routines written in other languages in your QB programs. You may never need these techniques, but you should be aware of the possibility of mixed-language programming.

Debugging Techniques

It is a rare program that runs properly the first time it is tried. Even the most experienced programmers encounter numerous bugs and errors in their programs during the development cycle. Inexperienced programmers, as you might expect, face even more. Bugs and errors are pretty much unavoidable, so you should not be discouraged when they crop up in your programs. The important lesson you can learn from such problems is how to deal with them efficiently.

Debugging a program is rarely, if ever, fun. It can be real torture, however, if you do not know how to go about it. Fortunately, QuickBASIC provides some powerful tools for finding and correcting program bugs. These tools are the subject of this chapter, which does the following:

❏ Explains the differences and relationship between *bugs* and *errors*

❏ Describes how to use the debugging facilities built into the QB environment

❏ Introduces the use of Microsoft's CodeView stand-alone debugger with QB programs

Most of the debugging tools are accessed via QB's Debug menu. Figure 3.1 shows the Debug menu pulled down over the display of a program you will see later when I demonstrate some debugging techniques.

Fig. 3.1. QuickBASIC's debugging tools are accessed via the Debug menu.

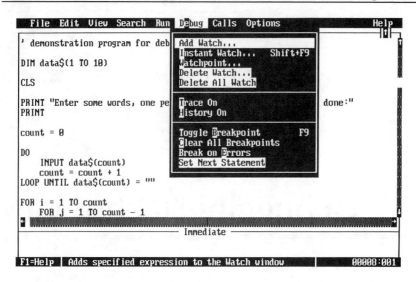

First, however, you need to understand the difference and relationship between *errors* and *bugs*.

Bugs and Errors, Errors and Bugs

You will notice that I have been using two different terms, *bugs* and *errors*, to describe problems with program execution. Whereas the two terms are related, they refer to different types of problems, and you should be aware of the difference.

❏ An *error* is a mistake in the program code or some aspect of the computer hardware that interferes with the program execution.

❏ A *bug* is a mistake in the program logic that causes the program to function incorrectly.

This distinction may not seem clear to you now. For the moment, this analogy may help. When you are driving a car, a flat tire is an error, whereas a wrong turn is a bug. Take a look at some examples.

Examples of errors are when a program does the following:

❏ Sends output to the printer when the printer is turned off or not connected

❏ Tries to divide by zero

❏ Tries to read data from a floppy disk when the drive door is open

❏ Attempts to set a video mode not supported by the installed hardware

The effect that an error has on the execution of your program depends on the specific error and the level of *error- handling code* in the program. Techniques for dealing with errors are covered in detail in Chapter 4.

In contrast, common program bugs occur when your program does the following:

❏ Uses the wrong variable in a calculation

❏ Increments a counter variable at the wrong point in a loop

❏ Sends execution to the wrong procedure

Some, but not all, bugs cause errors. Conversely, some, but not all, errors are caused by bugs. Consider a mistake in a program's source code that results in the wrong variable being used as the divisor in a calculation. If this variable is never 0, no error occurs, but the program gives incorrect results. This is a bug that does not cause an error. If the variable does become 0, however, a `Division by zero` error occurs.

In the remainder of this chapter I use the word *error* in its general sense: typographical error, logical error, and so on. When I refer specifically to an error that occurs during program execution, I use the phrase *run-time error*.

QuickBASIC's Built-In Debugging

Almost without exception, bugs are caused for one of the following two reasons (alone or in combination):

1. Variables are used incorrectly. Examples of this include using the wrong variable in an expression, assigning the wrong value to a variable, and not initializing a variable.

2. Program branching is performed incorrectly. Examples include calling the wrong procedure or executing a loop an incorrect number of times.

These two types of errors are not completely separate, of course—a variable error can be caused by an error in program branching and vice versa. The debugging tools in QB are designed so that you can track down both types of errors. Using the debugging tools, you can do the following:

❑ Examine the value of variables during program execution

❑ Modify variables during a run and see how the new values affect program execution

❑ Trace the sequence in which program lines and procedure calls are executed

❑ Alter the sequence of program execution

In this section, I first explain some debugging terms and concepts; then I describe the QB menu selections that are used in debugging (most, but not all, of these are on the Debug menu). Next I take you through a debugging session, using these tools to debug an actual program.

Before getting to the details of QB's debugging facilities, I want to emphasize the importance of program comments during debugging. When a section of code contains a bug, it is a lot easier to find and correct the bug if you understand what the code is doing and how it is doing it. Shortly after writing a program, the details may be fresh in your memory, but a month later they may start to fade. Don't make your comments too terse, or they will not be much help. By inserting clear and detailed comments in your code as you write it, you'll save a lot of headaches later when you are debugging or revising the program.

Keeping an Eye on Variables

As mentioned earlier, errors in variable use are a common cause of bugs. QB provides several ways for you to monitor the values of variables during program execution. These tools are found in the first part of the Debug menu.

Add Watch...

The Add Watch... command is used to continuously display the value of variables as the program executes. When you select this command, QB opens the dialog box shown in figure 3.2. Enter the name of the variable whose value you want to track. QB opens a *Watch window* at the top of the screen that lists the variables being watched and, during program execution, their values at any moment. Figure 3.2 also shows a Watch window; in this case a single variable, count, is being watched.

Fig. 3.2. *QuickBASIC's* Add Watch *dialog box.*

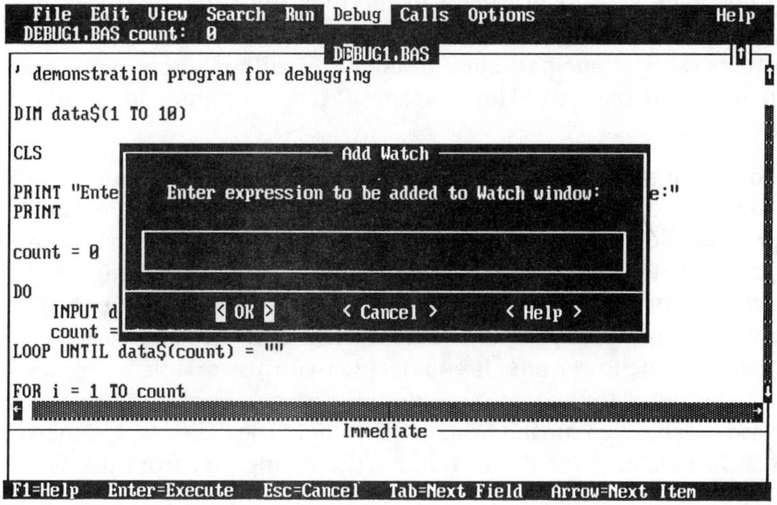

```
 File  Edit  View  Search  Run  Debug  Calls  Options          Help
 DEBUG1.BAS count:  0
──────────────────────────── DEBUG1.BAS ─────────────────────────────
' demonstration program for debugging

DIM data$(1 TO 10)

CLS                ┌──────────── Add Watch ────────────┐
                   │                                   │
PRINT "Ente        │ Enter expression to be added to Watch window:   e:"
PRINT              │                                   │
                   │ ┌───────────────────────────────┐ │
count = 0          │ │                               │ │
                   │ └───────────────────────────────┘ │
DO                 │                                   │
    INPUT d        │   ◄ OK ►      < Cancel >      < Help > │
    count =        │                                   │
LOOP UNTIL data$(count) = ""

FOR i = 1 TO count
──────────────────────────── Immediate ──────────────────────────────

 F1=Help   Enter=Execute   Esc=Cancel   Tab=Next Field   Arrow=Next Item
```

You can enter single variables or mathematical expressions involving two or more variables in the Watch window. You can also enter a logical expression; the Watch window displays whether the expression is true or false as the program executes. A display of 0 indicates false, whereas -1 indicates true.

Depending on the organization of your program, some variables may not be "watchable" during certain phases of program execution. The Watch window displays Not watchable next to the variable name rather than a value. A variable is available to the Watch window only while program execution is in that part of the program code from which the variable was added to the Watch window. Thus, a variable that was added to the Watch window before execution began or while execution was paused in module-level code is not watchable while execution is in procedure-level code. Likewise, a variable added to the Watch window while execution was paused in procedure-level code is not watchable while execution is in module-level code. Use of SHARED does not affect the "watchability" of variables.

Instant Watch...

Sometimes you do not need to monitor the value of a variable or expression constantly during program execution, but you would like to know its value at one particular moment (usually when program execution has been paused). The Instant Watch... command is used for this purpose.

To look at the value of a variable, put the QB editor's cursor on or just to the right of the variable's name in the source code. To evaluate an expression, select (that is, highlight) the expression using the mouse or the cursor keys. Next, select Instant Watch... from the Debug menu (or press the shortcut key, Shift-F9). A dialog box opens (see fig. 3.3) with the variable or expression in the upper text box, and the current value displayed in the lower box. If you decide that this variable or expression should be added to the Watch window for continuous monitoring, select the Add Watch... command from the bottom of the dialog box. Otherwise, select Cancel, or press Esc to remove the dialog box from the screen.

Fig. 3.3. *The logical expression* data$(count) = " " *has been selected for* Instant Watch. *This expression is true when* data$(count) *is equal to a null (empty) string.*

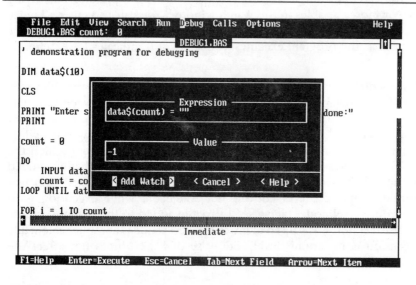

Delete Watch... and *Delete All Watch*

Delete Watch... removes a single item from the Watch window. When you select this command, a dialog box appears in which you select the item to delete. Delete All Watch deletes all items from the Watch window and closes the window.

Following and Controlling Program Execution

The other major cause of program bugs is errors in program branching or, in other words, errors in the path of program execution. It is a rare program that executes all of its statements in order from beginning to end. Loops, conditional statements, and procedure calls all offer opportunities for mistakes in program logic or source code to send execution where it does not belong. QB helps you examine and modify the course of program execution.

Trace On

QB's Trace feature provides an animated, slow-motion display of the path of program execution. When Trace On is active, the program is executed in slow motion, with program code being executed at a rate of several lines per second. As the program executes, QB displays the program's source code on the screen and moves a highlight bar from statement to statement as they are executed. If the program is writing to the screen, QB switches back and forth between the QB screen and the program output screen.

Trace On can be used with one or more Watch expressions. This enables you to observe changes in variable values as program execution proceeds.

Trace On is a toggle. When it is active, a bullet is displayed next to the command on the Debug menu. When a program is executed while Trace On is active, QB keeps a record of the last 20 statements executed. When program execution is paused, you can then use History Back and History Forward to review these statements. The History commands are discussed in greater detail in the next section.

The Trace On toggle can also be changed under program control. The TRON statement in a program toggles it on, whereas TROFF toggles it off.

Program execution with Trace On active is a bit too fast for a close examination of the execution path during actual execution. You can, however, pause the program just after execution has passed the program location where you suspect a problem might exist. Once the program is paused, use History Back and History Forward for a close look at the last 20 statements executed. The History Back and History Forward commands are not located on any menu but are activated with Shift-F8 and Shift-F10, respectively.

If you know in advance where you want to pause execution, you can set a *breakpoint*, discussed in detail later in this chapter. You can pause execution at any time by pressing Ctrl-Break. Selecting Continue from the Run menu (or pressing the corresponding shortcut key F5) restarts execution where it left off.

While execution is paused, you can use the Immediate window to change the value of variables. Press F6 until the Immediate window is active, then type in an assignment statement just as you would enter it in the program's source code:

```
j = 10
data(12) = 0
firstname$ = "John"
y = x/10
```

As soon as you press Enter, the new value takes effect. If the variable is being displayed in the Watch window, the change is displayed there as well. When you continue program execution, the new value is used.

The History Commands

Like Trace On, History On is a toggle. When active, as indicated by a bullet appearing next to the command on the debug menu, QB keeps a record of the last 20 program lines executed. As mentioned in the last section, History On is automatically activated whenever Trace On is active (although the menu bullet does not appear). Activating History On separately keeps a record of executed statements while slowing program execution only slightly.

The recorded program statements can be reviewed when program execution has terminated or whenever execution has been paused. History Back steps backward through the recorded statements, one at a time, moving the editing cursor from statement to statement. History Forward steps forward through the recorded statements. You must step back using History Back before you can use History Forward.

Because History On remembers only the last 20 program statements, to use it you must pause program execution at a location that is rather close to the region of source code you are interested in. When program execution is slowed by using Trace On, it might be possible to pause the program at the right spot with Ctrl-Break. At normal execution speed, however, this is next to impossible. You will need to use other methods of pausing program execution. These are discussed next.

Pausing Program Execution

QB has several debugging tools that give you precise control over pausing program execution. You can pause execution based on the following:

❏ A specific location in the source code

❏ The value of a variable

❏ The occurrence of an error condition

I cover each of these in turn, then discuss the debugging techniques that can be used while program execution is paused.

Breakpoints

A *breakpoint* is a specific location in a program where execution pauses. A program can have an essentially unlimited number of breakpoints. To set a breakpoint, move the cursor to the source code line where you want execution to pause, then select Toggle Breakpoint from the Debug menu or press the corresponding shortcut key, F9. Program lines where breakpoints are set are displayed in reverse video.

When execution reaches a breakpoint line, the program pauses with the QB screen displayed and the cursor on the breakpoint line. The line containing the breakpoint is not executed.

If the cursor is on a line that already has a breakpoint set, selecting Toggle Breakpoint or pressing F9 clears the breakpoint. To clear all breakpoints from a program, select Clear All Breakpoints from the Debug menu.

Watchpoints

A *watchpoint* is a BASIC expression that is monitored by QB during program execution. Program execution pauses when the expression becomes true. Watchpoints pause program execution based on the value of one or more variables.

To enter a watchpoint, select `Watchpoint...` from the Debug menu. A dialog box appears, as shown in figure 3.4.

***Fig. 3.4.** The* Watchpoint... *dialog box.*

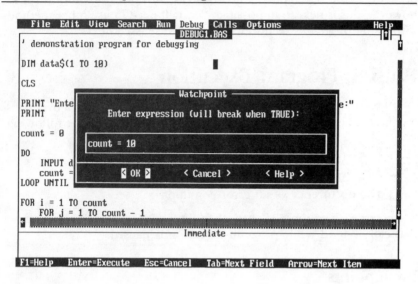

Enter the desired expression, then select `OK` to activate the watchpoint. Any valid QB expression can be entered. For example:

```
X = 10
DATA(20) > j + k
sin(x) + log (y) > 0.5
len(K$)
```

If, as in the last example in this list, a variable or expression is entered without a relational operator, QB assumes <> 0. Thus, execution pauses when len(k$) becomes nonzero.

Watchpoints are displayed in the Watch window followed by a colon and the current logical evaluation of the expression, <FALSE> or <TRUE>. This is shown in figure 3.5. <FALSE> is displayed in normal video, whereas <TRUE> is displayed in high-intensity video. If you have several watchpoints in the Watch window, the high-intensity display of <TRUE> helps you quickly determine which watchpoint caused execution to pause.

Fig. 3.5. A watchpoint, currently FALSE, displayed in the Watch window.

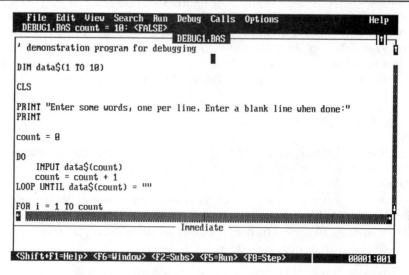

```
   File  Edit  View  Search  Run  Debug  Calls  Options            Help
   DEBUG1.BAS count = 10: <FALSE>
┌────────────────────────────── DEBUG1.BAS ──────────────────────────────┐
│ ' demonstration program for debugging         ▮                         │
│                                                                         │
│ DIM data$(1 TO 10)                                                      │
│                                                                         │
│ CLS                                                                     │
│                                                                         │
│ PRINT "Enter some words, one per line. Enter a blank line when done:"   │
│ PRINT                                                                   │
│                                                                         │
│ count = 0                                                               │
│                                                                         │
│ DO                                                                      │
│     INPUT data$(count)                                                  │
│     count = count + 1                                                   │
│ LOOP UNTIL data$(count) = ""                                            │
│                                                                         │
│ FOR i = 1 TO count                                                      │
│                                                ─────── Immediate ───────│
└─────────────────────────────────────────────────────────────────────────┘
 <Shift+F1=Help> <F6=Window> <F2=Subs> <F5=Run> <F8=Step>        00001:001
```

Watchpoint expressions are subject to the same "watchability" limitations discussed in the section on the Watch window earlier in this chapter. QB can evaluate a watchpoint expression as TRUE or FALSE only when program execution is in the section of code where the watchpoint was added. If, for example, you add a watchpoint while program execution is paused in a procedure, that watchpoint can be evaluated only while execution is in that procedure. While execution is in module-level code or in other procedures, Not Watchable will be displayed in the Watch window next to the expression. Use of SHARED does not affect watchability.

QB evaluates each watchpoint before the execution of each statement. When a watchpoint becomes true, execution pauses with the next statement highlighted and the cursor positioned on the first character of that statement. The "next statement" is the one immediately following the statement that caused the watchpoint to become TRUE.

Remember that all QB variables have the value of 0 (for numeric variables) or the null string (for string variables) until you explicitly assign values to them. Certain watchpoints, therefore, evaluate as TRUE from the beginning of program execution to the point where a value is assigned to one or more variables. For example, the watchpoint i = j + k is TRUE when the program first starts and all three variables are zero and possibly again during program execution after values have been assigned to the variables.

At times, however, you need to find the place in your program where a variable becomes zero (when you are looking for the cause of a divide-by-zero error, for example). To do this, set a watchpoint that stops the program when the variable becomes *nonzero*. If the program never pauses, you know the problem is simply that the variable is never assigned a nonzero value. If the program does pause, you can delete the original watchpoint and enter one that is TRUE when the variable becomes zero.

Break on Errors

Break on Errors is a toggle that applies only when debugging programs that use error handling (that is, contain one or more ON ERROR *label* statements). ON ERROR *label* causes program execution to branch to the statement identified by *label* when a run-time error occurs. When Break on Errors is enabled, an implicit breakpoint is set at the beginning of the error-handling routine. The breakpoint is set immediately after the *label* specified in the most recent ON ERROR statement.

Enabling Break on Errors also enables History On. When a run-time error occurs, program execution pauses, and you can use History Back to find the program statement that caused the error.

Execute to Cursor

The Execute to Cursor command is not on any menu but is activated by pressing F7. This command can be a bit confusing, because the QB manual does not correctly describe the way it works. The Execute to Cursor command is the equivalent of executing the following two commands:

1. Setting a breakpoint on the line containing the cursor (by pressing F9 or selecting Toggle Breakpoint from the Debug menu).

2. Continuing program execution (pressing F5 or selecting Continue from the Run menu).

Execute to Cursor works as described in the QB manual only if program execution is starting at the beginning (that is, execution has not been paused) and if there are no breakpoints or watchpoints that stop execution before it reaches the line containing the cursor. The usual use for Execute to Cursor is when you know the section of code that is causing a problem and want to execute the program from the beginning to a point just before the suspect code. In this case, the conditions mentioned in this paragraph are usually met.

While Your Program Is Paused

In itself, pausing program execution is of limited usefulness. It is the debugging procedures you can perform *while* the program is paused that are truly useful. While a program is paused, you can do the following:

❏ Delete and/or add breakpoints, watchpoints, and watch expressions

❏ If History is enabled, use History Back and History Forward to review the last 20 statements executed before the pause

❏ Examine the value of variables. This can be done using Instant Watch or the Immediate window.

❏ Change the value of variables by typing assignment statements in the Immediate window

❏ Edit the program

After you have used one or more of these techniques with your paused program, you will usually want to continue program execution. The various QB options for doing this are discussed next.

Continuing Execution After a Pause

There are several ways to continue program execution after a pause. Some of these techniques can also be used when the program is not paused (that is, from the beginning of execution), but they are most commonly used after execution is paused by a breakpoint, watchpoint, or similar technique.

Continue

The Continue command, located on the Run menu, causes a paused program to resume execution where it left off. The shortcut key for Continue is F5. If the program is not paused, execution starts at the beginning. If, during the pause, you make changes that prevent execution from continuing (for example, you delete the statement that would have been the next to execute), QB offers you the option of ignoring the change and continuing, or incorporating the change and starting the program from the beginning.

Set Next Statement

The Set Next Statement command specifies where program execution begins after a pause. It is used to skip over or reexecute a section of code. To use this command, place the cursor on the statement to be executed next and select Set Next Statement. When you select Continue, execution begins at the specified statement.

You cannot use Set Next Statement to shift execution from module-level code to the middle of a procedure. Use Set Next Statement with care, because skipping or reexecuting sections of code can cause errors.

Do not confuse this command with Next Statement on the View menu. Next Statement moves the cursor to the program statement that will be executed next if no changes are made.

Single-Step

QB's single-step feature enables you to execute one program statement at a time. One statement is executed with each press of the single-step key (there is no menu command for single step). As you single-step through a program, QB flashes back and forth between the program's output screen and the QB screen. On the QB screen, the next statement to be executed is highlighted.

There are actually two single-step keys, with slightly different functions. F8 is the "true" single-step key, executing a single statement no matter where you are in the program. F10 is the "procedure step" key. When the next program statement is anything other than a procedure call, F10 works the same as F8. When the next statement is a procedure call, F10 executes the call and the entire procedure at once. When you are single-stepping through a program and reach a call to a procedure that you know works properly, press F10.

Start

The Start command, located on the Run menu, causes a paused program to execute from the beginning. The shortcut key for Start is Shift-F5.

Restart

The Restart command, also on the Run menu, does everything that Start does *except* actually begin execution. When you select Restart, numeric variables are set to zero, string variables are set to zero-length strings, and the first program line is highlighted. Restart is most commonly used when you want to single-step through your program from the beginning.

The Calls Menu

When program execution is paused, the Calls menu provides a list of the procedure calls that were executed up to the current location. The Calls menu is particularly valuable when you are debugging a program that contains deeply nested procedure calls. You can use the Calls menu to determine the sequence of calls that led to a program crash or error and also to continue execution from the location where execution stopped up to any procedure listed on the Calls menu.

At a given point in program execution, the Calls menu does *not* contain a record of every procedure called since the program started. It lists only those procedures that have been called but not yet returned from. The procedure at the top of the Calls menu is the currently active procedure—the one executing when the program paused. The second procedure on the list is the one that called the procedure at the top of the list. At the bottom of the list is the name of the main module, which made the first procedure call. If you look at the Calls menu when no procedures are active, only the name of the main module is displayed.

Confused? Look at two examples for clarification. The program in listing 3.1 contains five procedures. Each procedure is called, in sequence, from the main module.

Listing 3.1. *CALLS1.BAS*

```
****************************************************************

DECLARE SUB Proc1 ()
DECLARE SUB Proc2 ()
DECLARE SUB Proc3 ()
DECLARE SUB Proc4 ()
DECLARE SUB Proc5 ()

' demonstration program for Calls menu

CALL Proc1
CALL Proc2
```

Listing 3.1 continues

Listing 3.1 *continued*

```
CALL Proc3
CALL Proc4
CALL Proc5

END


SUB Proc1

i = 1 / 1

END SUB


SUB Proc2

i = 1 / 1

END SUB


SUB Proc3

i = 1 / 1

END SUB


SUB Proc4

i = 1 / 1

END SUB


SUB Proc5

i = 1 / 0

END SUB
```
****

Note that `Proc5` tries to divide by zero. When CALLS1 is run, execution stops with a `Division by 0` error in `Proc5`. At this point, the Calls menu displays the list shown in figure 3.6. Note that only CALLS1.BAS (the main module) and `Proc5` are listed. The other four procedures are not listed. They were indeed called, but because execution *returned* from them, they have been removed from the Calls menu.

Fig. 3.6. *The Calls menu for the program in listing 3.1.*

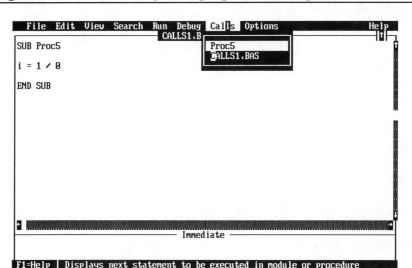

Program CALLS2.BAS in listing 3.2 also calls all five procedures in turn, with Proc5 again generating a `Division by 0` error. CALLS2.BAS differs from CALLS1.BAS in that each procedure is called by the last procedure; only Proc1 is called from the main module.

When CALLS2.BAS stops with a `Division by 0` error, the Calls menu appears as in figure 3.7.

Notice that the Calls menu now lists all five procedures plus the main module. Because of the way CALLS2.BAS is structured, with each procedure calling the next, execution has not returned from `Proc1`, `Proc2`, `Proc3`, or `Proc4` at the time the error occurs. Therefore, all 5 procedures are listed on the Calls menu.

When the Calls menu is displayed, you can select a procedure name and QB will display the procedure in the View window.

Listing 3.2. *CALLS2.BAS*

```
******************************************************************

DECLARE SUB Proc1 ()
DECLARE SUB Proc2 ()
DECLARE SUB Proc3 ()
DECLARE SUB Proc4 ()
DECLARE SUB Proc5 ()

' demonstration program for Calls menu

CALL Proc1

END


SUB Proc1

i = 1 / 1

CALL Proc2

END SUB


SUB Proc2

i = 1 / 1

CALL Proc3

END SUB

SUB Proc3

i = 1 / 1

CALL Proc4

END SUB
```

```
SUB Proc4

i = 1 / 1

CALL Proc5

END SUB


SUB Proc5

i = 1 / 0

END SUB
****************************************************************
```

Fig. 3.7. *The Calls menu for the program in listing 3.2.*

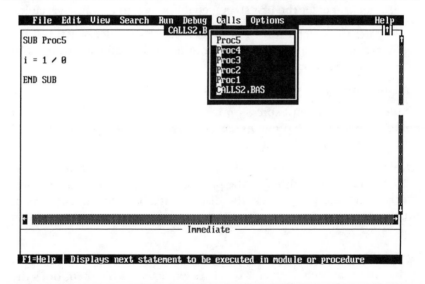

A Debugging Example

Now try working through a debugging example. It is impossible, of course, to demonstrate all the different types of bugs and debugging techniques, but even a short example will help you understand the use of QB's debugging facilities.

The program in listing 3.3 is intended to accept input strings, sort them alphabetically, and print the sorted list. Specifically, the program does the following:

1. Accepts one line of input at a time, putting each line in consecutive elements of a string array. The input loop terminates when a blank line is entered.

2. Sorts the array by comparing each element with the next. If the element with the lower array index is greater than the element with the higher array index, the two elements are swapped.

3. Goes through the array, printing each element.

If you enter the program and run it, you soon notice that it does not work properly; the program terminates as soon as you enter the first string. Because the program is supposed to stay in the input loop until a blank line is entered, you suspect the problem may be there. Try the following:

1. Insert a breakpoint immediately after the INPUT statement, that is, on the line that reads count = count + 1. This pauses the program after you enter the first string, enabling you to examine variables.

2. Enter the watch expression data$(count) = "". Because this is the expression that controls exit from the loop, you want to track its TRUE/FALSE value.

At this point your QB screen looks like the one in figure 3.8.

Note that the watch expression evaluates as −1 (TRUE). This is as it should be. Because the program has not started, string variables are null and the expression is indeed true.

Next, select Start from the Run menu. The program executes to the INPUT statement and "flips" to the program screen to accept user input. Enter a string and press Enter; the display flips back to the QB screen, and the program pauses at the breakpoint. The screen appears as in figure 3.9

Note that the watch expression is 0 (FALSE). Because you just entered a value into that array element, this is as expected. Why, then, does the loop terminate after one entry? Well, there is one more statement before the end of the loop. Press F8 (Single Step) to execute that one statement (count = count + 1). The screen now appears as in figure 3.10.

Listing 3.3. *DEBUG1.BAS*

```
**********************************************************

' demonstration program for debugging
' inputs strings from user, then sorts them alphabetically

DIM data$(10)

CLS

PRINT "Enter words, one per line. Enter a blank line when done:"
PRINT

count = 0

DO
    INPUT data$(count)
    count = count + 1
LOOP UNTIL data$(count) = ""

FOR i = 1 TO count
    FOR j = 1 TO count - 1
        IF data$(j) > data$(j + 1) THEN
            SWAP data$(j), data$(j + 1)
        END IF
    NEXT j
NEXT i

FOR i = 1 TO count
    PRINT data$(i)
NEXT i

END
**************************************************************
```

Fig. 3.8. *The QuickBASIC screen after setting the breakpoint and watch expression.*

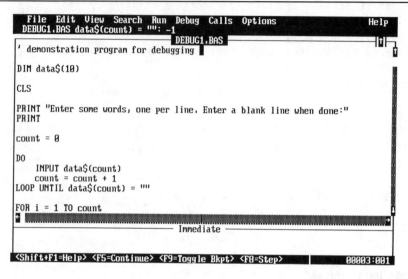

```
    File  Edit  View  Search  Run  Debug  Calls  Options          Help
  DEBUG1.BAS data$(count) = "": -1
┌──────────────────────────── DEBUG1.BAS ─────────────────────────────┤↑├┐
│ ' demonstration program for debugging                                  ↑│
│                                                                         │
│ DIM data$(10)                                                           │
│                                                                         │
│ CLS                                                                     │
│                                                                         │
│ PRINT "Enter some words, one per line. Enter a blank line when done:"   │
│ PRINT                                                                   │
│                                                                         │
│ count = 0                                                               │
│                                                                         │
│ DO                                                                      │
│     INPUT data$(count)                                                  │
│     count = count + 1                                                   │
│ LOOP UNTIL data$(count) = ""                                            │
│                                                                         │
│ FOR i = 1 TO count                                                     ↓│
├─────────────────────────── Immediate ─────────────────────────────────┤
│                                                                         │
└─────────────────────────────────────────────────────────────────────────┘
  <Shift+F1=Help> <F5=Continue> <F9=Toggle Bkpt> <F8=Step>     │ 00003:001
```

Fig. 3.9. *The program is paused at the breakpoint.*

```
    File  Edit  View  Search  Run  Debug  Calls  Options          Help
  DEBUG1.BAS data$(count) = "": 0
┌──────────────────────────── DEBUG1.BAS ─────────────────────────────┤↑├┐
│ ' demonstration program for debugging                                  ↑│
│                                                                         │
│ DIM data$(10)                                                           │
│                                                                         │
│ CLS                                                                     │
│                                                                         │
│ PRINT "Enter some words, one per line. Enter a blank line when done:"   │
│ PRINT                                                                   │
│                                                                         │
│ count = 0                                                               │
│                                                                         │
│ DO                                                                      │
│     INPUT data$(count)                                                  │
│     count = count + 1                                                   │
│ LOOP UNTIL data$(count) = ""                                            │
│                                                                         │
│ FOR i = 1 TO count                                                     ↓│
├─────────────────────────── Immediate ─────────────────────────────────┤
│                                                                         │
└─────────────────────────────────────────────────────────────────────────┘
  <Shift+F1=Help> <F5=Continue> <F9=Toggle Bkpt> <F8=Step>     │ 00014:005
```

Fig. 3.10. *After single-stepping one statement.*

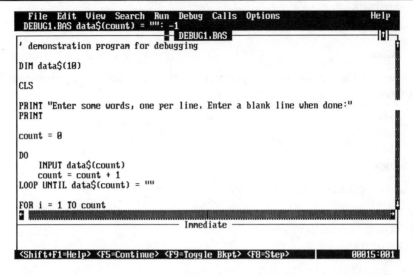

Notice that this single step has caused the watch expression to become −1 (TRUE). If this expression is true, the loop of course terminates. This explains the program's behavior. But why does this happen?

Examine this part of the code closely. The variable count is used as an index into the data$ array, both for inserting each input string and for evaluating the loop termination condition. Perhaps you have already noticed that count is incremented *after* the input statement but *before* the evaluation statement. This means that when input goes into array element *n*, the evaluation is performed on array element n+1. The first time through the loop, the input string goes into data$(0), and the evaluation is performed on data$(1). Because no input has been placed in data$(1), the statement data$(1) = "" is true, and the loop terminates.

This is easily fixed. Move the statement that increments count up two lines so that it is just *before* the input statement. Run the program again, and it seems to work fine. If you enter

    zebra
    aardvark
    lion
    eagle

the program prints out

> aardvark
> eagle
> lion
> zebra

But wait a minute; try the program with a mixture of uppercase and lowercase words. For example, enter

> Zebra
> aardvark
> Lion
> eagle

and you get back

> Lion
> Zebra
> aardvark
> eagle

Does QB not know its alphabet? There seems to be a problem with the sorting routine. Clearly, you are not finished debugging this program.

To deal with this bug, you must first decide which variables to watch. The data sorting is performed by a loop that uses j as an index and compares data$(j) with data$(j+1); if data$(j) is greater than data$(j+1), the two array elements are swapped. So, enter these two variables and the comparison statement as watch expressions. After doing so and selecting Restart, your screen will look like figure 3.11.

Note that both data$(j) and data$(j+1) are blank (that is, zero-length strings) and as a consequence, the comparison expression is false.

You want the program to execute through the data entry section, which seems to be working well, and to pause in the sort routine so that you can single step. Move the cursor to the line that reads

```
FOR j = 1 TO count -1
```

and press Execute to Cursor (F7). The program begins execution; enter the four upper- and lowercase words as just shown, then a blank line. Execution pauses, and the screen appears as in figure 3.12.

Fig. 3.11. *The program after watchpoints are set and* Restart *is selected.*

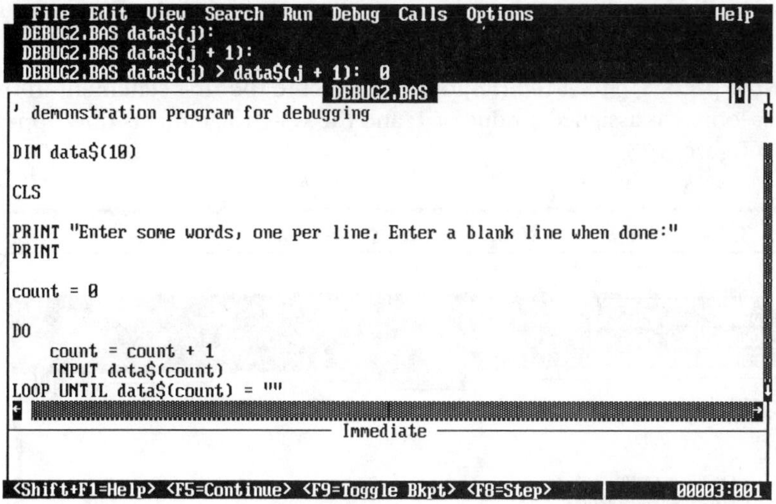

```
 File  Edit  View  Search  Run  Debug  Calls  Options        Help
DEBUG2.BAS data$(j):
DEBUG2.BAS data$(j + 1):
DEBUG2.BAS data$(j) > data$(j + 1):  0
                                  DEBUG2.BAS
' demonstration program for debugging

DIM data$(10)

CLS

PRINT "Enter some words, one per line. Enter a blank line when done:"
PRINT

count = 0

DO
    count = count + 1
    INPUT data$(count)
LOOP UNTIL data$(count) = ""

                              Immediate

<Shift+F1=Help> <F5=Continue> <F9=Toggle Bkpt> <F8=Step>    00003:001
```

Fig. 3.12. *The program paused in the sort loop.*

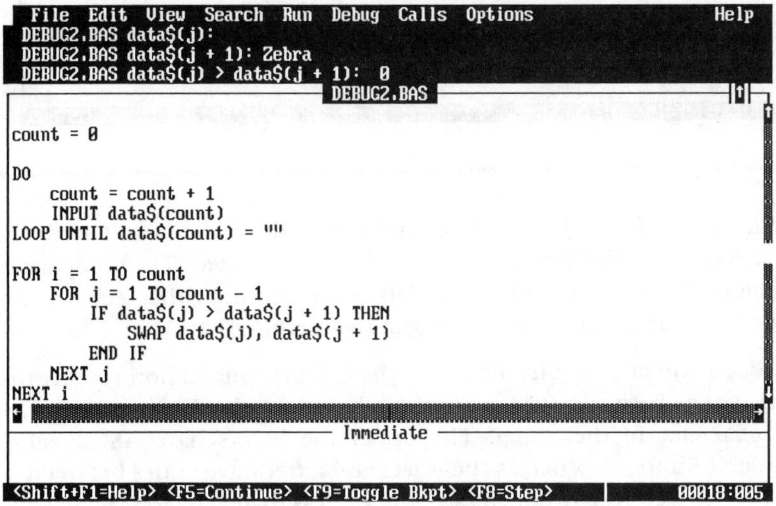

```
 File  Edit  View  Search  Run  Debug  Calls  Options        Help
DEBUG2.BAS data$(j):
DEBUG2.BAS data$(j + 1): Zebra
DEBUG2.BAS data$(j) > data$(j + 1):  0
                                  DEBUG2.BAS
count = 0

DO
    count = count + 1
    INPUT data$(count)
LOOP UNTIL data$(count) = ""

FOR i = 1 TO count
    FOR j = 1 TO count - 1
        IF data$(j) > data$(j + 1) THEN
            SWAP data$(j), data$(j + 1)
        END IF
    NEXT j
NEXT i

                              Immediate

<Shift+F1=Help> <F5=Continue> <F9=Toggle Bkpt> <F8=Step>    00018:005
```

Note that data$(j) is blank, data$(j+1) is Zebra, and the comparison is FALSE. Because j has not yet been assigned a value, it is 0. The data entry code does not use the 0th array element, putting the first entry in data$(1).

Now press Single Step (F8) once to execute the first statement in the inner loop. j is assigned a value of 1, and the watch statements now appear as in figure 3.13.

Fig. 3.13. *After single-stepping one statement.*

```
  File  Edit  View  Search  Run  Debug  Calls  Options            Help
 DEBUG2.BAS data$(j): Zebra
 DEBUG2.BAS data$(j + 1): aardvark
 DEBUG2.BAS data$(j) > data$(j + 1):  0
                    ┌───────── DEBUG2.BAS ─────────────────────────┐
                                                                   ▲
 count = 0                                                         ▒
                                                                   ▒
 DO                                                                ▒
     count = count + 1                                             ▒
     INPUT data$(count)                                            ▒
 LOOP UNTIL data$(count) = ""                                      ▒
                                                                   ▒
 FOR i = 1 TO count                                                ▒
     FOR j = 1 TO count - 1                                        ▒
         IF data$(j) > data$(j + 1) THEN                           ▒
             SWAP data$(j), data$(j + 1)                           ▒
         END IF                                                    ▒
     NEXT j                                                        ▒
 NEXT i                                                            ▼
 ◄ ▓▓▓▓▓▓▓▓▓▓▓▓▓▓▓▓▓▓▓▓▓▓▓▓▓▓▓▓▓▓▓▓▓▓▓▓▓▓▓▓▓▓▓▓▓▓▓▓▓▓▓▓▓▓▓▓▓▓▓▓▓▶
 ├────────────────────────── Immediate ─────────────────────────┤


 <Shift+F1=Help> <F5=Continue> <F9=Toggle Bkpt> <F8=Step>   00019:009
```

With j = 1, data$(j) and data$(j+1) now show Zebra and aardvark. These were your first two entries, so this is as expected. The comparison statement, however, is still FALSE. QB seems to think that Zebra is not greater than aardvark. Are you missing something here?

Indeed you are. A quick check of the QB documentation reveals that comparisons between strings are done based on the ASCII value of the first character in the string. The uppercase letters have ASCII values between 65 and 90, whereas the lowercase letter have codes between 97 and 122. Therefore, any uppercase letter is ''less than'' any lowercase letter. This explains the program's strange sort results.

The solution is simple. Use the UCASE$ function to convert each string to uppercase before the comparison. Change the IF statement to read

```
IF UCASE$(data$(j)) > UCASE$(data$(j + 1)) THEN
```

Rerun the program. It now alphabetizes properly no matter what the case of the entries. Your debugging has been successful.

Including Debugging Code in Your Program

Before the advent of debuggers, programmers had to rely on their own ingenuity to debug their programs. For the most part, the only way to debug a program was to include code in the program that would report on the path of execution and variable values as program execution proceeded. This method of debugging has largely been supplanted by stand-alone debugging programs (discussed later in this chapter) and by debugging facilities built into programming environments such as QB. Yet it is worthwhile to have at least a passing familiarity with what might be called "embedded code debugging," because these techniques can still at times be quite useful.

Using *BEEP*

Sometimes a debugging problem consists simply of needing to know whether program execution ever reaches a certain section of code. One or more strategically placed `BEEP` statements may be all you need to check this. By using single, double, and triple BEEPs, you can differentiate among several different execution paths.

Using *PRINT* and *LPRINT*

The `PRINT` and `LPRINT` statements can be used to display information about program execution. Variables, array elements, statement evaluations, and "tags" identifying execution location can be sent to either the screen or the printer. The output device you use depends on the program. If the program makes heavy use of the display, the printer is the best destination for debugging information, and vice versa.

Conditional Debugging Code

If you include more than a line or two of debugging code in your program, it is a good idea to make the code execution conditional. This means that the debugging statements, such as the `BEEP`s just mentioned, are executed only if a certain variable is TRUE (nonzero); if the variable is FALSE, the statements are not executed.

You could, for example, use the term debug, either defined as a constant at the beginning of the source code or as a variable with a value assigned by an assignment statement or a user input statement. Your debugging code would then take the form

```
IF DEBUG THEN
    .
    .
    debugging code here
    .
    .
END IF
```

During program development, set `DEBUG = 1`; once the program is thoroughly debugged, set `DEBUG = 0` before you compile the final version of the program. Of course, the debugging code remains part of the program, increasing its size. In some cases this is a problem, requiring you to actually remove the debugging statements from the source code. By using your editor's SEARCH function to find occurrences of the `DEBUG` variable, the task is less onerous.

Now run through a quick example of using embedded debugging code with the example program presented earlier. When tracing down the bug that causes the program to sort incorrectly, you could insert conditional debugging code in the program, as shown in listing 3.4 (only parts of the program are shown here). With each iteration of the sort loop, the debugging code prints the two strings being compared and whether the program is swapping them.

When the program is run with `DEBUG = 1`, the first part of the output looks like this:

```
j = 1
data$(j) = Zebra
data$(j+1) = aardvark
not swapping

j = 2
data$(j) = aardvark
data$(j+1) = Lion
swapping
```

Examining this output clearly reveals the problem, just as does using the QB environment's debugging tools.

Listing 3.4. DEBUG3.BAS

```
'***************************************************************
' demonstration program for debugging
' inputs strings from user, then sorts them alphabetically

CONST DEBUG = 1


    .
    .
    .


FOR i = 1 TO count
    FOR j = 1 TO count - 1

' ****** debugging code
    IF DEBUG THEN
        LPRINT "j ="; j
        LPRINT "data$(j) = ", data$(j)
        LPRINT "data$(j+1) = ", data$(j + 1)
        IF data$(j) > data$(j + 1) THEN
            LPRINT "swapping"
        ELSE
            LPRINT "not swapping"
        END IF
        LPRINT
    END IF
' ****** end debugging code

        IF data$(j) > data$(j + 1) THEN
            SWAP data$(j), data$(j + 1)
        END IF
    NEXT j
NEXT i


    .
    .
    .


END
'***************************************************************
```

The Microsoft CodeView Debugger

As powerful and convenient as the QB environment's debugging facilities are, there are even more powerful debugging tools available. *Stand-alone debuggers* are programs whose sole function is debugging other programs. These stand-alone debuggers provide significantly more debugging functionality than is available in QB.

For QB programs, the stand-alone debugger of choice is Microsoft CodeView. CodeView must be purchased separately—it is not part of the QB package. It is provided with Microsoft Macro Assembler and Microsoft C, however, so if you have either of those packages you already have CodeView.

CodeView is an extremely powerful and somewhat complicated program. Some of its features are specific to debugging programs in C, Fortran, assembly language, or Pascal, and are of no relevance to BASIC programmers. Even so, it would require an entire book to completely cover using CodeView to debug QB programs. Obviously, I cannot do so in a few pages. Rather, this section provides a quick tour of CodeView, emphasizing the features that are not available within the QB environment. If you then decide to try CodeView, you can use its documentation to obtain a more detailed understanding of its functions.

Preparing QuickBASIC Programs for CodeView

When you write a QB program that will be debugged with CodeView, there are two points to keep in mind.

❑ Source code in INCLUDE files cannot be debugged, so keep all your source code in one or more modules (this is good practice even when not writing for CodeView).

❑ Whereas putting multiple statements on a single line is perfectly legal in BASIC, such formats can make the program difficult to debug. This is because CodeView sees your multiple statement lines as single units. For example, the following BASIC code runs perfectly well:

```
i = 0 : WHILE i < 20 : INPUT data(i) : i = i + 1 : WEND
```

Because these five statements are placed on a single line, CodeView cannot access them individually. You cannot, for example, pause program execution at the input statement. The preferred arrangement of source code would be

```
i = 0
WHILE i < 20
 INPUT data(i)
 i = i + 1
WEND
```

Not only does this arrangement make debugging easier, it also makes the source code easier to read and understand.

To be debugged with CodeView, a QB program must exist on disk as an executable (.EXE) file. Furthermore, that .EXE file must have been created using the stand-alone method of programming development (discussed in Chapter 1). You cannot use CodeView to debug any .EXE file created from within the QB environment.

You must use the /ZI compiler option and the /CO linker option when you create a program for CodeView. For example, to compile and link a BASIC source file named DEMO.BAS for debugging with CodeView, use the following command lines:

```
BC /ZI DEMO;
LINK /CO DEMO;
```

These options cause the compiler and linker to include information needed by CodeView in the .EXE file. This information makes the file somewhat larger, so once your program is thoroughly debugged, you should recompile and link without the CodeView options.

Starting CodeView

To begin a CodeView debugging session, the following files must be available (usually in the current directory):

- ❏ CODEVIEW.EXE, the CodeView program file
- ❏ CODEVIEW.HLP, the CodeView help file
- ❏ PROGRAM.EXE, the program to be debugged
- ❏ PROGRAM.BAS, the program source code

CodeView makes excellent use of a mouse, although it can be used without one. If you have a mouse, be sure to install the mouse driver before you start CodeView. To start CodeView, enter the startup command in the following format at the DOS prompt:

```
CodeView [options] program [arguments]
```

The *arguments* are the command-line arguments that would normally be passed to the program. These are the arguments accessed via the Basic `COMMAND$` function. Include *arguments* in the CodeView startup command only if your program accepts them.

The *options* are an optional list of one or more CodeView options. Each CodeView option is preceded by a slash. The 14 CodeView options are explained in detail in the CodeView documentation. The ones you are most likely to use are

/B	Runs CodeView in monochrome mode. Use this option if you have a monochrome monitor connected to a color graphics adapter.
/43	Runs CodeView in 43-line display mode. This option can be used only if you have an EGA or VGA video adapter and an enhanced color monitor.
/E	Instructs CodeView to use expanded memory, making more room in standard memory available for the program being debugged. Use this option only if your system has expanded memory that adheres to the Lotus/Intel/Microsoft EMS specification.

When CodeView starts, it displays the program's source code, as shown in figure 3.14. As with the QB environment, CodeView enables you to set breakpoints and watchpoints, open a Watch window, display the value of variables, and single-step through the program. Any debugging task you can do in QB can also be done in CodeView.

CodeView's power lies in the features not available in QB. In *assembly* display mode, for example, CodeView displays the program in assembly language, as shown in figure 3.15.

The columns at the left of the screen are the relative addresses and the actual hexadecimal machine language instructions that were read from the .EXE file. In the right part of the screen, CodeView displays the *disassembled* program code. *Disassembled* means that CodeView has converted the machine-language instructions to their assembly language equivalents. By viewing the disassembled code you can see exactly how your BASIC program is controlling the computer's CPU. Do not worry if the assembly language code makes no sense to you. You will not be using this debugging mode unless you understand assembly language.

CodeView's third display mode, *mixed*, is perhaps its most powerful. In mixed display mode CodeView displays the BASIC source code statements *and* the corresponding assembly language instructions. The

Fig. 3.14. *The CodeView screen displaying the source code of the*
demonstration program.

```
File  View  Search  Run  Watch  Options  Language  Calls  Help  | F8=Trace F5=Go
                          DBUGDEMO.BAS
 1:      ' demonstration program for debugging
 2:
 3:      DIM data$(10)
 4:
 5:      CLS
 6:
 7:      PRINT "Enter some words, one per line. Enter a blank line when done:"
 8:      PRINT
 9:
10:      count = 0
11:                                       ▌
12:      DO
13:          count = count + 1
14:          INPUT data$(count)
15:      LOOP UNTIL data$(count) = ""
16:
17:      FOR i = 1 TO count
18:          FOR j = 1 TO count - 1

Microsoft (R) CodeView (R) Version 2.2
(C) Copyright Microsoft Corp. 1986-1988.  All rights reserved.
>
```

Fig. 3.15. *CodeView in assembly display mode.*

```
File  View  Search  Run  Watch  Options  Language  Calls  Help  | F8=Trace F5=Go
                          DBUGDEMO.BAS
5B24:00CC BF8D5B         MOV     DI,5B8D
5B24:00CF A10200         MOV     AX,Word Ptr [0002]
5B24:00D2 2EA33200       MOV     Word Ptr CS:[0032],AX
5B24:00D6 2BC7           SUB     AX,DI
5B24:00D8 3D0010         CMP     AX,1000
5B24:00DB 7203           JB      00E0
5B24:00DD B80010         MOV     AX,1000
5B24:00E0 FA             CLI
5B24:00E1 8ED7           MOV     SS,DI
5B24:00E3 81C4BE0E       ADD     SP,0EBE
5B24:00E7 FB             STI
5B24:00E8 96             XCHG    AX,SI
5B24:00E9 9F             LAHF
5B24:00EA 2E88263400     MOV     Byte Ptr CS:[0034],AH
5B24:00EF 96             XCHG    AX,SI
5B24:00F0 83E4FE         AND     SP,-02
5B24:00F3 03C7           ADD     AX,DI
5B24:00F5 A30200         MOV     Word Ptr [0002],AX

Microsoft (R) CodeView (R) Version 2.2
(C) Copyright Microsoft Corp. 1986-1988.  All rights reserved.
>
```

BASIC statements are interspersed among the assembly code, so you can see which BASIC statement corresponds to each section of assembly code. Mixed display mode is shown in figure 3.16. Another CodeView option, also shown in figure 3.16, is a display of the CPU register contents.

Fig. 3.16. *The CodeView "mixed" display; the register display has also been turned on.*

```
 File  View  Search  Run  Watch  Options  Language  Calls  Help |F8=Trace F5=Go
                    | DBUGDEMO.BAS |
5AD8:00C5 CD351EF60D   INT    35 ;FSTP     DWord Ptr [0DF6]    AX = 0DD6
5AD8:00CA CD3D         INT    3D ;FWAIT                        BX = 0E52
5AD8:00CC CD35065A0E   INT    35 ;FLD      DWord Ptr [0E5A]    CX = 0000
5AD8:00D1 E9C000       JMP    0194                             DX = 0000
18:          FOR j = 1 TO count - 1                            SP = 16AE
5AD8:00D4 CD3506F20D   INT    35 ;FLD      DWord Ptr [COUNT! (0  BP = 16B8
5AD8:00D9 CD34065E0E   INT    34 ;FADD     DWord Ptr [0E5E]    SI = 0E04
5AD8:00DE CD351EFA0D   INT    35 ;FSTP     DWord Ptr [0DFA]    DI = 0EAC
5AD8:00E3 CD3D         INT    3D ;FWAIT                        DS = 5B0D
5AD8:00E5 CD35065A0E   INT    35 ;FLD      DWord Ptr [0E5A]    ES = 5B0D
5AD8:00EA E98000       JMP    016D                             SS = 5B0D
5AD8:00ED 90           NOP                                     CS = 5AD8
19:          IF UCASE$(data$(j)) > UCASE$(data$(j + 1)) THEN   IP = 00C0
5AD8:00EE CD3506FE0D   INT    35 ;FLD      DWord Ptr [J! (0DFE)
5AD8:00F3 9A7002F95A   CALL   B$FIS2 (5AF9:0270)               NV UP
5AD8:00F8 D1E0         SHL    AX,1                             EI PL
5AD8:00FA D1E0         SHL    AX,1                             ZR NA
5AD8:00FC 81C0C60D     ADD    AX,0DC6                          PE NC
                                                        ‡
>S&                                                            DS:0DF2
mixed                                                          00008040
>
>
```

When CodeView is in assembly or mixed display, breakpoints can be set on individual lines of assembly code.

Here are some other CodeView features not available in QB:

❏ You can set tracepoints; a *tracepoint* pauses program execution when the value of an expression or a range of memory changes.

❏ The Calls menu shows not only the sequence of procedures calls, but the current value of each procedure's arguments.

❏ You can display and modify the values of the CPU registers.

❏ You can display the contents of the registers in 8087/80287 math coprocessor chips.

❏ You can search areas of the computer's memory for specific byte values.

❏ You can "dump" the contents of specified memory areas, displaying the contents in a variety of formats.

These and other features make CodeView a powerful debugging tool. Most QB programmers will never need these abilities, because the debugging facilities in the QB environment are adequate for most tasks. If you are writing and debugging long, complex programs, you may find CodeView to be a lifesaver.

Summary

If you are just getting started with QB, you may have been tempted to skip over this chapter, because you were probably anxious to get started writing actual programs. Program bugs seem of little concern before you write and run your first program! I predict, however, that readers who skipped this chapter will so come back to it! Like it or not, bugs are an unavoidable part of programming. The better you are able to find and correct them, the greater the programming productivity you can achieve. You also can enjoy it more. There is nothing more frustrating than spending hours tracking down a bug that could have been found in minutes with the right tools!

Part II

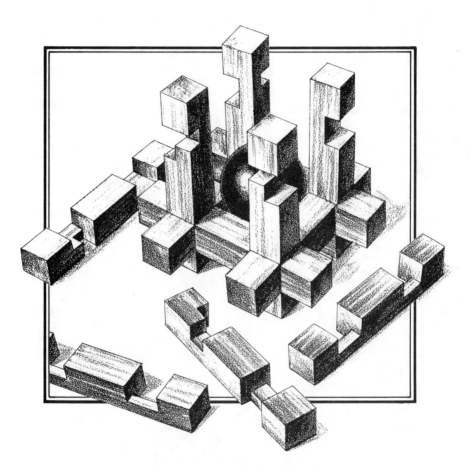

Programming Topics

4

Error Handling

The last chapter dealt with program bugs—what they are, how to find them, and their relationship to program errors. As a jog to your memory, I will repeat the definitions developed in that chapter:

❏ An *error* is a mistake in the program code, or some aspect of the computer hardware or user input, that interferes with program execution.

❏ A *bug* is a mistake in the program logic that causes the program to function incorrectly.

Again drawing from Chapter 3, you can use the following analogy: When you are driving a car, a flat tire is an error, whereas a wrong turn is a bug. Errors, like bugs, are an unavoidable part of program development. This chapter deals with QuickBASIC run-time errors and does the following:

❏ Explains the types of run-time errors that can occur and how QB reacts to them

❏ Shows how to include error-trapping code in your programs

❏ Demonstrates how to creatively use run-time errors as a programming tool

❏ Presents a run-time error-handling routine that allows a program to recover gracefully from run-time errors while providing an informative error message to the user

121

Types of Errors

One type of error *not* covered in this chapter (beyond these two paragraphs) is *compile-time errors*. A compile-time error occurs during program compilation and is caused by errors in the source code. A misspelled BASIC keyword, missing parenthesis, or data type mismatch are examples of problems that cause a compile-time error.

If you are working in the QB environment, some errors are caught by the "smart" editor as soon as you move the cursor off the offending line of source code. Others are caught when you try to run the program. If you are using the BC stand-alone compiler, all compile-time errors are caught during compilation. In either case—QB environment or stand-alone compilation—QB flags all compile-time errors with an informative error message and an indication of where in the source code the error is located. With all of this help, dealing with compile-time errors is fairly straightforward.

Another type of error this chapter does not deal with is *link-time errors*. These occur during the link stage of stand-alone program development and, like compile-time errors, are accompanied by informative error messages. You do not have to be concerned with link-time errors if you are working in the QB environment.

The type of error of interest here is the *run-time error*. As the name implies, run-time errors occur while a program is running. They can be caused by a variety of factors: the hardware, the program, the user, or a combination of these factors. There is really no way to avoid run-time errors. Thorough debugging can completely rid your program of bugs, there is no way to guarantee that *somebody* using your program eventually will not leave a disk drive door open or forget to turn on the printer. Because of the human factor—and this is particularly true if you are distributing your program for use by others—it is important to make your program as "crash-proof" as possible. A fully crash-proof program is one where nothing the user can do short of turning the computer off can crash the program and cause data loss.

As in the last chapter, here I use the term *run-time error* to refer specifically to the program execution errors that can be trapped while a QB program is running. The word *error* used alone refers to more general types of errors.

Avoiding Run-Time Errors

Before you explore QB's facilities for dealing with run-time errors, look at the best way to deal with run-time errors—avoiding them altogether, or "cutting them off at the pass," so to speak. Many run-time errors cannot be avoided, but some, particularly those caused by improper user input or hardware incompatibilities, can be.

Verifying User Input

No matter how much effort you put into designing your program's data entry screens, there is no way to prevent users from making improper entries. Most of the time, an improper entry will simply be a mistake that does not cause a run-time error—if users type 21 when they should have entered 12, there is really nothing you or your program can do about it. At times, however, an improper entry *can* cause a run-time error. One common example is if a value of 0 is mistakenly entered for a variable that will be used as the divisor in a calculation. A Division by 0 error occurs if the mistaken entry is not caught first. Catching this error is easy, as shown in the following code fragment:

```
    .
    .
    .
DO
    INPUT X
    IF X <> 0 THEN EXIT LOOP
    BEEP
    PRINT "Nonzero value required."
LOOP
    .
    .
    .
```

Similar code can be used to ensure a positive input, as required for a variable to be used as the argument to a LOG or LN function.

QuickBASIC's Error Trapping

Error trapping is the ability to detect the occurrence of a run-time error and pass program execution to an error handler. An *error handler* is a section of code that deals with the error that occurred. In most situations, the code in the error handler can correct the problem that caused the error, often by prompting the user to take certain action, such as turning on the printer. Even if the error condition cannot be corrected, error-handling code can be used to gracefully terminate the program without loss of data and provide information to the user about the error that occurred.

The QB statements and functions that are used in error trapping are

ON ERROR GOTO	Enables error trapping and specifies the location of the error handler
RESUME	Returns execution to a specified location in the main program after the error-handling code has executed
ERR	Returns a numerical code for the most recent run-time error
ERL	Returns the line number nearest the code location that caused the most recent run-time error
ERROR	Simulates an error under program control
ERDEV, ERDEV$	Provides device-specific error information

This section looks at each of these QB features in detail

ON ERROR GOTO

The statement that enables error trapping and specifies the location of the error handler is ON ERROR GOTO. The syntax of this statement is

```
ON ERROR GOTO linenumber
```

or

```
ON ERROR GOTO label
```

The location of the first line of the error handler is given by *linenumber* or *label*. You can use either a line number or an alphanumeric label. The ON ERROR GOTO statement must be executed before error trapping is enabled. A simple example of error trapping is shown in listing 4.1.

Run this program, entering different values at the prompt. If you enter a nonzero value, no error occurs, and the program prints "OK". Execution never reaches the code following the label errorhandler:. If you enter 0, however, the division 1/x causes a divide by 0 error. Execution passes to errorhandler: and the program prints "Not OK".

Listing 4.1. ERROR1.BAS

```
' fundamental error trapping

ON ERROR GOTO errorhandler

INPUT x
y = 1 / x
PRINT "OK"
END

errorhandler:

PRINT "Not OK"
END
```

Because the ON ERROR GOTO statement must be executed before error trapping is enabled, it should be placed near the beginning of the program's executable code. In fact, making ON ERROR GOTO the first executable statement in your programs is a good habit to develop. You can have additional ON ERROR GOTO statements in your program, specifying different error-handling routines for different program sections. When an error occurs, execution branches to the location specified by the most recently executed ON ERROR GOTO statement.

ON ERROR GOTO statements can be located anywhere in your program, including procedure-level code. The error-handling code, however, must be located at the module level.

The statement ON ERROR GOTO 0 has a special meaning. If it is executed outside of an error-handling routine, it disables error trapping. Subsequent errors will halt program execution and display QB's normal error message. If ON ERROR GOTO 0 is executed within an error-handling routine, the program halts, and the usual error message is displayed. By making ON ERROR GOTO the last line in the error-handling code (after all RESUME statements, as explained later), you will enable your program to respond to errors that you did not anticipate.

Note that the scope of error trapping is limited to a single module. In a multiple module program, each module must contain its own ON ERROR GOTO statement(s) and error-handling routine(s).

RESUME

Error trapping would be of limited usefulness if, as in the example given in listing 4.1, an error handler could only print a message, then end program execution. Fortunately, this is not the case. Much of the real power of QB's error trapping lies in the fact that your program can continue executing, without loss of valuable data, following trapping of an error. This is done with the RESUME statement, which has three forms:

RESUME	Causes program execution to continue with the same statement that caused the error
RESUME NEXT	Causes program execution to continue with the statement immediately following the one that caused the error
RESUME *line*	Causes program execution to continue with the statement identified by *line*, which can be either a line number or line label. *line* must designate a line at the module level.

RESUME and RESUME NEXT can return execution to either module- or procedure-level code. The statement you use depends on whether you want the error causing statement reexecuted. If the condition causing the error was corrected, such as by turning the printer on, use RESUME. If the condition cannot be corrected, use RESUME NEXT.

RESUME *line* must be used with caution. Because *line* must be at the module level, RESUME *line* following an error occurring at the procedure level causes execution to continue at the module level *without* having properly returned from the procedure where the error occurred. You can use the ERL function, described later, to ensure that RESUME *line* is executed only when an error has occurred at the module level. Otherwise, it is best to limit yourself to RESUME and RESUME NEXT.

RESUME statements can appear only in an error handler. If a RESUME is encountered outside of an error handler, a run-time error RESUME without error occurs. The code in an error handler must either end the program with an END statement or transfer execution out of the error handler with a RESUME statement. If an error handler simply "runs out" of code, a run-time error is generated. It is legal to transfer execution out of an error handler with GOTO and other control statements, but the practice should be avoided.

The error-handler code must be situated in your source code so that it cannot be executed during normal program execution. Error-handling code is not privileged as is code in procedures, and execution can fall right into it. Look at this code fragment:

```
ON ERROR GOTO errorhandler
.
. (program code)
.

errorhandler:
.
. (error-handling code)
.

END
```

The error-handling code will be executed every time the program runs, even if no error occurs. The best location for error handlers is following the **END** statement in the main module.

> Note: Errors that occur *within* an error handler cannot be trapped. If an error occurs while the error handler is dealing with another error, an error message is displayed, and the program terminates.

ERR

ERR is a function that returns a numerical code for the most recent run-time error. The codes and their associated errors are listed in the appendix of the QB documentation. By using ERR, your error-handling routine can take appropriate action based on the specific error that occurred.

For example, two errors that commonly occur when a program tries to send output to the printer are the printer being turned off or being out of paper. The ERR code returned when a program tries to print to a turned-off printer is 25 Device fault; when the printer is on but out of paper, error 27 Out of paper is generated. A program could use ERR to detect these conditions and prompt the user to take action to correct the problem, as shown in listing 4.2.

Listing 4.2. PRINTERR.BAS

```
' ERR function demonstration

ON ERROR GOTO errorhandler

LPRINT "QuickBASIC Advanced Techniques"

END

errorhandler:

IF ERR = 25 THEN
    PRINT "ERROR--turn printer on, then press any key."
ELSE IF ERR = 27 THEN
    PRINT "ERROR--out of paper; correct, then press any key."
END IF

WHILE INKEY$ = "": WEND

RESUME
```

ERR can be called multiple times. It returns the same value each time as long as another error has not occurred in the meantime.

ERL

The ERL function returns the line number of the program line that caused the most recent error. If the error-causing line has no number, the number of the most recently executed numbered line is returned. If no numbered line was executed between the start of the program and the error, ERL returns 0.

Unfortunately, ERL cannot return a line label. Line numbers are a throwback to the unlamented days of interpreted BASIC and have no place in a QB program other than for use by ERL. Knowing where in the program an error occurred can be quite useful, both for dealing with real errors, as you will see next, and as a program tool, discussed later in this chapter.

Here is an example. Error 25, Device fault, can occur with various hardware peripherals such as printers and communications ports. Using ERL to determine where in the program an error 25 has occurred, you can alert the user to the source of the problem, as shown in this code fragment:

```
ON ERROR GOTO errorhandler
.
.
1000 FOR i = 1 TO 50
         LPRINT DATA$(i)
     NEXT i
.
.
2000 OPEN "COM1: 1200,,,2" FOR OUTPUT AS #1
     FOR I = 1 TO 50
         WRITE #1, DATA$(i)
     NEXT i
.
.END
.
errorhandler:

IF ERR = 25 THEN
    IF ERL = 1000 THEN
        PRINT "Printer device fault"
    ELSE IF ERL = 2000 THEN
        PRINT "Communications port device fault"
    END IF
END IF
.
.
.(remainder of error-handling code with RESUME)
```

For **ERL** to be of any use, your program must contain line numbers. If your error handler uses **ERL**, you should place line numbers at strategic locations throughout your program—at the beginning of each procedure, perhaps, and every 10 or 15 lines in module-level code. If an error occurs, you will at least know the section of code that caused it. If necessary, you can then add additional line numbers in that section to further localize the line that causes the error.

ERROR

The **ERROR** statement is used to simulate run-time errors during program development. The syntax is

```
ERROR errorcode
```

where *errorcode* is an integer expression in the range 0 to 255. If *error-code* is one of QB's defined error codes, executing ERROR causes the program to behave exactly as if the corresponding error actually occurred; execution passes to the defined error handler or, if none is defined, QB prints its usual error message. If *errorcode* is not one of QB's defined error codes, ERR returns *errorcode*, or, if no error handler is defined, QB reports an Unprintable error.

The most important use for ERROR is during development of your error-handling code. By simulating various errors in the program, you can test the functioning of your error handler.

ERROR can also be used when you create custom error codes to use during program execution. For example, a mailing list program might check state and ZIP code entries for length, ensuring that the state field is 2 characters and the ZIP is 5 characters. Upon detection of an improper entry, a custom error code would be issued. Look at this code fragment:

```
ON ERROR GOTO errorhandler
    .
    .
GetState:
     INPUT "Enter state: ", state$
     IF LEN(state$) <> 2 THEN ERROR 200

GetZip:
     INPUT "Enter zip code: ",zip$
     IF LEN(zip$) <> 5 THEN ERROR 201
    .
    .
    .
errorhandler:
    .
    .
    .
IF ERR = 200 THEN
     BEEP
     PRINT "State entry must be two characters long."
     WHILE i = 1 TO 10000              ' pause briefly
     RESUME GetState
END IF
```

```
IF ERR = 201 THEN
     BEEP
     PRINT "Zip code entry must be five characters long."
     WHILE i = 1 TO 10000          ' pause briefly
     RESUME GetZip
END IF
     .
     .
     .
```

The advantage to using custom error codes is that all your program's error handling code can be kept together in the section of code defined by the ON ERROR GOTO statement.

ERDEV and *ERDEV$*

The ERDEV and ERDEV$ functions return information about errors generated by devices. ERDEV returns an integer error code identifying the error, whereas ERDEV$ returns a string identifying the device that caused the error.

The error codes returned by ERDEV are listed in table 4.1, and the device names returned by ERDEV$ are listed in table 4.2.

Table 4.1. ERDEV Error Codes

Errorcode	Meaning
0	write protect error
1	unknown device
2	disk drive not ready
3	unknown command
4	disk data error
5	bad request structure length
6	disk seek error
7	unknown media type
8	disk sector not found
9	out of paper
10	write fault
11	read fault
12	general failure

Table 4.2. ERDEV$ Device Names

Device Name	Physical Device
X:	disk drive X: (X: = A:, B:, and so on)
LPT1:	printer 1
LPT2:	printer 2
LPT3:	printer 3
PRN	logical printer
CON	console (keyboard and screen)
KYBD	keyboard
SCRN	screen
COM1	serial port 1
COM2	serial port 2
AUX	auxiliary device (usually same as COM1)
CLOCK$	system clock

Note: If the error occurs in a user-installed software device driver, ERDEV$ returns the device name established by that device driver.

The simple example in listing 4.3 illustrates the use of ERDEV and ERDEV$. Run the program with the door to drive B: open.

Listing 4.3. ERDEV.BAS

```
ON ERROR GOTO errorhandler

' leave drive B: open

FILES "B:"
END



errorhandler:

PRINT "Error"; ERDEV; "in device "; ERDEV$

END
```

The output is

```
Error 2 in device B:
```

You may have noticed that most of the errors handled by ERDEV and ERDEV$ can also be dealt with by the regular error-handling procedures using ERR and ERL. When dealing with device errors, the ERDEV/ERDEV$ method offers the advantage of providing the device name as well as a numerical error code.

Errors as Programming Tools

Errors are generally thought of as completely negative—conditions to be avoided if at all possible, and if unavoidable, to be handled as expeditiously as possible. With some imaginative thinking, however, you can make certain types of errors serve as powerful programming tools.

How can errors serve as useful tools? They provide information about the hardware configuration and status of the computer system and about the contents of disks. Therefore, the occurrence or nonoccurrence of certain errors can be used to guide program execution and to warn the user of conditions that might later cause data loss or other serious problems. Consider these examples.

- ❏ Printer errors can be used to determine whether a required printer is attached and functioning.

- ❏ Disk errors can be used to verify that a required disk and/or needed files are available.

- ❏ Video errors can be used to determine whether needed video hardware is installed.

- ❏ Device errors can be used to verify that a serial port is installed and functioning.

Now look at three concrete examples. Assume that you have written a graphics program that requires an enhanced graphics adapter (EGA) to run. Despite the very clear program instructions that explain this, you can count on some users trying to run the program on systems not equipped with an EGA. The following code provides a warning message and exits the program.

```
ON ERROR GOTO errorhandler

' attempt to set an EGA screen mode
```

```
100 SCREEN 9
.
. remainder of program code
.
END

errorhandler:

IF ERR = 5 AND ERL = 100 THEN
    CLS
    BEEP
    PRINT "This program requires an enhanced graphics adapter."
    END
END IF
.
. (remainder of error-handling code)
.
```

The line numbered 100 tries to set screen mode 9, which can be set only if an EGA or VGA video adapter is installed. If some "lower-level" video adapter is installed, the SCREEN 9 statement causes an Illegal function call error (number 5). Execution passes to the error-handling routine, which prints a message and ends the program. Note that the IF statement checks not only for ERR = 5, but also for ERL = 100. This ensures that an Illegal function call error in another part of the program does not cause the error message to be displayed and the program to terminate. Chapter 11 develops a real-world program that uses error trapping as part of a routine to check video hardware.

For the second example, consider a program that uses a set of configuration parameters to control various aspects of its operation. The program has a set of default parameters that can be modified by the user and saved in a disk file. When the program starts, it should perform the following tasks in the order shown.

1. Check the disk for a configuration file.

2. If such a file exists, input the program parameters from the file.

3. If a configuration file is not found, use the default parameters defined in the program code.

This is easily done using the fact that trying to OPEN a disk file that does not exist causes a File not found error (number 53). The following code shows how to do this, reading parameters from the disk file if it exists, and setting default parameters if the file does not exist. In this example,

the configuration file is named `config.dat`, and the program parameters
are stored in the array `params()`.

```
DIM params(10)

ON ERROR GOTO errorhandler

100 OPEN "config.dat" FOR INPUT AS #1
    FOR i = 1 TO 10
         INPUT #1, param(i)
    NEXT i
    CLOSE #1
nofile:
    .
    . (remainder of program code)
    .
END

errorhandler:

IF ERR = 53 AND ERL = 100 THEN
' set default parameters

    param(1) = 1
    .
    .
    param(10) = 250
    RESUME nofile
  .
.(remainder of error-handling code)
  .
```

The final example of using errors as programming tools also deals with
files. When a program stores data on disk, the usual practice is to ask the
user to enter a name for a *filename*. If *filename* already exists, however,
you want to give the user the option of overwriting the existing file with
the new one or leaving the existing file intact and entering a new name
for the file. The steps for doing this are as follows:

1. Prompt the user for *filename*.

2. Try to OPEN *filename* for input.

3. If a file not found error occurs, *filename* does not exist and there
   is no danger of overwriting existing data. Open *filename* for output
   and proceed with saving the data.

4. If a file not found error does *not* occur, *filename* already exists. Close the file, and ask the user whether the file should be overwritten.

5. If YES, OPEN *filename* for output, and proceed with saving the data (this replaces any existing file). If NO, return to step 1.

Following is the code to perform these tasks:

```
CONST NO = 0, YES = 1

ON ERROR GOTO errorhandler

.
.
FILE_EXISTS = YES.

DO

    INPUT "Enter name for data file: ",filename$
    .
    . (you might want to include code to verify that
    . (filename$ is a valid DOS file name)
    .
100 OPEN filename$ FOR INPUT AS #1

    IF FILE_EXISTS = NO THEN EXIT LOOP

' execution reaches here only if filename$ exists

    CLOSE #1
    PRINT "File ";filename$;" already exists."
    PRINT "Press R to replace, any other key for new name."
    DO
        k$ = inkey$
    LOOP UNTIL k$ <> ""
    IF UCASE$(k$) = "R" THEN EXIT LOOP

LOOP

    OPEN filename$ FOR OUTPUT AS #1
    .
    .(data saving statements)
    .
    CLOSE #1
```

```
errorhandler:

IF ERR = 53 AND ERL = 100 THEN FILE_EXISTS = NO : RESUME NEXT
   .
   .
   .
```

These are just some of the ways you can use file-related errors as programming tools.

A General Error-Handling Routine

Writing error handlers is a task that many programmers tend to avoid. The real challenge seems to be those parts of the program that perform the tasks for which the program is intended. These parts of the program get most of the programmer's attention, and error-handling code is ignored as long as possible. Unfortunately, this approach is not wise. It is much easier to design error handling into a program from the start than it is to add it later.

To help with this problem, the remainder of this chapter presents a generic error-handling routine that you can incorporate into your QB program from the very beginning. Then, as your program develops, you can add to and modify this error handler to meet the specific needs of your program.

At the heart of the generic error handler is a string array that contains the various QB error messages. The array index for each message is the corresponding error number. When an error occurs, the error handler does the following:

1. Prints the error message, error number, and error line.

2. Offers the user the option of printing the error information on the printer to create a running log of errors.

3. Presents the user with choices to RESUME, RESUME NEXT, or terminate the program.

The code for the generic error handler is presented in listing 4.4.

Listing 4.4. ERROR3.BAS

```
' generic error-handling routine

DECLARE SUB DefineErrorMessages ()

DIM SHARED error$(76)

ON ERROR GOTO errorhandler

CALL DefineErrorMessages

' ******* begin user code

CLS

INPUT "Enter desired error code: ", x%
100 ERROR x%

' ******* end user code

END


errorhandler:

' use error$(1)to hold current error message. If no error
' message exists for ERR, it is an UNKNOWN ERROR
IF LEN(error$(ERR)) > 0 THEN

     error$(1) = error$(ERR)
ELSE
     error$(1) = "Unknown error"
END IF

LOCATE 18, 1

PRINT "Error number"; ERR; "("; error$(1); ")";
     " in line"; ERL
PRINT
PRINT "Options: Type P to print error information."
PRINT "              R to RESUME."
PRINT "              N to RESUME NEXT."
```

```
PRINT "              E to end program."

DO
    DO
        K$ = INKEY$
    LOOP UNTIL K$ <> ""

SELECT CASE K$
    CASE "P", "p"
        LPRINT "Error number"; ERR; "("; error$(1); ")";
                " in line"; ERL
        LPRINT
    CASE "R", "r"
        RESUME
    CASE "N", "n"
        RESUME NEXT
    CASE "E", "e"
        END
END SELECT

LOOP        ' end of error handler

SUB DefineErrorMessages

' loads array error$() with QB error messages.

error$(3) = "RETURN without GOSUB"
error$(5) = "Illegal function call"
error$(6) = "Overflow"
error$(7) = "Out of memory"
error$(9) = "Subscript out of range"
error$(11) = "Division by 0"
error$(14) = "Out of string space"
error$(16) = "String formula too complex"
error$(19) = "No RESUME" error$(20) = "RESUME without error"
error$(24) = "Device timeout"
error$(25) = "Device fault"
error$(27) = "Out of paper"
error$(39) = "CASE ELSE expected"
error$(50) = "FIELD overflow"
error$(51) = "Internal error"
```

Listing **4.4** *continues*

Listing 4.4 *continued*

```
error$(52) = "Bad file name or number"
error$(53) = "File not found"
error$(54) = "Bad file mode"
error$(55) = "File already open"
error$(56) = "FIELD statement active"
error$(57) = "Device I/O error"
error$(58) = "File already exists"
error$(59) = "Bad record length"
error$(61) = "Disk full"
error$(62) = "Input past end of file"
error$(63) = "Bad record number"
error$(64) = "Bad file name"
error$(67) = "Too many files"
error$(68) = "Device unavailable"
error$(69) = "Communications buffer overflow"
error$(70) = "Permission denied"
error$(71) = "Disk not ready"
error$(72) = "Disk media error"
error$(73) = "Advanced feature unavailable"
error$(74) = "Rename across disks"
error$(75) = "Path/file access error"
error$(76) = "Path not found"


END SUB
```

The "user code" section of listing 4.4 contains a few lines to demonstrate the error handler. The user is prompted to input an error code, and the ERROR statement is used to simulate that error. Be aware that when you run the demonstration, selecting R to Resume from the error handler message returns execution to the ERROR statement, causing another error.

As you develop your program, you will probably want to modify the error handler to deal with error situations that are specific to your program. For example, you might want to add code to use file errors to check for a configuration file, as discussed earlier in the chapter. Place any additions at the beginning of the error handler. This way, errors that are not "caught" by your additions will be handled by the generic error handler.

Summary

This chapter was intended to bring home to you the importance of good error handling. Nothing infuriates users more than a program that cannot recover from simple errors. Whereas QB's error-handling abilities are limited, they are nonetheless adequate for most situations. By putting a reasonable amount of attention into your programs' error-handling code, you can ensure that your programs will be able to handle most—if not all—of the errors that may occur.

Accessing DOS Services

QuickBASIC programs can access DOS services to perform tasks that cannot be accomplished directly through QuickBASIC. QuickBASIC accesses DOS services by issuing interrupts.

Interrupts and the PC

An *interrupt* is a special category of signal that causes the computer's central processing unit (CPU) to temporarily suspend its current activity and pass control to a program called an *interrupt handler* or interrupt service routine (ISR). The code in the interrupt handler determines the cause of the interrupt, takes appropriate action, then returns control to the original, suspended process.

Interrupts are an extremely powerful feature of the Intel 8086 family of CPUs used in IBM PCs and compatibles. This book is not the place for a detailed treatment of interrupts; for details, refer to one of the various MS-DOS technical programming reference books available. I cover interrupts briefly here, however, discussing those aspects you need to know to use interrupts in your QuickBASIC programs. This chapter does the following:

❑ Explains the basics of hardware and software interrupts

❏ Describes the built-in operating system services that can be accessed with an interrupt

❏ Shows how to use QB statements and data types to access the services

❏ Gives reference information on interrupts that provide services not available in QB itself

❏ Develops a set of QB procedures that you follow to access system services from your QB programs

Please be aware that the sections of this chapter that deal with technical aspects of DOS and the PC hardware are *far* from complete. My goal is to provide only enough information for you to understand and use the QB procedures and functions in this chapter.

Hardware and Software Interrupts

Interrupts on the PC are divided into three categories:

❏ *Internal hardware interrupts*. These interrupts are caused by certain errors or events that occur within the CPU during program execution. An example of a condition that causes an internal hardware interrupt is attempting to divide by zero. These interrupts are of little direct concern to programmers, because the interrupts are essentially "hard-wired" into the CPU and thus are not modifiable.

❏ *External hardware interrupts*. This type of interrupt is generated by a hardware device external to the CPU, such as a serial port, hard disk, or keyboard. External hardware interrupts are used just about every time a program receives data from a peripheral device. These interrupts can be manipulated by a program to maximize control over incoming data. This chapter does not cover external hardware interrupts.

❏ *Software interrupts*. A software interrupt is triggered not by a hardware event but, as the name implies, a software statement. Almost all programming languages include one or more statements used to trigger, or call, software interrupts. In QB, these statements are INTERRUPT and INTERRUPTX. Using software interrupts, you can bring a great deal of added functionality to your QB programs. In fact, the interrupts provide capabilities that are not included in QB itself—all with relatively little programming effort. The next section clarifies how to use these interrupts.

DOS and BIOS Interrupt Services

Some beginning programmers think of hardware and software as two totally separate categories. The computer sitting on your desk is the hardware; by itself it can do nothing. The program that you load from diskettes—the word processor, spreadsheet, or whatever—contains all of the instructions that control the operation of the computer.

This is not accurate. Before you load your program, there is already a great deal of powerful software in the computer. This software is built-in at two distinct levels: ROM BIOS and DOS.

ROM BIOS

ROM BIOS stands for Read-Only Memory Basic Input/Output System. The ROM BIOS is a set of software routines contained in read-only memory on the computer's system board. (Read-only memory cannot be modified and does not lose information when the power is turned off.) As the name implies, ROM BIOS routines are concerned mainly with data input and output.

DOS

DOS, of course, is the abbreviation for disk operating system. If you are using an IBM PC or compatible, you are almost surely using either MS-DOS (Microsoft DOS) or IBM PC DOS, which are essentially identical. Essential parts of DOS are loaded from diskettes or a fixed disk into your computer's memory at boot time, so it is not literally built in like the ROM BIOS. It might as well be built in, however, because DOS commands and features are always present when a program is running. Because DOS is not built-in, it can be improved and expanded as needs change. This is exactly what has happened as MS-DOS has evolved from the original version, 1.0, to the current versions 3.3 and 4.0.

Both DOS and the BIOS contain many interrupt service routines (ISRs) that programs use to interact with the computer hardware by issuing an interrupt service request. This, in fact, is one of the main purposes of DOS and the BIOS—to provide a standardized interface between programs and the hardware. The DOS and BIOS routines also greatly simplify the task of writing compilers such as QB. Rather than having to deal directly with, say, the intricacies of a hard disk interface, a compiler need only deal with the relevant DOS and BIOS routines. The difficult job of programming directly for the hardware has already been taken care of.

Programs written in QB (or any other language) already rely heavily on the DOS and BIOS routines. Some DOS and BIOS services, however, are not available directly with QB statements. For example, DOS includes an interrupt service routine for changing a file's attributes, but there is no corresponding statement in QB. The remainder of this chapter shows you how to use some of these services in your QB programs. First, however, you need to know the fundamentals of how the CPU in your computer deals with data and memory addresses.

CPU Registers and Memory Addressing

What follows is an extremely abbreviated description of the 8088/8086 CPU family. Entire books have been written about these fascinating chips, and in these few paragraphs I do nothing more than give you a few fundamental facts. Note also that the material here is, strictly speaking, true only for the 8088/8086 CPUs used in IBM PCs, XTs, and compatibles. The 80286 and 80386 chips found in PC/AT and PS/2 computers are more complicated, but because these advanced CPUs can emulate the earlier chips, this information applies to them as well.

Registers

Your computer's CPU contains a small number of data storage locations called *registers*. Each register can hold 16 bits, or 2 bytes, of data. The registers in the 8088/8086 CPU are listed here. Each register is referred to by a two-letter code as well as by a descriptive name.

Data registers:

AX	accumulator
BX	base
CX	count
DX	data

Pointer and index registers:

SP	stack pointer
BP	base pointer
SI	source index
DI	destination index

Segment registers:

CS	code segment
DS	data segment
SS	stack segment
ES	extra segment

Others:

IP	instruction pointer
-	status flags

The names assigned to the registers reflect their dedicated or usual functions. Many of these registers have specialized functions that are important to know when you are programming in assembly language. The *data registers* are used to hold data being manipulated. The *segment registers* in combination with the *pointer registers* are used for memory addressing, with the segment:offset addressing scheme explained in the next discussion. The *instruction pointer* points to the address of the next instruction to be executed by the CPU. For this chapter's purposes, all you need to know is that several of the processor registers pass information to, and receive information from, BIOS and DOS interrupt service routines.

The *status flags* register is a special case. Rather than containing two bytes of data, the flags consist of single-bit "flags" that can be set to either 0 or 1. The flags register contains 16 bits, but only 9 of them are used in the 8088/8086. Six of these bits are status flags that report various internal CPU conditions. Three are control flags that allow a program to control certain aspects of the CPU's behavior.

The only flag that you need be concerned with is the *carry flag*, which is located at bit position 0 in the flags register. During arithmetic operations, the CPU sets the carry flag to 1 if an addition produces a carry or a subtraction produces a borrow; otherwise, it is 0. The carry flag is also used by some DOS and BIOS interrupt routines to signal an error; if a function succeeds in execution, the carry flag is clear (0); if the function fails, the carry flag is set (1).

Each of the four data registers can operate either as a single 16-bit register or as two 8-bit registers. The 8-bit registers are referred to with the suffix letters H or L, indicating either the high byte or the low byte of the corresponding 16-bit register. Thus, the 16-bit AX register is made up of two 8-bit registers, AL and AH; BX consists of BL and BH, and so on. QB does not provide direct access to the 8-bit registers, but as you will see, these values are easily extracted from the 16-bit registers.

Memory Addressing

As you have seen, the CPUs used in IBM compatible PCs manipulate data in 16-bit chunks. This data comprises not only program code and data but also the memory addresses that the processor uses to store and retrieve data in RAM. A 16-bit address can specify only 2^{16}, or 65536, different memory addresses. This is not nearly enough, so the CPU developers had to find a way around this limitation.

The solution used by Intel was to use two 16-bit registers to specify an address. The contents of one register are multiplied by 16 (or, in binary terms, shifted left by 4 bits) to form a 20-bit *segment address*. The contents of the second register give the *offset address* relative to the segment address. In other words, the offset address is added to the segment address to create the *physical address* actually used to specify a particular location in RAM. The physical address is a 20-bit quantity, so the total address space for the PC is 2^{20} or 1048576 bytes.

Take a look at an example.

Contents of segment register	10010101 11010101
Shifted left 4 bits	1001 01011101 01010000
Added to contents of offset register	+ 00101101 01011000
Final 20-bit physical address	1001 10001010 10101000

There are four segment registers in the 8088/8086 CPU, enabling you to access as many as four different memory segments at one time. As you can see in the routines listed later in the chapter, it is sometimes necessary to pass the segment and offset of a variable to an interrupt routine. These values can be obtained with the QB functions VARSEG, VARPTR, and SADD.

Hexadecimal Notation

Before going any further, you need to understand hexadecimal notation. Hexadecimal notation is a number system that is particularly useful for dealing with binary computers. It uses base 16, rather than the base 10 used by the everyday decimal notation everyone is familiar with. In decimal notation:

456 (decimal)

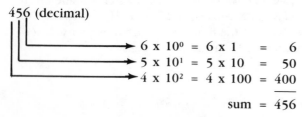

$$6 \times 10^0 = 6 \times 1 = 6$$
$$5 \times 10^1 = 5 \times 10 = 50$$
$$4 \times 10^2 = 4 \times 100 = 400$$
$$\text{sum} = 456$$

Hexadecimal notation works the same way, except that each position in the number represents a power of 16:

456 (hexadecimal)

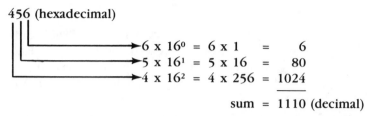

$$6 \times 16^0 = 6 \times 1 \quad = \quad 6$$
$$5 \times 16^1 = 5 \times 16 \quad = \quad 80$$
$$4 \times 16^2 = 4 \times 256 = 1024$$

$$\text{sum} = 1110 \text{ (decimal)}$$

Because the hexadecimal system uses powers of 16, it needs single digits for the numbers up to 15 (decimal). The regular digits 0 through 9 are used, plus the letters A through F to represent the (decimal) numbers 10 through 15. Thus, counting up from 0 in hexadecimal (with decimal equivalents):

Hex: 1 ... 9 A B C D E F 10 11 12 ... 1E 1F 20 ... FF 100

Dec: 1 ... 9 10 11 12 13 14 15 16 17 18 ... 30 31 32 ... 255 256

and, as used in larger numbers:

FCB (hexadecimal)

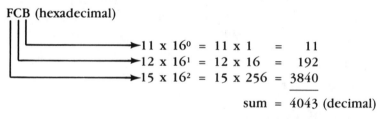

$$11 \times 16^0 = 11 \times 1 \quad = \quad 11$$
$$12 \times 16^1 = 12 \times 16 \quad = \quad 192$$
$$15 \times 16^2 = 15 \times 256 = 3840$$

$$\text{sum} = 4043 \text{ (decimal)}$$

Hexadecimal notation is a favorite among programmers, because the binary bit patterns used internally by computers translate directly into hex digits. A single hex digit can represent one nybble (4 bits), a pair of hex digits can represent one byte, and 4 hex digits are perfect for representing 16-bit memory addresses:

Decimal	Hex	Binary
0	00	0000 0000
1	01	0000 0001
.	.	.
.	.	.
254	FE	1111 1110
255	FF	1111 1111
.	.	.
.	.	.
65534	FFFE	1111 1111 1111 1110
65535	FFFF	1111 1111 1111 1111

Hexadecimal numbers are written in QB with the prefix &H.

Calling Interrupt Service Routines from QuickBASIC

Interrupts are called from QB with two statements: INTERRUPT and INTERRUPTX. These two statements are identical except for the type of data structures used (as detailed in the next section). The declarations of these procedures are located in the include file QB.BI, supplied with your QB package. The declarations are

```
DECLARE SUB INTERRUPT (intnum AS INTEGER, inreg AS RegType,
        outreg AS RegType)
DECLARE SUB INTERRUPTX (intnum AS INTEGER, inreg AS RegTypeX,
        outreg AS RegTypeX)
```

The code for these procedures is located in the default quick library QB.QLB, which must be loaded if you are going to use INTERRUPT or INTERRUPTX from within the QB environment. Both procedures take three arguments. The first, *intnum*, is an integer that specifies which interrupt is called. The other two arguments, inregs and outregs, are data structures used to place data in, and retrieve data from, the processor registers. INTERRUPT and INTERRUPTX differ only in that the former uses a data structure of type RegType, whereas the latter uses the type RegTypeX. These data structures are also defined in QB.BI, as follows:

```
TYPE RegType
        ax    AS INTEGER
        bx    AS INTEGER
        cx    AS INTEGER
        dx    AS INTEGER
        bp    AS INTEGER
        si    AS INTEGER
        di    AS INTEGER
        flags AS INTEGER
END TYPE

TYPE RegTypeX
        ax    AS INTEGER
        bx    AS INTEGER
        cx    AS INTEGER
        dx    AS INTEGER
        bp    AS INTEGER
        si    AS INTEGER
        di    AS INTEGER
```

```
        flags AS INTEGER
        ds    AS INTEGER
        es    AS INTEGER
END TYPE
```

Note that RegType and RegTypeX are identical except that RegTypeX permits access to the ES and DS segment registers, whereas RegType does not. Note also that neither data structure allows access to the IP, SP, CS, and SS registers. Rarely does a program need access to these registers, and you are best off leaving them alone.

To use the QB INTERRUPT(X) statement, follow this procedure:

1. Load the quick library QB.QLB by starting QuickBASIC with the command QB /L.

2. Include the file QB.BI in your program with an $INCLUDE metastatement.

3. DIMension two data structures of the appropriate type—RegType if you plan to use INTERRUPT, RegTypeX if you plan to use INTERRUPTX. The names inreg and outreg, or something similar, make the function of the two structures clear.

4. Load inreg with the register values needed for whatever interrupt function you are calling. To use a register's current value, load the corresponding structure element with −1.

5. Call the subroutine with the desired interrupt number as the first parameter, and inreg and outreg as the other parameters.

6. Read the structure elements in outreg to obtain any values returned by the interrupt service routine.

You can use a single structure of type RegType (or RegTypeX) for both sending values to and receiving values from the registers. Use the following format:

```
DIM regs AS RegType
    .
    .
    .
CALL INTERRUPT(intnum, regs, regs)
```

It is preferable, however, to use two separate structures so that the results of one call are not inadvertently passed as arguments to the next call.

Now that you understand the mechanics of calling an interrupt service routine, take a look at the details of some of the DOS and BIOS services.

DOS and BIOS Interrupt Reference

This is not intended to be a complete reference to all of the DOS and BIOS interrupt functions. I have not included those interrupt functions that duplicate capabilities available with QB statements. Neither have I included functions that are specific for multitasking or network environments, nor other functions unlikely to be of interest to most QB programmers. Rather, this discussion concentrates on interrupt functions that provide capabilities not available in QB or that significantly improve on QB functions. Following this section, I explain code that makes these functions available to your QB programs.

INT &H21, Function &H0B

Purpose: Checks for keyboard character.

Action: Checks whether a character is available from the standard input device but does not actually read the character.

Call: AH = &H0B

Return: AL = 0 if no character available.
AL = &HFF if a character is available.

Comments: The standard input device is the keyboard unless input has been redirected. This function determines whether a character is waiting in the type-ahead buffer without removing the character from the buffer.

INT &H21, Function &H0E

Purpose: Sets default disk drive.

Action: Sets the default disk drive and returns the number of logical drives in the system.

Call: AH = &H0E
DL = code for drive (0 = A, 1 = B, and so on)

Return: AL = number of logical drives.

Comments: "Logical drives" do not always correspond to physical drives. RAM disks are counted, as are multiple partitions on hard disks.

If you try to make a nonexistent drive the default drive, no error occurs. The original default remains unchanged, and the function nevertheless returns the correct number of logical drives.

INT &H21, Function &H19

Purpose: Gets the default disk drive.

Action: Returns the current default drive.

Call: AH = &H19

Return: AL = drive code (0 = A, 1 = B, and so on)

Comments: None.

INT &H21, Function &H1C

Purpose: Gets drive allocation information.

Action: Returns information about the specified disk drive and a pointer to a copy of the identification byte from the drive's File Allocation Table (FAT).

Call: AH = &H1C
DL = drive code (0 = default, 1 = A, and so on)

Return: AL = number of segments per cluster
CX = bytes per physical sector
DX = total number of clusters
DS:BX = address (segment:offset) of FAT identification byte

Comments: Total disk capacity in bytes can be calculated as

```
AL * CX * DX
```

Note that this interrupt gives the total capacity, *not* the available space (which can be obtained with function &H36).

The FAT identification byte has the following meanings:

&HFF	Dual-sided floppy, 8 sectors per track
&HFE	Single-sided floppy, 8 sectors per track
&HFD	Dual-sided floppy, 9 sectors per track
&HFC	Single-sided floppy, 9 sectors per track
&HF9	Dual-sided floppy, 15 sectors per track (high-density PC/AT drives)
&HF8	Hard disk

INT &H21, Function &H2E

Purpose: Sets/clears the verify flag.

Action: Sets or clears the operating system flag for read-after-write data verification during disk writes.

Call: AH = &H2E
     AL = &H00 to clear verify flag
        = &H01 to set verify flag
     DL = &H00 for DOS versions < 3.x only

Return: Nothing

Comments: This function has the same effect as the DOS command-line commands VERIFY ON and VERIFY OFF.

When the verify flag is ON, the operating system verifies disk writes by reading the data from the disk immediately after they are written. This operation does not verify that the correct data was written, only that whatever was written can be read. Having the verify flag ON slows down disk operations.

Use function &H54 to determine the state of the verify flag.

INT &H21, Function &H30

Purpose: Gets the DOS version number.

Action: Returns the version number of the MS-DOS release being used.

Call: AH = &H30

Return: AL = integer part of version number
      AH = decimal part of version number
          for example, for DOS 2.1, AL = &H02 (2 decimal) and
          AH = &H0A (decimal 10)

Comments: If 0 is returned in AL, the DOS version is 1.x.

INT &H21, Function &H36

Purpose: Gets the free disk space.

Action: Returns information about the specified disk drive; the information can be used to calculate the amount of free space on the drive.

Call: AH = &H36
       DL = drive code (0 = default, 1 = A, and so on)

Return: AX = sectors per cluster (or &HFFFF if drive invalid)
          BX = number of free clusters
          CX = sector size (in bytes)
          DX = total clusters per drive

Comments: Free disk space can be calculated as

```
AX * BX * CX
```

The amount of disk space in use can be calculated as

```
(DX - BX) * AX * CX
```

INT &H21, Function &H43

Purpose: Gets/sets file attributes.

Action: Reads or sets a file's attributes (archive, hidden, read-only, and system).

Call: AH = &H43
      AL = &H00 to read attributes
         = &H01 to set attributes
      CX = new attribute (if AL = 1)
         Bit 0 = read-only
           1 = hidden
           2 = system
           5 = archive
      DS:DX segment:offset of ASCIIZ file specification

Return: If function succeeded:
         carry flag = clear
         CX = attributes (if AL = 0 on call)
      If function failed:
         carry flag = set
         AX = error code:
             1 = function code invalid
             2 = file not found
             3 = path not found/file does not exist
             5 = attribute cannot be changed

Comments: When it reads a file's attributes, CX returns them in the same bit positions that are used for setting them.

INT &H21, Function &H47

Purpose: Gets the current directory.

Action: Returns an ASCIIZ string specifying the path to the current directory.

Call: AH = &H47
  DL = drive code (0 = default, 1 = A, and so on)
  DS:SI = segment:offset of 64 byte buffer

Return: If function succeeded:
      carry flag = clear
      buffer contains the path to the current directory
    If function failed:
      carry flag = set
      AX = &H0F

Comments: This function places the path name as an ASCIIZ string in the buffer pointed to by DS:SI. The path name is the full path from the root directory to the current directory on the specified drive. The returned path name does not include the drive identifier or a leading \. If the root directory is current, the first byte in the buffer is a zero (that is, CHR$(0)).

INT &H21, Function &H56

Purpose: Renames/moves a file.

Action: Renames a file and/or moves it to a different directory on the same disk.

Call: AH = &H56
  DS:DX = segment:offset of ASCIIZ string with current path/file name.
  ES:DI = segment:offset of ASCIIZ string with new path/file name.

Return: If function succeeded:
      carry flag = clear
    If function failed:
      carry flag = set
      AX = error code:
          2 = file not found
          3 = path not found/file does not exist
          5 = access denied
          &H11 = not same device

Comments: Wild-card characters are not allowed in either the current or the new file specification. This function fails if

❏ you try to move a file to a full directory.

❏ you try to move a file to a different disk.

❏ a file with the new path/file name already exists.

Moving a file consists simply of moving its directory entry to a different directory; the file itself is not moved. For this reason, moving a file is much faster, particularly for large files, than copying it to the new location and deleting it from the old location. For the same reason, files cannot be "moved" between disks. This interrupt service routine duplicates the QB **NAME** statement, but this routine allows errors to be handled without an **ON ERROR GOTO** statement.

INT &H10, Function &H03

Purpose: Reads the cursor type and position.

Action: Reads the current cursor position—in text coordinates—and the starting and stopping cursor scan lines (that is, the cursor's shape).

Call: AH = &H03
     BH = page number

Return: CH = starting scan line
       CL = ending scan line
       DH = row (Y coordinate)
       DL = column (X coordinate)

Comments: The monochrome display adapter has only one display page. Other display adapters have multiple display pages (for example, the CGA has four). Each display page has its own cursor, which has a position and shape that can be read with this function even when the page is not displayed.

INT &H10, Function &H0F

Purpose: Gets the current display mode.

Action: Returns the current display mode of the video adapter.

Call: AH = &H0F

Return: AH = number of character columns on the screen.

AL = display mode
&H00 = 40 x 25 monochrome text, color adapter
&H01 = 40 x 25 color text
&H02 = 80 x 25 monochrome text
&H03 = 80 x 25 color text
&H04 = 320 x 200 4-color graphics
&H05 = 320 x 200 4-color graphics (color burst off)
&H06 = 640 x 200 2-color graphics
&H07 = monochrome adapter text display
&H08 = 160 x 200 16-color graphics (PCjr)
&H09 = 320 x 200 16-color graphics (PCjr)
&H0A = 640 x 200 4-color graphics (PCjr)
&H0D = 320 x 200 16-color graphics (EGA)
&H0E = 640 x 200 16-color graphics (EGA)
&H0F = 640 x 350 monochrome graphics (EGA)
&H10 = 640 x 350 4- or 16-color graphics (EGA; number of colors depends on amount of video RAM installed
&H11 = 640 x 480 monochrome graphics (MCGA, VGA)
&H12 = 640 x 480 16-color graphics (VGA)
&H13 = 320 x 200 256-color graphics (MCGA, VGA)

BH = active display page.

Comments: None

INT &H16, Function &H02

Purpose: Reads keyboard flags.

Action: Returns information about the various keyboard toggle and shift keys.

Call: AH = &H02

Return: AL = the ROM BIOS keyboard flag byte.

The bits in this byte correspond to the following keys: if the bit is 1, the key is ON (for toggles) or down (for Shift, Ctrl, and Alt).

bit 0 = right shift key
bit 1 = left shift key
bit 2 = Ctrl key
bit 3 = Alt key

bit 4 = Scroll Lock key
bit 5 = Num Lock key
bit 6 = Caps Lock key
bit 7 = Ins key

Comments: Note that this function can distinguish between the right and left shift keys.

DOS and BIOS Call Procedures

You are now ready to develop QB code for the procedures to access the DOS and BIOS interrupt service routines. The code itself is presented later in the chapter. I will present some general information about these procedures, then discuss each individual procedure in turn.

Drive Specifiers

Those interrupt service routines that deal with disk drives must be told which drive to use. The drive is passed as an argument, using the following numerical code:

```
0 = default drive
1 = A:
2 = B:
.
.
26 = Z:
```

The QB procedures for these interrupt service routines are written to take a drive letter as an argument. The drive letter argument may be passed as a letter alone (C) or with a colon (C:). The procedure code converts the letter into the appropriate numerical code. If no drive letter is passed or if it is outside the range of A through Z, the function automatically assumes the default drive (code = 0).

The Carry Flag

Several of the interrupt service routines use the carry flag to signal success or failure; upon return from the interrupt service routine, a clear carry flag signifies success, and a set carry flag signifies failure. The carry flag is the first bit in the flags register and can be extracted as follows:

```
IF OutRegs.flags AND 1 THEN
     ' carry flag set; error occurred
ELSE IF
     ' carry flag not set; no error
END IF
```

Extracting Single Bytes from Registers

Some ISRs return byte values in the "high" and "low" registers. For example, INT $H10 function 3 (Get Cursor Information) returns the cursor row in register CH (the high byte of CX) and the cursor column in register CL (the low byte of CX). QB does not provide direct access to the byte registers, but the values can easily be extracted as follows:

```
LOW BYTE = REGISTER AND &HFF
HIGH BYTE = REGISTER \ &HFF
```

Extracting Single Bits from Registers

It is sometimes necessary to extract single bits from a register—for example, INT &H21, function 43 (Get File Attributes). A given bit can be extracted as follows (remember that the first bit is bit 0):

```
BIT N = (REGISTER \ (2^N)) AND 1
```

Thus,

```
BIT 0 = REGISTER AND 1
BIT 1 = (REGISTER \ 2) AND 1
BIT 2 = (REGISTER \ 4) AND 1
  .
  .
BIT 7 = (REGISTER \ 128) AND 1
```

ASCIIZ Strings

An *ASCIIZ string* is simply a string of ASCII characters that is terminated by a byte with a value of zero. A variable-length QB string is converted into an ASCIIZ string using the following format:

```
ASCIIZ$ = OLDSTRING$ + CHR$(0)
```

Information on Individual Procedures

This section provides a brief summary of each of the QB procedures that access the DOS and BIOS interrupt routines. Some of the functions return error codes. For the meaning of specific error codes, see the entry for the relevant interrupt function in the preceding reference section.

GetCurrentDir

GetCurrentDir returns a string, maximum length 64 characters, giving the path from the root directory to the current directory on the designated disk drive. The drive is passed as an argument to the function. If no argument is passed, the current default drive is used. If GetCurrentDir fails, a null string is returned.

GetCursor

This procedure obtains position and shape information about the screen cursor. The information is put in a user-defined data structure of type CursorInfo, defined as follows:

```
TYPE CursorInfo
     row AS INTEGER
     col AS INTEGER
     startline AS INTEGER
     stopline AS INTEGER
END TYPE
```

The calling program must define the data structure, which is also used by SetCursor.

SetCursor

SetCursor uses information in a data structure of type CursorInfo to set the position and shape of the screen cursor. SetCursor does not use an interrupt call directly, because you can set the cursor position and shape with the QB LOCATE statement. This procedure was designed to use the same data structure as GetCursor, so the two procedures can be used together to save the cursor status and then later restore it, as in this example:

```
DIM Cursor as CursorInfo
' save cursor shape and location
GetCursor (Cursor)
' other code here that changes cursor shape and/or position
  .
  .
  .
' now restore original cursor shape/position
SetCursor (Cursor)
```

GetDefaultDriveLetter

This function returns a two-character string consisting of the letter of the current default drive followed by a colon.

SetDefaultDrive

This function sets the default drive to the letter passed as an argument. If the specified drive does not exist, no change is made. The return value gives the total number of logical drives in the system.

GetDriveInfo

GetDriveInfo obtains technical information about the drive whose letter is passed as an argument. The data is put in a user-defined data structure of type DriveInfo, which must be defined by the calling program as follows:

```
TYPE DriveInfo
      SectorsPerCluster AS INTEGER
      SectorSize AS INTEGER
      Clusters AS LONG
      Capacity AS LONG
      SpaceAvailable AS LONG
      Ident AS INTEGER
END TYPE
```

The structure element SpaceAvailable is not used by GetDriveInfo.

GetDriveSpace

`GetDriveSpace` obtains the same technical information as `GetDriveInfo`. `GetDriveSpace` also determines the total amount of free space available on the drive. This can be very useful in determining whether a disk has enough space for your program to store data. If not, your code can prompt users to change diskettes or take other action.

Even if you need only the technical drive information and are not interested in free space, using `GetDriveSpace` is preferable to using `GetDriveInfo`, because `GetDriveSpace` returns a code if an error occurs and 0 on success. Note that `GetDriveInfo` returns a drive identification byte, whereas `GetDriveSpace` does not.

GetFileAttr

This function determines the attributes of the specified file and puts them in a user-defined data structure of type `FileAttributes`. This data structure must be defined by the calling program, as follows:

```
TYPE FileAttributes
      ReadOnly AS INTEGER
      Archive AS INTEGER
      Hidden AS INTEGER
      Systm AS INTEGER
END TYPE
```

The function returns 0 on success and an error code on failure.

SetFileAttr

This procedure sets a file's attributes according to an "attribute string" that is passed as an argument. The details of how to set up the attribute string argument are given in comments in the source code in listing 5.1. If a given attribute is not specified in the attribute string, it is left unchanged.

GetVideoMode

This function returns an integer code indicating the currently set video mode. The codes and the corresponding modes are listed in the reference section earlier in this chapter.

KBStatus

KBStatus returns the status of the keyboard status and shift keys. The function uses a data structure of type KeyboardInfo that must be defined in the calling program as follows:

```
TYPE KeyboardInfo
        insert AS INTEGER
        capslock AS INTEGER
        numlock AS INTEGER
        scrollock AS INTEGER
        alt AS INTEGER
        ctrl AS INTEGER
        leftshift AS INTEGER
        rightshift AS INTEGER
END TYPE
```

A structure element is set to 1 if the corresponding key is DOWN or ON at the time of the call; otherwise, it is set to 0.

KeyInBuf

This function returns 0 if no key is waiting in the type-ahead buffer and returns 1 if a key is waiting. Unlike INKEY$, KeyInBuf does not remove the keystroke from the buffer.

MSDOSVersion

This function returns a single precision number giving the version of DOS that is currently loaded.

Rename

The Rename function can be used to rename a file or to move it to a different directory on the same disk. It *cannot* be used to move a file to a different disk. Rename returns 0 upon success and an error code upon failure.

VerifyOn, VerifyOff

These procedures set or clear the DOS verify flag. When the flag is ON, DOS checks the integrity of data written to disk. When the flag is OFF, no checking is performed.

Now you are finally ready to get to the code itself. Listing 5.1 presents the QB code for the DOS BIOS call procedures.

Listing 5.1. *DOS and BIOS Calls Procedures*

```
**********************************************************************
FUNCTION GetCurrentDir$ (driveletter$)

' Set up buffer to receive path name.

buffer$ = STRING$(64, " ")

' Convert drive letter to code.

IF driveletter$ = "" THEN
      InRegs.dx = 0
ELSE
      InRegs.dx = ASC(UCASE$(driveletter$)) - 64
END IF

' Be sure InRegs.dx is in the range 0-26.

IF InRegs.dx < 0 OR InRegs.dx > 26 THEN
      InRegs.dx = 0
END IF

InRegs.ax = &H4700

' Get segment:offset of buffer.

InRegs.ds = VARSEG(buffer$)
InRegs.si = SADD(buffer$)

CALL Interruptx(&H21, InRegs, OutRegs)

' If carry flag is set, return empty string.
```

Listing 5.1 *continues*

Listing 5.1 continued

```
IF (OutRegs.flags AND 1) THEN
    GetCurrentDir$ = ""
    EXIT FUNCTION
END IF

' Return path name preceded by \.

GetCurrentDir$ = "\" + LEFT$(buffer$, INSTR(buffer$, " ") - 2)

END FUNCTION        ' end of GetCurrentDir


SUB GetCursor (cursor AS CursorInfo)

InRegs.ax = &H300
InRegs.bx = 0

CALL Interruptx(&H10, InRegs, OutRegs)

' Row is in DH.

cursor.row = (OutRegs.dx \ &HFF) + 1

' Column is in DL.

cursor.col = (OutRegs.dx AND &HFF) + 1

' Startline is in CH.

cursor.startline = OutRegs.cx \ &HFF

' Stopline is in CL.

cursor.stopline = OutRegs.cx AND &HFF

END SUB      ' end of GetCursor


FUNCTION GetDefaultDriveLetter$

InRegs.ax = &H1900
```

```
CALL Interruptx(&H21, InRegs, OutRegs)

' Return drive letter plus ":".

GetDefaultDriveLetter$ = CHR$((OutRegs.ax AND &HFF) + 65) + ":"

END FUNCTION          ' end of GetDefaultdriveletter$


SUB GetDriveInfo (driveletter$)

SHARED Drive AS DriveInfo

InRegs.ax = &H1C00

' Convert drive letter into code.

IF LEN(driveletter$) = 0 THEN
     InRegs.dx = 0
ELSE
     InRegs.dx = ASC(UCASE$(driveletter$)) - 64
END IF

' Be sure InRegs.dx is in the range 0-26.

IF InRegs.dx < 0 OR InRegs.dx > 26 THEN
     InRegs.dx = 0
END IF

CALL Interruptx(&H21, InRegs, OutRegs)

Drive.SectorsPerCluster = OutRegs.ax
Drive.SectorSize = OutRegs.cx

' Convert unsigned integer returned by the interrupt to the
' signed integer format used by QB.

IF OutRegs.dx >= 0 THEN
     Drive.Clusters = OutRegs.dx
ELSE
     Drive.Clusters = OutRegs.dx + 65536
```

Listing 5.1 continues

Listing 5.1 continued

```
END IF

' Address DS:BX points to drive identifier byte.

DEF SEG = OutRegs.ds
Drive.Ident = PEEK(OutRegs.bx)
DEF SEG

END SUB      ' end of GetDriveInfo


FUNCTION GetDriveSpace (driveletter$)

SHARED Drive AS DriveInfo

InRegs.ax = &H3600

' Convert drive letter to code.

IF LEN(driveletter$) = 0 THEN
     InRegs.dx = 0
ELSE
     InRegs.dx = ASC(UCASE$(driveletter$)) - 64
END IF

' Be sure InRegs.dx is in the range 0-26.

IF InRegs.dx < 0 OR InRegs.dx > 26 THEN
     InRegs.dx = 0
END IF

CALL Interruptx(&H21, InRegs, OutRegs)

' If function failed, return error code.

IF OutRegs.ax = &HFFFF THEN
     GetDriveSpace = OutRegs.ax
     EXIT FUNCTION
END IF

Drive.SectorsPerCluster = OutRegs.ax
Drive.SectorSize = OutRegs.cx
```

```
' Convert unsigned integer returned by the interrupt to the
' signed integer format used by QB.

IF OutRegs.dx >= 0 THEN
      Drive.Clusters = OutRegs.dx
ELSE
      Drive.Clusters = OutRegs.dx + 65536
END IF

' Calculate total drive capacity.

Drive.Capacity = Drive.Clusters * OutRegs.ax * OutRegs.cx

' Calculate available space (in bytes).  The multiplications
' are done in two steps to avoid overflow.

IF OutRegs.bx >= 0 THEN
      Drive.SpaceAvailable = OutRegs.bx
      Drive.SpaceAvailable = Drive.SpaceAvailable * OutRegs.ax *
OutRegs.cx
ELSE
      Drive.SpaceAvailable = (OutRegs.bx + 65536)
      Drive.SpaceAvailable = Drive.SpaceAvailable * OutRegs.ax *
OutRegs.cx
END IF

' Return 0 because procedure succeeded.

GetDriveSpace = 0

END FUNCTION          ' end of GetDriveSpace


FUNCTION GetFileAttr (FileName$)

SHARED File AS FileAttributes

' Convert FileName$ to ASCIIZ string.

TempFileName$ = FileName$ + CHR$(0)

InRegs.ax = &H4300
```

Listing 5.1 continues

Listing 5.1 *continued*

```
' Get segment:offset of file specifier.

InRegs.ds = VARSEG(TempFileName$)
InRegs.dx = SADD(TempFileName$)

CALL Interruptx(&H21, InRegs, OutRegs)

' Return errorcode if function failed.

IF (OutRegs.flags AND 1) THEN
     GetFileAttr = OutRegs.ax
     EXIT FUNCTION
END IF

' Read only = bit 0.
' Hidden = bit 1.
' System = bit 2.
' Archive = bit 5.

File.ReadOnly = OutRegs.cx AND 1
File.Hidden = (OutRegs.cx \ 2) AND 1
File.Systm = (OutRegs.cx \ 4) AND 1
File.Archive = (OutRegs.cx \ 32) AND 1

' Return 0.

GetFileAttr = 0

END FUNCTION       ' end of GetFileAttr


FUNCTION GetVideoMode

InRegs.ax = &HF00

CALL Interruptx(&H10, InRegs, OutRegs)

' Video mode is in AL.

GetVideoMode = OutRegs.ax AND &HFF
```

```
END FUNCTION        ' end of GetVideoMode


SUB KBStatus

' Returns the status of the keyboard toggle and shift keys
' at the time of the call.

SHARED keyboard AS KeyboardInfo

InRegs.ax = &H200

CALL Interruptx(&H16, InRegs, OutRegs)

OutRegs.ax = OutRegs.ax AND &HFF

' Extract bits 7 thru 0 in order.

        keyboard.insert = OutRegs.ax \ 128
        keyboard.capslock = (OutRegs.ax AND &H40) \ 64
        keyboard.numlock = (OutRegs.ax AND &H20) \ 32
        keyboard.scrollock = (OutRegs.ax AND &H10) \ 16
        keyboard.alt = (OutRegs.ax AND &H8) \ 8
        keyboard.ctrl = (OutRegs.ax AND &H4) \ 4
        keyboard.leftshift = (OutRegs.ax AND &H2) \ 2
        keyboard.rightshift = (OutRegs.ax AND 1)

END SUB      ' end of KBStatus


FUNCTION KeyInBuf

' Returns 0 if there is no character waiting in the type-ahead
' buffer, nonzero if there is a character waiting.

' Does not remove character from buffer.

InRegs.ax = &HB00

CALL Interruptx(&H21, InRegs, OutRegs)
```

Listing 5.1 continues

Listing 5.1 *continued*

```
KeyInBuf = OutRegs.ax AND &HFF

END FUNCTION


FUNCTION MSDOSVersion!

' Returns the version number of MS-DOS that is loaded.

InRegs.ax = &H3000

CALL Interruptx(&H21, InRegs, OutRegs)

' Major version number is in AL, minor is in AH.

major = OutRegs.ax AND &HFF
minor = OutRegs.ax \ &HFF

' Put together final version number.

MSDOSVersion = major + minor / 100

END FUNCTION


FUNCTION Rename (old$, new$) STATIC

' Renames a file and/or moves it to a different directory on
' the same disk.

' Converts arguments to ASCIIZ strings.

tempold$ = old$ + CHR$(0)
tempnew$ = new$ + CHR$(0)

InRegs.ax = &H5600

' Set registers to segment:offset of arguments.

InRegs.dx = SADD(tempold$)
InRegs.di = SADD(tempnew$)
```

```
InRegs.es = VARSEG(tempnew$)
InRegs.ds = VARSEG(tempold$)

CALL Interruptx(&H21, InRegs, OutRegs)

' If function succeeded (that is, carry flag is clear), return 0.
' Otherwise, return error code from AX.

IF (OutRegs.flags AND &H1) = 0 THEN
     Rename = 0
ELSE
     Rename = OutRegs.ax
END IF

END FUNCTION          ' end of Rename


SUB SetCursor (cursor AS CursorInfo)

' Uses the LOCATE statement to set the text cursor position
' and shape, per information in a CursorInfo data structure.

LOCATE cursor.row, cursor.col, , cursor.startline, cursor.stopline

END SUB          ' end of SetCursor


FUNCTION SetDefaultDrive (driveletter$)

' Sets the default disk drive.

' If the specified drive does not exist, no error occurs
' and no change is made.

InRegs.ax = &HE00

' Convert drive letter to a code.

InRegs.dx = ASC(UCASE$(driveletter$)) - 65

' Be sure it is between 0 and 26.
```

Listing 5.1 continues

Listing 5.1 *continued*

```
IF InRegs.dx < 0 OR InRegs.dx > 26 THEN
      SetDefaultDrive = 0
      EXIT FUNCTION
END IF

CALL Interruptx(&H21, InRegs, OutRegs)

' Return number of logical drives.

SetDefaultDrive = OutRegs.ax AND &HFF

END FUNCTION          ' end of SetDefaultDrive


FUNCTION SetFileAttr (FileName$, attributes$)

' Changes attributes of the file FileName$.

' The argument attributes$ is interpreted as follows:

' If it contains an "R," the read-only attribute is set ON.
' If it contains an "r," the read-only attribute is set OFF.
' If it contains neither "R" nor "r," the read-only
'    attribute is unchanged.

' The same applies to "S" and "s" for the system attribute,
' "A" and "a" for the archive attribute, and "H" and "h" for
' the hidden attribute.

' If attributes$ contains any of the relevant letters in
' both uppercase and lowercase, the one closest to the start
' of the string is used.

SHARED File AS FileAttributes

' Call GetFileAttributes to determine the
' current attributes of Filename$.

iserror = GetFileAttr(FileName$)

' If function failed, return the error code.
```

```
IF iserror THEN
      SetFileAttr = iserror
      EXIT FUNCTION
END IF

' Now parse the argument attributes$.

' The variables R, S, A, and H are set to YES, NO, or the
' current corresponding attribute depending on the argument
' attributes.

IF INSTR(attributes$, "R") > 0 THEN
      R = YES
ELSEIF INSTR(attributes$, "r") > 0 THEN
      R = NO
ELSE
      R = File.ReadOnly
END IF

IF INSTR(attributes$, "S") > 0 THEN
      S = YES
ELSEIF INSTR(attributes$, "s") > 0 THEN
      S = NO
ELSE
      S = File.Systm
END IF

IF INSTR(attributes$, "H") > 0 THEN
      H = YES
ELSEIF INSTR(attributes$, "h") > 0 THEN
      H = NO
ELSE
      H = File.Hidden
END IF

IF INSTR(attributes$, "A") > 0 THEN
      A = YES
ELSEIF INSTR(attributes$, "a") > 0 THEN
      A = NO
ELSE
      A = File.Archive
END IF
```

Listing 5.1 continues

Listing 5.1 continued

```
' Now set up registers CX and AX.

InRegs.cx = (R * 1) + (H * 2) + (S * 4) + (A * 32)
InRegs.ax = &H4301

'Convert FileName$ to an ASCIIZ string.

TempFileName$ = FileName$ + CHR$(0)

' Get its segment:offset.

InRegs.ds = VARSEG(TempFileName$)
InRegs.dx = SADD(TempFileName$)

CALL Interruptx(&H21, InRegs, OutRegs)

' If function failed, return the error code.

IF (OutRegs.flags AND 1) THEN
     SetFileAttr = OutRegs.ax
     EXIT FUNCTION
END IF

' Otherwise, return 0.

SetFileAttr = 0

END FUNCTION        ' end of SetFileAttr


SUB VerifyOff

' Turns the DOS VERIFY flag off.

InRegs.ax = &H2E00
InRegs.dx = 0

CALL Interruptx(&H21, InRegs, OutRegs)

END SUB             ' end of VerifyOff
```

```
SUB VerifyOn

' Turns the DOS verify flag on.

InRegs.ax = &H2E01
InRegs.dx = 0

CALL Interruptx(&H21, InRegs, OutRegs)

END SUB            ' end of VerifyOn
```

****

A Demonstration

The QB program in listing 5.2, DOSCALLS.BAS, demonstrates most of the procedures developed in this chapter. Note that the demonstration program uses a subroutine called WaitKey, whose code is at the end of the listing. WaitKey waits for any key to be pressed and may display a message, depending on the argument passed.

Listing 5.2. *DOSCALLS.BAS.*

```
**********************************************************************
DECLARE FUNCTION KeyInBuf% ()
DECLARE SUB WaitKey (message%)
DECLARE SUB VerifyOn ()
DECLARE SUB VerifyOff ()
DECLARE SUB KBStatus ()
DECLARE SUB GetCursor (cursor AS ANY)
DECLARE SUB GetDriveInfo (driveletter$)
DECLARE SUB SetCursor (cursor AS ANY)
DECLARE FUNCTION GetCurrentDir$ (driveletter$)
DECLARE FUNCTION SetFileAttr% (FileName$, attributes$)
DECLARE FUNCTION GetFileAttr% (FileName$)
DECLARE FUNCTION MSDOSVersion! ()
DECLARE FUNCTION GetDriveSpace% (driveletter$)
DECLARE FUNCTION GetDefaultDriveLetter$ ()
DECLARE FUNCTION Rename (old$, new$)
```

Listing 5.2 continues

Listing 5.2 continued

```
DECLARE FUNCTION SetDefaultDrive% (driveletter$)
DECLARE FUNCTION GetVideoMode% ()

'$INCLUDE: 'QB.BI'.

DEFINT A-Z

CONST YES = 1, NO = 0

' Define data structure for disk drive information.

TYPE DriveInfo
      SectorsPerCluster AS INTEGER
      SectorSize AS INTEGER
      Clusters AS LONG
      Capacity AS LONG
      SpaceAvailable AS LONG
      Ident AS INTEGER
END TYPE

DIM Drive AS DriveInfo

' Define data structure for file attributes.

TYPE FileAttributes
      ReadOnly AS INTEGER
      Archive AS INTEGER
      Hidden AS INTEGER
      Systm AS INTEGER
END TYPE

DIM File AS FileAttributes

' Define data structure for cursor information.

TYPE CursorInfo
      row AS INTEGER
      col AS INTEGER
      startline AS INTEGER
      stopline AS INTEGER
END TYPE
```

```
DIM cursor AS CursorInfo

' Define data structure for keyboard status information.

TYPE KeyboardInfo
      insert AS INTEGER
      capslock AS INTEGER
      numlock AS INTEGER
      scrollock AS INTEGER
      alt AS INTEGER
      ctrl AS INTEGER
      leftshift AS INTEGER
      rightshift AS INTEGER
END TYPE

DIM keyboard AS KeyboardInfo

DIM SHARED InRegs AS RegTypeX, OutRegs AS RegTypeX

' Start execution.

' Display information about the state of the computer
' and the default disk drive.

CLS

PRINT "Quick Basic DOS and BIOS interrupt procedures demo program"
PRINT

WaitKey (YES)

CLS

PRINT "Here's some information about your system:"

PRINT
PRINT
PRINT "You are running DOS version "; MSDOSVersion
PRINT
PRINT "The default disk drive is "; GetDefaultDriveLetter$
PRINT
```

Listing 5.2 continues

Listing 5.2 continued

```
PRINT "The current directory is "; GetCurrentDir("")
PRINT
PRINT "The current video mode is "; GetVideoMode
PRINT
PRINT "For the default drive:"
PRINT

IF GetDriveSpace("") THEN
      PRINT "Function failed"
ELSE
      PRINT "    Clusters ="; Drive.Clusters
      PRINT "    Sectors per cluster ="; Drive.SectorsPerCluster
      PRINT "    Sector size ="; Drive.SectorSize; "bytes."
      PRINT "    Total capacity ="; Drive.Capacity; "bytes."
      PRINT "    Drive space ="; Drive.SpaceAvailable; "bytes."
      PRINT
END IF

PRINT

WaitKey (YES)

CLS

PRINT "Demonstrating GetCursor and SetCursor."
PRINT "Here is the original cursor."

LOCATE 10, 10, 1, 0, 7

CALL GetCursor(cursor)

WaitKey (NO)

LOCATE 2, 1
PRINT "Now the cursor's position and shape have been modified."
LOCATE 20, 50, 1, 6, 7

WaitKey (NO)

LOCATE 2, 1
PRINT "Now you have restored the original cursor shape and position."
```

```
CALL SetCursor(cursor)

WaitKey (NO)

CLS
PRINT "Demonstrating KBStatus."
PRINT
PRINT "Try the keyboard toggles and shifts (Ctrl, Num Lock, etc.)."
PRINT "Press Q to quit"
DO

        KBStatus
        LOCATE 6, 1, 0

' INSERT toggle on?

        IF keyboard.insert THEN
                PRINT "INSERT"
        ELSE
                PRINT "          "
        END IF

' CAPS LOCK toggle on?

        IF keyboard.capslock THEN
                PRINT "CAPSLOCK"
        ELSE
                PRINT "          "
        END IF


' NUM LOCK toggle on?

        IF keyboard.numlock THEN
                PRINT "NUMLOCK"
        ELSE
                PRINT "          "
        END IF


' SCROLL LOCK toggle on?
```

Listing 5.2 continues

Listing 5.2 *continued*

```
        IF keyboard.scrollock THEN
                PRINT "SCROLL LOCK"
        ELSE
                PRINT "            "
        END IF


' ALT key pressed?

        IF keyboard.alt THEN
                PRINT "ALT"
        ELSE
                PRINT "    "
        END IF


' CTRL key pressed?

        IF keyboard.ctrl THEN
                PRINT "CTRL"
        ELSE
                PRINT "     "
        END IF


' LEFT SHIFT key pressed?

        IF keyboard.leftshift THEN
                PRINT "LEFT SHIFT"
        ELSE
                PRINT "          "
        END IF


' RIGHT SHIFT key pressed?

        IF keyboard.rightshift THEN
                PRINT "RIGHT SHIFT"
        ELSE
                PRINT "           "
        END IF
```

```
LOOP UNTIL INKEY$ = "q" OR INKEY$ = "Q"

CLS

PRINT "Creating temporary file JUNK.XXX on default drive."

OPEN "JUNK.XXX" FOR OUTPUT AS #1
WRITE #1, "Test data"
CLOSE #1

PRINT
PRINT "Current attributes for JUNK.XXX are"
PRINT

x = GetFileAttr("junk.xxx")

IF (x <> 0) THEN
    PRINT "Function failed with code"; x
ELSE
    PRINT "  Hidden ="; File.Hidden
    PRINT "  System ="; File.Systm
    PRINT "  Archive ="; File.Archive
    PRINT "  Read only ="; File.ReadOnly
END IF

PRINT
WaitKey (YES)
PRINT

PRINT "Enter new attributes for JUNK.XXX as follows:"
PRINT
PRINT "    R = set read-only, r = clear read-only, neither = unchanged."
PRINT "    H = set hidden,    h = clear hidden,    neither = unchanged."
PRINT "    A = set archive,   a = clear archive,   neither = unchanged."
PRINT "    S = set system,    s = clear system,    neither = unchanged."
PRINT
PRINT "Sample attribute strings:"
PRINT
PRINT "    Ra    set read-only, clear archive, leave others unchanged."
PRINT "    RASH  set all"
PRINT "    aSH   set system and hidden, clear archive"
```

Listing 5.2 continues

***Listing 5.2** continued*

```
PRINT
INPUT "Enter attributes"; attr$
PRINT


x = SetFileAttr("junk.xxx", attr$)


IF x <> 0 THEN
    PRINT "Function failed with error code "; x
END IF


x = GetFileAttr("junk.xxx")
PRINT


IF (x <> 0) THEN
    PRINT "Function failed with code"; x
ELSE
    PRINT "Current attributes for JUNK.XXX:"
    PRINT "  Hidden ="; File.Hidden
    PRINT "  System ="; File.Systm
    PRINT "  Archive ="; File.Archive
    PRINT "  Read only ="; File.ReadOnly
END IF

PRINT


IF File.Hidden THEN
    PRINT
    PRINT "Clearing hidden attribute on JUNK.XXX to make file"
    PRINT "visible for the next part of the demonstration."
    x = SetFileAttr("JUNK.XXX", "h")
    PRINT
END IF

WaitKey (YES)
PRINT

PRINT "Directory of default disk/directory:"
PRINT
FILES
PRINT
WaitKey (YES)
```

```
PRINT
INPUT "Enter new name for JUNK.XXX"; newname$

PRINT
PRINT "Renaming JUNK.XXX to "; newname$
PRINT

x = Rename("JUNK.XXX", newname$)

IF x = 0 THEN
    PRINT "Renaming successful; new directory listing:"
    PRINT
    FILES
ELSE
    PRINT "Function failed with error code"; x
END IF

PRINT
WaitKey (YES)

CLS

PRINT "End of DOS and BIOS interrupt procedures demonstration program"

END            ' end of doscalls.bas


SUB WaitKey (message%)

' Waits for a keystroke. Prints message if argument <> 0.

IF message THEN
     PRINT "Press any key to continue..."
END IF

WHILE INKEY$ = ""
WEND

END SUB          ' end of WaitKey
*****************************************************************
```

Summary

This chapter has shown you how to use QB to perform programming tasks that cannot be done with QB. That paradoxical statement is meant simply to emphasize that QB's INTERRUPT and INTERRUPTX statements, by enabling you to access operating system services, also enable your QB programs to perform tasks that cannot be accomplished directly through QB. As new versions of DOS are developed, your programs will always have access to new capabilities even though QB itself may not incorporate these features.

6

Data Structures

A lmost all computer programs manipulate data in some form. Whereas individual variables are important, of course, repeated data types seem to be at the heart of most data-intensive programs. *Repeated data type* refers to data storage in which a large number of identical data elements are stored in a manner such that a relationship between the individual elements is maintained. The term *identical* refers to the structure of the data elements, not, of course, to their contents.

The most familiar kind of repeated data storage is the array. Arrays are perhaps the most important type of repeated data storage, and you should be thoroughly familiar with their use in QB. This chapter does not deal further with arrays except to note the following two characteristics of arrays:

❑ The relationship among individual elements of an array is defined by their storage location in memory. Array element *n* is stored adjacent to element *n* + 1. To modify the relationship between two array elements, you must move one or both elements.

❑ Storage space in an array is defined by the array's dimensions. During program execution, if you fill an array, you cannot make it larger without using REDIM, which erases the array's contents. If you use only part of an array, the unused space is wasted.

I mention these characteristics of arrays because in some applications they can become limitations. The methods for repeated data storage covered in this chapter avoid these limitations (but have their own limitations). The type of storage in which a program keeps repeated data has a major influence on what can—and cannot—be done with the data. By becoming familiar with various techniques of repeated data storage, you can select the method that is best for your program. This chapter shows how to program the following:

- ❏ Linked lists
- ❏ Binary trees
- ❏ Indexed lists
- ❏ Stacks
- ❏ Queues

The first three items on this list are powerful and widely used methods for storing repeated data. The last two items are techniques for temporary storage of small numbers of data items during program execution. This chapter uses standard database terminology to refer to different types of data items. A *record* is a functional unit of data that often consists of multiple data items. In an address database, for example, one record is all the information for one individual: name, address, city, and so on. A *field* is a single item of data within a record. In the address database, name, address, and city are each fields.

Linked Lists

A very powerful and flexible type of data structure is the *linked list*. A linked list is a one-dimensional structure in which the relationships between the individual list elements, or records, are contained in the records themselves and not in a memory structure set up by the compiler (as is the case with arrays). How does this work? Quite simply, the first record points to the second record, the second record points to the third record, and so on. This is illustrated schematically in figure 6.1.

Fig. 6.1. *The basic structure of a linked list.*

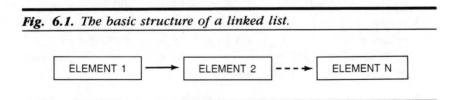

Each record in the list must contain space for a pointer as well as for the data. The simplest records contain two parts: one pointer field and one data field. More complex elements are possible, containing multiple fields. Clearly, QB's user-defined data structures, created with TYPE...END TYPE statements, are ideal for defining records. So, for a mailing list maintained as a linked list, you might define the list record as follows:

```
TYPE person
      lastname AS STRING * 16
      firstname AS STRING * 12
      address1 AS STRING * 20
      address2 AS STRING * 20
      city AS STRING * 12
      state AS STRING * 2
      zip AS STRING * 5
      pointer AS INTEGER
END TYPE
```

The beginning of a linked list is indicated by a *head pointer,* which points to the first record. The head pointer is a simple variable maintained independently of the list itself. The end of the list is indicated by the last record having a pointer value of zero. If the list is empty, the head pointer is zero. In more detail, the structure of a linked list is shown in figure 6.2.

Fig. 6.2. *A linked list showing data and pointer fields.*

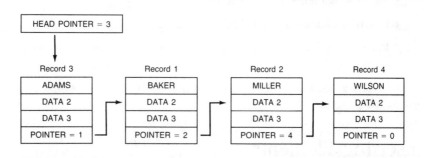

For some applications, linked lists have a number of advantages over arrays. It is easier to maintain a linked list in sorted order than to maintain a sorted array. Inserting an element into the middle of a linked list requires only changing a couple of pointers, whereas inserting an element in the middle of an array requires shifting many array elements. In addition, the size of an array is limited by its dimensions, but the size of a linked list has no restriction beyond available storage capacity.

Perhaps you have been wondering how to implement a linked list in BASIC. How can you make one variable "point" to another variable? In fact, this points out one of the few serious limitations of BASIC (pun intended!). Some other languages, such as C and Pascal, have a special *pointer* data type to point to other variables. More precisely, in C and Pascal a pointer contains the address of a variable. Using these pointers, linked lists are quite easily established.

Unfortunately, BASIC does not have a pointer variable type, making it impossible to establish true linked lists in memory. Some programmers have implemented BASIC linked lists in arrays, using the array index as the pointer. This is a poor approach, however, because forcing a linked list into an array structure negates most of the list's advantages.

A better approach is to use a random disk file to hold the list. Each record in a random file has an "address," its record number, that can be pointed to by an integer variable in a list record. The size of a random file is essentially unlimited, restricted only by your disk capacity. If access time is a problem, use a RAM disk (such as VDISK, supplied with DOS) to hold the file, copying it to a physical disk only at the end of a session. As you will see, QB's random files can implement fully functional linked lists.

There are four basic operations required for linked lists.

❏ Inserting new elements into the list

❏ Finding elements within the list

❏ Deleting elements from the list

❏ Reclaiming the space of deleted elements (why this is necessary becomes clear soon)

This section examines these tasks individually, then develops a QB linked list program.

Inserting Elements

Although they are not required to be, linked lists are usually maintained in sorted order. The first list element, the one pointed to by the head pointer, is "lowest" in terms of the sort criterion, and the last list element is "highest." Sorting is usually done during insertion, meaning that when a new element is inserted, it is put in its "proper" location.

When you start a linked list, the head pointer is zero. Inserting the first element is simple. Set the head pointer to point at the new list element, and set the new element's pointer to 0 (because it is last in the list).

If the list is not empty, do the following to insert a new element:

1. Starting at the head of the list, compare the new element with each existing element until its proper location is found.

2. Insert the element by adjusting pointers. Say the new record, number 20, is to be inserted between records 7 and 12. Before the insertion, record 7 points to record 12. After the insertion, record 7 points to the new record, 20, and the new record points to record 12. This is shown graphically in figure 6.3. Remember here that *record number* refers to a record's position in the random disk file, not to its position in the linked list.

Fig. 6.3. *Steps in inserting a new record into a linked list.*

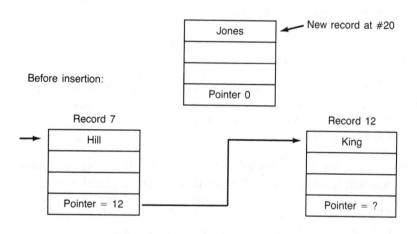

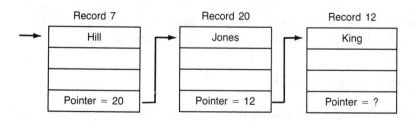

If the new record is first in the list, the head pointer must be pointed to the new record, and the new record pointed to the old first record. If the new record is last in the list, its pointer must be set to zero.

Finding Records

Finding a record in a linked list is simple. Starting at the head of the list, retrieve each record and compare it with your "find" template. Each record examined points to the next one to be examined. When you find a zero pointer, you have reached the end of the list.

Searching is one of the weak points of linked lists. Because each search must start at the head of the list, every search, on average, has to examine half of the list records before finding the target. As is shown later in this chapter, other methods of data organization offer advantages over linked lists when search speed is important.

Deleting Records

Deleting a record from a linked list is conceptually similar to inserting one. After finding the record to be deleted, you simply adjust pointers so the previous record points to the following record. This is illustrated for deleting record 20 in figure 6.4.

Notice that when a record is deleted from a linked list, it is not actually erased; it is simply taken "out of the chain," so to speak. The storage space used by the deleted record is still occupied. After numerous deletions, a linked list can waste a significant amount of space on deleted records. When you want to reclaim this space, use the procedure shown in the next discussion.

Even though a deleted list record is out of the chain, it is a good idea to mark it in some way. One technique is to include a data field in each list record that indicates whether the record has been deleted. Another technique, used in the sample program developed in this section, is to fill a data field in each deleted record with a special character.

Reclaiming Space

As just mentioned, deleted records in a linked list still occupy storage space. In a disk-file-based list, such wasted space should be reclaimed periodically. The technique to do this is

---

Fig. 6.4. *Deleting a record from a linked list.*

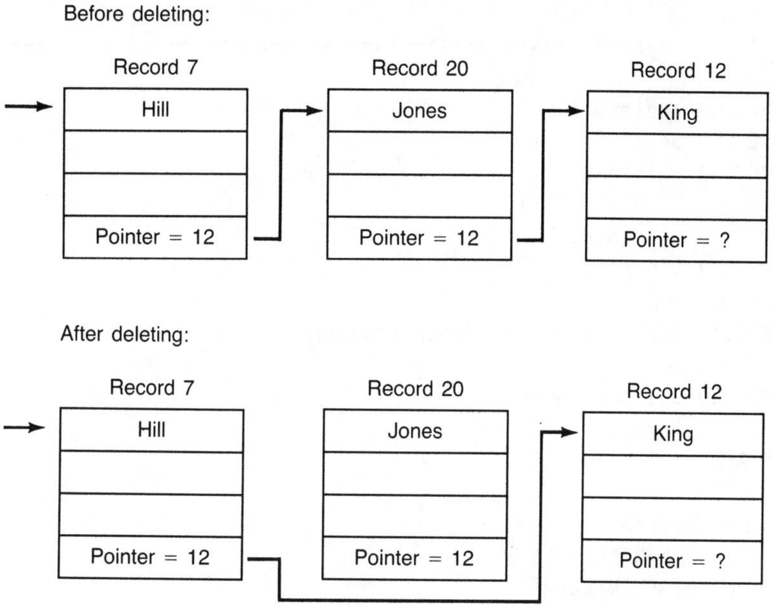

Before deleting:

Record 7	Record 20	Record 12
Hill	Jones	King
Pointer = 12	Pointer = 12	Pointer = ?

After deleting:

Record 7	Record 20	Record 12
Hill	Jones	King
Pointer = 12	Pointer = 12	Pointer = ?

---

1. Copy all undeleted records from the original file to a new file.

2. Delete the original file.

3. Rename the new file to the original file name.

Now you are ready to examine a linked list application. LINKED.BAS, in listing 6.1, uses a random file to hold a linked list of names. For the sake of simplicity, each list record contains only one data item in addition to the pointer. You could easily add more items to the TYPE structure to create a full-fledged address database. Note that the find and delete routines in this program deal with only the first occurrence of a target.

Listing 6.1. *LINKED.BAS*

```
******************************************************************

DECLARE SUB reclaim ()
DECLARE SUB deletedata ()
DECLARE SUB printdata ()
DECLARE FUNCTION menu$ ()
DECLARE SUB dataentry ()
DECLARE SUB linkrecords ()

' LINKLIST.BAS, linked list demonstration.

ON ERROR GOTO errorhandler

DEFINT A-Z

TYPE personrecord
    named AS STRING * 16
    nextname AS INTEGER
END TYPE

' The variable person holds new input. The variables
' oldperson1 and oldperson2 hold existing records during
' the list insertion routine.

DIM SHARED person AS personrecord
DIM SHARED oldperson1 AS personrecord
DIM SHARED oldperson2 AS personrecord

' Try to open header file.

100 OPEN "datafile.hdr" FOR INPUT AS #1
    INPUT #1, FirstRecord, NumOfRecords
    CLOSE #1

200

' Open the data file.

OPEN "datafile.dat" FOR RANDOM AS #1 LEN = LEN(person)
```

```
' Point NextRecord to the end of the file.

NextRecord = LOF(1) \ LEN(person) + 1

CLS

DO

SELECT CASE menu$
    CASE "E"
        CALL dataentry
    CASE "X"
        ' write value of firstrecord to file
        OPEN "datafile.hdr" FOR OUTPUT AS #2
        WRITE #2, FirstRecord, NumOfRecords
        CLOSE #2
        CLOSE #1
        CLS
        END
    CASE "P"
        CALL printdata
    CASE "D"
        CALL deletedata
    CASE "R"
        CALL reclaim
END SELECT

LOOP

END      ' end of linklist.bas


errorhandler:

    IF ERR = 53 AND ERL = 100 THEN FirstRecord = 1: RESUME 200

    PRINT "Error"; ERR
    PRINT "Press any key to exit program."
    WHILE INKEY$ = "": WEND
    END
```

Listing 6.1 continues

Listing 6.1 *continued*

```
SUB dataentry

SHARED NumOfRecords

CLS

DO
    INPUT "Enter name (blank to exit): ", temp$

    IF temp$ = "" THEN
        EXIT DO
    ELSE
        person.named = temp$
    END IF

    NumOfRecords = NumOfRecords + 1
' If nextrecord = 1, you are starting a new data file.

    IF NextRecord = 1 THEN
        person.nextname = 0
        PUT #1, NextRecord, person
        NextRecord = NextRecord + 1
    ELSE
        CALL linkrecords
    END IF

LOOP

END SUB


SUB deletedata

SHARED NextRecord, FirstRecord, NumOfRecords

DIM target AS STRING * 16

NumDeleted = 0

CLS
```

```
INPUT "Enter name to delete:"; target
PRINT

j = FirstRecord

DO

    GET #1, j, person

    IF person.named = target THEN
        person.named = "????????????????"
        nextone = person.nextname
        NumDeleted = 1
        NumOfRecords = NumOfRecords - 1

        IF j = FirstRecord THEN
            FirstRecord = person.nextname
            PUT #1, j, person
        ELSE
            PUT #1, j, person
            GET #1, LastRecord, person
            person.nextname = nextone
            PUT #1, LastRecord, person
        END IF

        EXIT DO

    ELSE
        LastRecord = j
        j = person.nextname
        IF j = 0 THEN EXIT DO
    END IF

LOOP

IF NumDeleted = 0 THEN
    PRINT "Not found"
ELSE
    PRINT "Found and deleted."
END IF
```

Listing 6.1 continues

Listing 6.1 continued

```
PRINT
PRINT "Press any key"

WHILE INKEY$ = "": WEND

END SUB          ' end of deletedata


SUB linkrecords

' Inserts a record into a random file linked list.

SHARED NextRecord, FirstRecord, NumOfRecords

' Firstrecord points at the first record in the linked list,
' which is not necessarily the first record in the file.

i = FirstRecord

DO

' Get the first record in the list.

    GET #1, i, oldperson2

' Should the new entry come before it?

   IF UCASE$(person.named) < UCASE$(oldperson2.named) THEN

' If i = FirstRecord, the new record becomes the first one
' in the list.

        IF i = FirstRecord THEN
            person.nextname = FirstRecord
            FirstRecord = NextRecord
            PUT #1, NextRecord, person
            NextRecord = NextRecord + 1          EXIT DO

' If i <> firstrecord, place the new record between two existing
' records.
```

```
            ELSE
                person.nextname = oldperson1.nextname
                oldperson1.nextname = NextRecord
                PUT #1, LastRecord, oldperson1
                PUT #1, NextRecord, person
                NextRecord = NextRecord + 1
                EXIT DO
            END IF

        ELSE

' If you have not reached the end of the file, save current
' record then loop back to get next one.

            IF oldperson2.nextname > 0 THEN
                LastRecord = i
                i = oldperson2.nextname
                oldperson1 = oldperson2

' If you have reached the end of the file, the new record must be
' "larger" than all existing records and should therefore become
' the last record in the list.

            ELSE
                oldperson2.nextname = NextRecord
                PUT #1, i, oldperson2
                person.nextname = 0
                PUT #1, NextRecord, person
                NextRecord = NextRecord + 1
                EXIT DO
            END IF

        END IF
LOOP

END SUB      'end of linkrecords


FUNCTION menu$

' Displays a menu and returns the key pressed.
```

Listing 6.1 continues

Listing 6.1 *continued*

```
CLS
LOCATE 5, 10
PRINT "QuickBASIC linked list demonstration program"
LOCATE 6, 10
PRINT "===========================================
LOCATE 7, 12
PRINT "E -> enter data"
LOCATE 8, 12
PRINT "D -> delete data"
LOCATE 9, 12
PRINT "P -> print data on screen"
LOCATE 10, 12
PRINT "R -> reclaim deleted records"
LOCATE 11, 12
PRINT "X -> exit program"

    DO
        k$ = INKEY$
    LOOP UNTIL k$ <> ""

menu$ = UCASE$(k$)

END FUNCTION



SUB printdata

SHARED NextRecord, FirstRecord, NumOfRecords

CLS

j = FirstRecord

' Display records on screen in sorted order.

FOR i = 1 TO NumOfRecords
    GET #1, j, person
    PRINT "Record #"; j; ": "; person.named
    j = person.nextname
NEXT i
```

```
WHILE INKEY$ = ""
WEND

END SUB      ' end of printdata


SUB reclaim

' Reclaim empty records in linked list random file.

 SHARED FirstRecord, NextRecord

' Set up a temporary file with an unlikely name.

OPEN "tempZZZZ.000" FOR RANDOM AS #2 LEN = LEN(person)

j = FirstRecord
OutCounter = 1
CLS
DO
    GET #1, j, person
    PRINT ".";
    j = person.nextname

    IF j = 0 THEN
        person.nextname = 0
    ELSE
        person.nextname = OutCounter + 1
    END IF

    PUT #2, OutCounter, person
    OutCounter = OutCounter + 1
LOOP UNTIL j = 0

CLOSE

PRINT : PRINT
PRINT NextRecord - OutCounter; " record(s) reclaimed"

FirstRecord = 1
NextRecord = OutCounter
```

Listing 6.1 continues

Listing 6.1 continued

```
WHILE INKEY$ = "": WEND

' Discard original data file.

KILL "datafile.dat"

' Rename temporary file and reopen it.

NAME "tempzzzz.000" AS "datafile.dat"

OPEN "datafile.dat" FOR RANDOM AS #1 LEN = LEN(person)

END SUB     ' end of reclaim
```

****

Doubly Linked Lists

The type of linked list shown up to now is singly linked, meaning that there is only a single link—one pointer—between adjacent pairs of elements. Another type of linked list is *doubly linked*. As its name implies, each element in a doubly linked list has two pointers, one to the next element and one to the previous element. In addition to a head pointer, a doubly linked list has a *tail pointer* that points to the list's last element.

The advantage of a doubly linked list is that you can move along the list in both directions, not just bottom-to-top as with a singly linked list. Listing 6.1 could, with a moderate amount of work, be converted to use doubly linked lists. This is left as an exercise for you.

Binary Trees

A *binary tree* is like a linked list in that each data record points to following records. It is different in that each record, or *node*, in the tree points to two following records—hence the name binary. The organization of a binary tree makes it an extremely fast and efficient storage organization for many data applications. In a binary tree,

❑ Each record, or node, contains data plus two pointers, the *left pointer* and the *right pointer*.

❏ The left pointer points to a node containing data whose value is less than the data in the current node.

❏ The right pointer points to a node containing data whose value is greater than or equal to the data in the current node. The "value" of a node depends on the contents of the field on which the tree is ordered.

A binary tree is illustrated in figure 6.5. The first or uppermost node is called the *root node*.

Fig. 6.5. *Structure of a binary tree.*

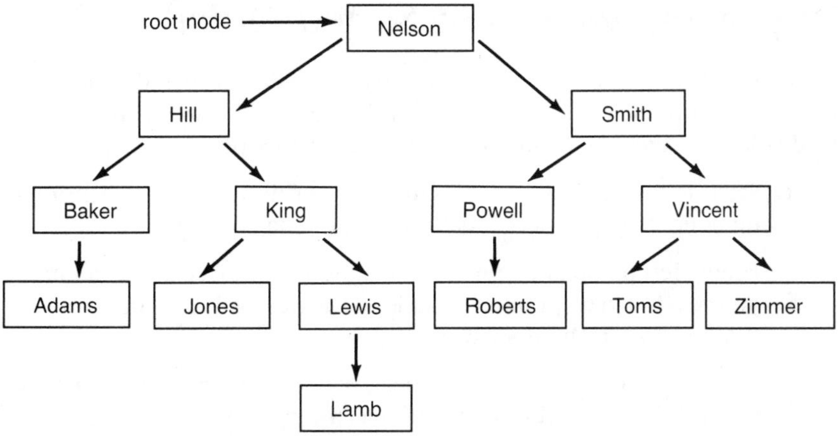

Inserting Records in a Binary Tree

Unlike a linked list, a binary tree does not need a head pointer. The root node is defined by being located in the first physical storage location—in the example here, in random file record 1.

A new record is always added at the "tips of the twigs" in a binary tree. The only task the insertion routine must perform is to find the correct twig. The steps are

1. Starting with the root node, compare the new record with existing data records. Follow the left pointer if the new record's value is less than the existing record; follow the right pointer if the value is greater than or equal to the existing record.

2. When you find a zero pointer, you have found the correct twig. Set that pointer to point to the new record. Both of the new records' pointers are, of course, zero.

Finding a Record in a Binary Tree

Finding a record is similar to inserting one. Simply start at the root node and compare the search template with each existing record. If they do not match, follow the left or right pointer accordingly. If you reach a zero pointer, the template is not in the tree.

Displaying Records in Sorted Order

The records in a binary tree are not actually kept in sorted order, but an order is implicitly contained in the relationships between the nodes. To display the records in sorted order, follow this procedure.

1. Start at the root node, n, which has node number 1 (a node's number is its physical location in the data structure).

2. Follow left pointers, keeping track of node numbers as you go, until you reach a zero pointer. This is the lowest value in the tree, so it is the first to be displayed.

3. Using the record of node numbers, back up one node and display it (this is the second-lowest value). If the right pointer of this node is zero, repeat this step.

4. If the right pointer is not zero, follow it down one node. If this node has a nonzero left pointer, return to step 2. If this node has a zero left pointer and a nonzero right pointer, repeat step 4. If both pointers are zero, display the node and go to step 3.

5. Continue until all nodes have been displayed.

Deleting a Record from a Binary Tree

Deleting a record from a binary tree can be rather complicated. Unless a record is at the end of a twig (has both left and right pointers of zero), actually deleting it requires some rather complicated reshuffling of pointers and node locations. For this reason, the usual practice is to mark records as deleted while you leave them and their pointers in the tree. In the earlier example you saw how to define a one-character field in each record to serve as the "deleted" flag. The contents of records marked as deleted are ignored by search-and-display routines.

Reclaiming the Storage Space of Deleted Records

After numerous deletions, the amount of storage space taken up by deleted records becomes significant. The simplest way to reclaim this space is to create a new binary tree that contains only undeleted records. Use the following procedure:

1. Assign the original file a new name.

2. Open a new, empty file under the original name.

3. One at a time, read all of the records from the original file.

4. If a record is not marked as "deleted," place it in the new file.

5. When all undeleted records are in the new file, delete the original file.

The demonstration program, BTREE.BAS, is shown in listing 6.2. Because BTREE.BAS was written following the principles of structured programming covered in Chapter 2, the task of reclaiming space is greatly simplified. Each undeleted record from the original file is simply passed to the data entry routine in the same way as data entered from the keyboard. Note that the find routine in BTREE.BAS locates only the first occurrence of duplicate records.

Listing 6.2. *BTREE.BAS*

```
*********************************************************************

DECLARE SUB insertdata (temp$)
DECLARE SUB reclaim ()
DECLARE SUB sortorder ()
DECLARE SUB recordorder ()
DECLARE SUB find ()
DECLARE SUB printdata ()
DECLARE FUNCTION menu2$ ()
DECLARE SUB dataentry ()
DECLARE SUB insertnode ()

' BTREE.BAS - binary tree demonstration.
```

Listing 6.2 continues

Listing 6.2 continued

```
DEFINT A-Z

CONST LEFTWARD = 1, RIGHTWARD = 2, YES = 1, NO = 0

TYPE datarecord
    named AS STRING * 16
    left AS INTEGER
    right AS INTEGER
    deleted AS STRING * 1
END TYPE

DIM SHARED person AS datarecord
DIM SHARED person1 AS datarecord

OPEN "btree.dat" FOR RANDOM AS #1 LEN = LEN(person)

NextRecord = LOF(1) \ LEN(person) + 1

DO

    SELECT CASE menu2$
        CASE "E"
            CALL dataentry
        CASE "P"
            CALL printdata
        CASE "R"
            CALL reclaim
        CASE "F"
            CALL find
        CASE "X"
            CLOSE
            CLS
            END
    END SELECT

LOOP

END      ' end of BTREE.BAS


SUB dataentry
```

```
    SHARED NextRecord

DO
    CLS
    LOCATE 5, 5
    PRINT "Enter name; enter a blank when done ";
    INPUT temp$
    IF temp$ = "" THEN EXIT DO
    CALL insertdata(temp$)
LOOP

END SUB      ' end of dataentry


SUB find

DIM template AS STRING * 16

CLS

INPUT "Enter name to find: ", template

NextRecord = 1
found = NO

DO
    GET #1, NextRecord, person
    IF person.named = template THEN
        found = YES
        EXIT DO
    ELSE
        IF UCASE$(person.named) < UCASE$(template) THEN
            NextRecord = person.right
        ELSE
            NextRecord = person.left
        END IF
    END IF

    IF NextRecord = 0 THEN EXIT DO
LOOP
```

Listing 6.2 continues

Listing 6.2 continued

```
PRINT

IF found THEN
    PRINT "Search successful at record #"; NextRecord
    PRINT
    PRINT "Type D to delete, any other to continue"

    DO
        K$ = INKEY$
    LOOP UNTIL K$ <> ""

    IF UCASE$(K$) = "D" THEN
        person.deleted = "Y"
        PUT #1, NextRecord, person
    END IF
ELSE
    PRINT template; "not found"
    PRINT "Press any key to continue"
    WHILE INKEY$ = "": WEND
END IF

END SUB       ' end of find


SUB insertdata (temp$)

SHARED NextRecord

    person.named = temp$
    person.deleted = "N"
    person.left = 0
    person.right = 0
    PUT #1, NextRecord, person
    IF NextRecord > 1 THEN CALL insertnode
    NextRecord = NextRecord + 1

END SUB       'end of insertdata


SUB insertnode
```

```
SHARED NextRecord

NextNode = 1

DO
    GET #1, NextNode, person1
    LastNode =  NextNode
    IF UCASE$(person.named) < UCASE$(person1.named) THEN
        direction = LEFTWARD
        NextNode = person1.left
    ELSE
        direction = RIGHTWARD
        NextNode = person1.right
    END IF
LOOP UNTIL NextNode = 0

IF direction = LEFTWARD THEN
    person1.left = NextRecord
ELSE
    person1.right = NextRecord
END IF

PUT #1, LastNode, person1

END SUB      ' end of insertnode


FUNCTION menu2$

' Displays menu and returns keystroke.
CLS

LOCATE 5, 10
PRINT "QuickBASIC binary tree demonstration program"
LOCATE 6, 10
PRINT "==========================================="
LOCATE 7, 12
PRINT "E -> enter data"
LOCATE 8, 12
PRINT "P -> print data on screen"
LOCATE 9, 12
```

Listing 6.2 continues

___

Listing 6.2 *continued*

___

```
PRINT "F -> find a name"
LOCATE 10, 12
PRINT "R -> reclaim space of deleted nodes"
LOCATE 12, 12
PRINT "X -> exit program"

DO
    K$ = INKEY$
LOOP UNTIL K$ <> ""

menu2$ = UCASE$(K$)

END FUNCTION          'end of menu2$


SUB printdata

CLS

PRINT "Type R to print in RECORD order, S for SORTED order"

DO
    K$ = INKEY$
LOOP UNTIL UCASE$(K$) = "S" OR UCASE$(K$) = "R"

SELECT CASE K$
    CASE "S", "s"
        CALL sortorder
    CASE "R", "r"
        CALL recordorder
END SELECT

END SUB      ' end of printdata


SUB reclaim

SHARED NextRecord
NextRecord = 1
CLOSE #1
```

```
NAME "btree.dat" AS "temp%%%%.@@@"

' Rename original data file.

OPEN "temp%%%%.@@@" FOR RANDOM AS #2 LEN = LEN(person)

' Open new data file.

OPEN "btree.dat" FOR RANDOM AS #1 LEN = LEN(person)

NumRecords = LOF(2) \ LEN(person)

FOR i = 1 TO NumRecords
    GET #2, i, person
    IF person.deleted = "N" THEN
        CALL insertdata(person.named)
    END IF
NEXT i

' Close, then delete, temporary file.

CLOSE #2
KILL "temp%%%%.@@@"

END SUB        ' end of reclaim


SUB recordorder

SHARED NextRecord

CLS

PRINT "Record #", "Name", , "Left pointer", "Right pointer"
PRINT "========================================================================="

FOR i = 1 TO NextRecord - 1
    GET #1, i, person
    IF person.deleted = "N" THEN
        PRINT i, person.named, person.left, person.right
    END IF
```

Listing 6.2 continues

Listing 6.2 continued

```
NEXT i

WHILE INKEY$ = "": WEND

END SUB      ' end of recordorder


SUB sortorder

DIM keeptrack((LOF(1) \ LEN(person)) / 2)

NextRecord = 1
count = 0

keeptrack(0) = 0
index = 1

CLS
PRINT "Record #", "Name", , "Left pointer", "Right pointer"
PRINT "===================================================================="

DO
    DO WHILE index > 0
        GET #1, index, person
        count = count + 1
        keeptrack(count) = index
        index = person.left
        NextRecord = index
    LOOP

    NextRecord = keeptrack(count)
    count = count - 1

    IF NextRecord = 0 THEN EXIT DO

    GET #1, NextRecord, person

    IF person.deleted = "N" THEN
        PRINT NextRecord, person.named, person.left, person.right
    END IF
```

```
        index = person.right
        NextRecord = index
LOOP

WHILE INKEY$ = "": WEND

END SUB      ' end of sortorder
```

****

Unbalanced Trees

The structure of a particular binary tree depends on the order of data entry. If an entry of data items is random in relation to the tree's sort order, the resulting tree is *balanced*, meaning that all of its branches are of approximately equal lengths. If, by chance or design, data entry is not random, the tree can become unbalanced. Some branches will be much longer than others, as shown in figure 6.6.

Fig. 6.6. *An unbalanced binary tree.*

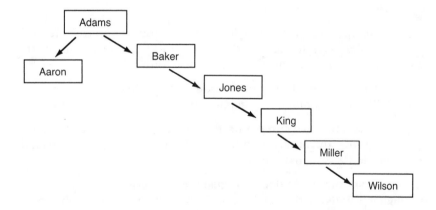

An unbalanced tree results, for example, from entering data in alphabetical order into a tree that sorts alphabetically. Each entry is "greater than" the last, so only right pointers are used in constructing the tree. The result is a tree whose rightmost branch is enormous, but whose other branches are small or nonexistent.

The problem with unbalanced trees is that they compromise search efficiency. The maximum number of nodes a search routine has to examine is equal to the number of nodes, or levels, in the tree's longest branch. In a completely balanced tree containing a total of x records, the number of levels is approximately equal to $\log_2(x)$. In a completely unbalanced tree the number of levels would equal x. A 1000 node tree has 9 levels if balanced and as many as 1000 levels if completely unbalanced. That is a 100-to-1 ratio!

To deal with unbalanced trees, you first determine how unbalanced a given tree is and then if necessary bring it into balance. The programming for these tasks is left as an exercise for you, but here are the steps to take to determine the "balance" state of a tree of x nodes.

1. Using the $\log_2(x)$ formula, calculate the branch length for a perfectly balanced tree.

2. Determine the actual maximum branch length in your tree. This is done by actually traversing all of the branches to their endpoints and keeping track of the number of nodes passed.

3. The ratio (actual maximum length)/(theoretical maximum length) gives a measure of your tree's balance.

There is no rule that states with certainty when a binary tree requires rebalancing, but a ratio of 2 or greater can be used as a general guideline. To rebalance a tree, follow these steps:

1. Using the same method as described for displaying a tree's records in order, copy all the records in order to a new file. In this file the physical order is the same as the sort order.

2. Retrieve records from this file one at a time in random order. Use QB's random-number generator to control record retrieval.

3. Start a new binary tree with the first record retrieved, then add each subsequent record to the tree. When this process is finished, delete the original file.

Using a random order does not guarantee a perfectly balanced tree. Although it is unlikely, the new tree might be equally or more unbalanced than the original! You might want to evaluate the balance ratio of the new tree and rerun the balancing routine if necessary. A more complicated balancing algorithm could guarantee a perfect balance; this is left as an exercise for interested readers.

Indexed Lists

In linked lists and binary trees, the relationship between individual data elements—the sort order—is maintained by the data elements themselves. In both cases, one or two pointers contained as part of each data element serve as the links that specify the order of elements within the list or tree.

It is also possible to maintain a collection of like data elements in which the sort order is maintained independently of the data list itself. This type of data storage is called an *indexed list*. The data elements are contained in one array or file, and the sort order is maintained in a separate array or file called, as you might expect, the *index*. The index file is kept in sorted order, whereas the data file is not. Usually, the data file elements are simply left in the order in which they were entered. Each record in the index file contains two fields. One corresponds to the field in the data file on which the index is based, and the other is a value pointing to a record in the data file. The relationship between a data file and its index file is shown in figure 6.7.

Fig. 6.7. *The relationship between an index file and its data file.*

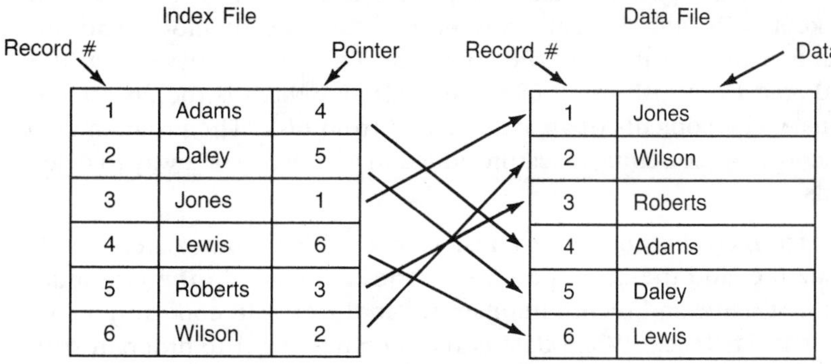

You may be wondering what the advantages of index files are. Why not just sort the data file and be done with it? There are two main advantages to indexed files.

One has to do with sorting efficiency. Indexed files are usually used when each data file record contains numerous fields—in a mailing list file, for example, each record might contain seven or eight fields. In contrast, the corresponding index file contains only two fields per record. Because the time required to sort a file is proportional to the amount of data in each record, it is clearly faster to sort an index file than to sort the data file itself.

The second advantage is that you can keep more than one index file for a given data file, with each index file based on a different data field. With a mailing list, for example, you could keep one index based on last name and another based on ZIP code. This enables you to print out the data records quickly in either order without re-sorting the data file.

In addition, having multiple index files can be a great help when you search a data file. As Chapter 7 shows, searching a data file for a particular entry is much faster if the records are sorted on the search field than if the records are unsorted. In Chapter 7 this kind of search is done with an indexed list.

Now examine how to develop an actual application that uses indexed lists. INDEX.BAS in listing 6.3 maintains a data file of people using index files for both last name and ZIP code fields. For simplicity's sake, the data file records contain only last name, first name, and ZIP code—you could easily add the other fields required for a real mailing list application.

The records for the data file and the two index files are implemented as user-defined types. The data is kept in a random file. The indexes are each kept in a 100-element array—for a data file of more than 100 elements, you must increase the array size. The index arrays are written to and read from disk using BSAVE and BLOAD, which is the fastest way to transfer the contents of an array to and from disk. The program does not incorporate searching (a feature added in Chapter 7) or a way to delete records.

As each record is entered from the keyboard it is immediately PUT in the data file, and the corresponding entries are made in the two index arrays: last name and record number in NameIndex, ZIP code and record number in ZipIndex. When data entry is completed, the program sorts the two index arrays. The sort method used is the *bubble sort*, which is explained in detail in Chapter 7.

Printing records in order is simple. The program simply goes through the index array (ZIP or last name) in order and uses the pointer in each index array record to select the data record to print next.

Listing 6.3. INDEX.BAS

```
*****************************************************************

' INDEX.BAS-indexed list demo.

DECLARE SUB test ()
DECLARE SUB printdata ()
DECLARE SUB sortindices ()
DECLARE FUNCTION menu1$ ()
DECLARE SUB enterdata ()

DEFINT A-Z

ON ERROR GOTO errorhandler

' Data structure for address records.

TYPE DataRecord
    lastname AS STRING * 16
    firstname AS STRING * 12
    zip AS STRING * 5
END TYPE

' Data structure for zip code index file.

TYPE ZipIndex
    zip AS STRING * 5
    pointer AS INTEGER
END TYPE

' Data structure for last name index file.

TYPE NameIndex
    lastname AS STRING * 16
    pointer AS INTEGER
END TYPE

DIM SHARED person AS DataRecord
```

Listing 6.3 continues

***Listing 6.3** continued*

```
' Dimension indexing arrays.

DIM SHARED NameIndex(100) AS NameIndex
DIM SHARED ZipIndex(100) AS ZipIndex

' Try to open name index file; if it is not found, error
' handler sends execution to line 200.

100 OPEN "name.ndx" FOR INPUT AS #1

' File exists.

CLOSE #1

' BLOAD the index files in their respective arrays.

x = VARSEG(NameIndex(0))
DEF SEG = x
y = VARPTR(NameIndex(0))
BLOAD "name.ndx", y
x = VARSEG(ZipIndex(0))
DEF SEG = x
y = VARPTR(ZipIndex(0))
BLOAD "zip.ndx", y
DEF SEG

NumOfRecords = NameIndex(0).pointer

200

' Open the data file.

OPEN "address.lst" FOR RANDOM AS #1 LEN = LEN(person)

DO

SELECT CASE menu1$
    CASE "E"
        CALL enterdata
    CASE "P"
        CALL printdata
```

```
        CASE "X"
            CLOSE #1
            x = VARSEG(NameIndex(0))
            DEF SEG = x
            BSAVE "name.ndx", VARPTR(NameIndex(0)), 101 * LEN(NameIndex(0))
            x = VARSEG(ZipIndex(0))
            DEF SEG = x
            BSAVE "zip.ndx", VARPTR(ZipIndex(0)), 101 * LEN(ZipIndex(0))
            DEF SEG
            CLS
            END
END SELECT


LOOP


errorhandler:

IF ERR = 53 AND ERL = 100 THEN NumOfRecords = 0: RESUME 200


SUB enterdata

' Accepts entries and enters them in the data file and both
' index arrays.

SHARED NumOfRecords

DO
    CLS

    LOCATE 2, 5
    PRINT "Enter a blank last name when finished"
    LOCATE 5, 10
    INPUT "Last name "; person.lastname
    IF person.lastname = "                " THEN EXIT DO
    LOCATE 6, 10
    INPUT "First name "; person.firstname
    LOCATE 7, 10
    INPUT "Zip code "; person.zip
```

Listing 6.3 continues

Listing 6.3 *continued*

```
    NumOfRecords = NumOfRecords + 1

    PUT #1, NumOfRecords, person

    NameIndex(NumOfRecords).lastname = person.lastname
    NameIndex(NumOfRecords).pointer = NumOfRecords
    ZipIndex(NumOfRecords).zip = person.zip
    ZipIndex(NumOfRecords).pointer = NumOfRecords

LOOP

NameIndex(0).pointer = NumOfRecords

' Now sort the index arrays.

CALL sortindices

END SUB      ' end of enterdata


FUNCTION menu1$

' Displays menu and returns keystroke.
CLS

LOCATE 5, 10
PRINT "QuickBASIC indexed list demonstration program"
LOCATE 6, 10
PRINT "==========================================="
LOCATE 7, 12
PRINT "E -> enter data"
LOCATE 8, 12
PRINT "P -> print data on screen"
LOCATE 10, 12
PRINT "X -> exit program"

DO
    K$ = INKEY$
LOOP UNTIL K$ <> ""

menu1$ = UCASE$(K$)
```

```
END FUNCTION          ' end of menu1$


SUB printdata

' Prints out records sorted by name or zip.

SHARED NumOfRecords

CLS

    PRINT "Type N to sort by names, Z to sort by ZIPs"
    DO
        K$ = INKEY$
    LOOP UNTIL UCASE$(K$) = "N" OR UCASE$(K$) = "Z"
    K$ = UCASE$(K$)

CLS

FOR i = 1 TO NumOfRecords

    IF K$ = "Z" THEN
        j = ZipIndex(i).pointer
    ELSEIF K$ = "N" THEN
        j = NameIndex(i).pointer
    END IF

    GET #1, j, person
    PRINT person.lastname; person.firstname; person.zip

NEXT i
WHILE INKEY$ = "": WEND

END SUB      ' end of printdata


SUB sortindices

' Sorts the index arrays.
```

Listing 6.3 continues

Listing 6.3 continued

```
SHARED NumOfRecords

FOR i = 1 TO NumOfRecords
    FOR j = 1 TO NumOfRecords - 1

    IF NameIndex(j).lastname > NameIndex(j + 1).lastname THEN
        SWAP NameIndex(j), NameIndex(j + 1)
    END IF

    IF ZipIndex(j).zip > ZipIndex(j + 1).zip THEN
        SWAP ZipIndex(j), ZipIndex(j + 1)
    END IF

    NEXT j
NEXT i

END SUB      ' end of sortindices
```

****

When you use an indexed list (or other kinds of data storage, for that matter), be aware of the difference between *key fields* and *nonkey fields*. A key field is one in which there is no duplication of entries—every entry is unique. In a nonkey field, duplication is permitted. In a data file of employee records, for example, Social Security Number would be a key field, because no two individuals have the same number. Last Name, on the other hand, would not be a key field, because two people could certainly have the same last name.

Be aware of the distinction between a key field, as just defined, and a sort key, which is a field on which the database has been sorted. A sort key may or may not be a key field.

When you search a nonkey field, remember that finding one instance of the search template does not mean you have found them all. As you or your users enter data into a key field, it is wise to search the field for the new entry to ensure that a duplication does not occur.

Stacks

A *stack* is a method of data storage in which the most recently stored item is the first one retrieved. In other words, a stack operates on the last-in, first-out (LIFO) principle. The favorite analogy for a stack is the plate holders found in many cafeterias. As plates are added to the top, the stack sinks; as plates are removed, the stack rises. If you have had any experience with assembly language programming, you are familiar with stacks. The same concept can be implemented in BASIC and can be quite useful in certain situations.

Access to a stack is limited to the top of the stack. Adding an item to the stack is called *pushing*, which always adds the item to the top of the stack. Retrieving an item is called *popping*, which always retrieves the item on the top of the stack. The stack is implemented as a linear memory segment—in this case, as an array. The *stack pointer* indicates the current top of the stack—the next unused location. Pushing a data item onto the stack consists of copying it to the location pointed to by the stack pointer, then incrementing the stack pointer. Popping a data item off the stack consists of decrementing the stack pointer, then retrieving the value pointed to by the stack pointer. A stack for integer variables is implemented in listing 6.4.

Listing 6.4. *STACK.BAS*

```
***********************************************************************

' STACK.BAS: first-in, last-out storage.

DECLARE SUB pop (value%)
DECLARE SUB push (value%)

DEFINT A-Z

CONST MAXSTACK = 99
DIM SHARED stack(MAXSTACK) AS INTEGER
stackpointer = 0
counter = 0

CLS
PRINT "Enter some values; enter 0 when done"
```

Listing 6.4 continues

Listing 6.4 continued

```
DO
    INPUT x
    IF x = 0 THEN EXIT DO
    counter = counter + 1
    push x
LOOP

FOR i = 1 TO counter
    pop x
    PRINT x
NEXT i
END



SUB pop (value)

SHARED stackpointer

stackpointer = stackpointer - 1
value = stack(stackpointer)

END SUB      'end of pop


SUB push (value)

SHARED stackpointer

stack(stackpointer) = value
stackpointer = stackpointer + 1

END SUB      ' end of push
```

****

The push and pop routines in STACK.BAS do not check the stack pointer. The calling program must keep track of the pointer and ensure that it does not exceed the stack array limits. Note that this code uses the alternate QB syntax for calling subroutines: push x instead of CALL push(x). This is to make the syntax more closely resemble that used in assembly language. If you prefer, you can revert to the syntax using the CALL keyword.

Queues

A *queue* is similar to a stack in that it provides temporary storage for variables. Unlike a stack, a queue works on a first- in, first-out (FIFO) basis. Depending on the specific temporary storage application, a queue may be more appropriate than a stack.

The program QUEUE.BAS in listing 6.5 implements a queue for integers in a 100-element array. Two pointers are kept: one each for the head and tail of the queue. The head of the queue is where the next queued item is placed; the tail is where the next item is retrieved. Both head and tail pointers are circular in that when they reach the end of the array, they return to the beginning. If more than MAXQUEUE items are put in the queue at one time, the newest items overwrite the oldset items.

Listing 6.5. *QUEUE.BAS*

```
******************************************************************
' QUEUE.BAS: first-in, first-out storage.

DECLARE SUB outqueue (value%)
DECLARE SUB inqueue (value%)

DEFINT A-Z

CONST MAXQUEUE = 99
DIM SHARED queue(MAXQUEUE) AS INTEGER

counter = 0

CLS
PRINT "Enter some values; enter 0 when done"

DO
    INPUT x
    IF x = 0 THEN EXIT DO
    counter = counter + 1
    inqueue x
LOOP
```

Listing 6.5 *continues*

Listing 6.5 continued

```
FOR i = 1 TO counter
    outqueue x
    PRINT x
NEXT i

END     'end of QUEUE.BAS


SUB inqueue (value)

STATIC queuehead

queue(queuehead) = value
queuehead = queuehead + 1
IF queuehead = MAXQUEUE + 1 THEN queuehead = 0

END SUB     ' end of inqueue


SUB outqueue (value)

STATIC queuetail

value = queue(queuetail)
queuetail = queuetail + 1
IF queuetail = MAXQUEUE + 1 THEN queuetail = 0
 END SUB       'end of outqueue
```

****

Because no pointer checking is done, it is quite possible for the tail pointer to overtake the head pointer. If this happens, the integrity of the queue is lost. The calling program is responsible for keeping track of calls to inqueue and outqueue to ensure this does not happen.

Summary

As you can see, there are several different methods of storing repetitive data. The best one for your program depends on the specifics of your application. For example, if fast searches are a priority, a binary tree is preferable; if you need multiple sort keys, an indexed list is recommended. Decide which data representation to use very early in the program development cycle. If you change your mind halfway through, you are likely to have wasted a lot of programming effort.

CHAPTER 7

Data Sorting and Searching

The last chapter showed several methods for storing data in your QB programs. These methods share the common trait of *ordering*, but not *sorting*, the data. This means that pointers are used to indicate the ordering of the data elements, but this order is not reflected in the items' physical storage locations. For example, you can retrieve items from a linked list in order, but they are not stored on disk in that order. For many applications this type of data organization—ordered but not sorted—is fine.

Other applications require data to be stored, in memory or on disk, in sorted order. Because your data is very unlikely to be input in sorted order, you need some way to sort a data list. There are numerous methods, or *algorithms*, for sorting data, and the main business of this chapter is to explain how some of the methods work and to present code for sorting. The chapter covers these five sorting algorithms:

❏ Quicksort

❏ Bubble sort

❏ Insertion sort

❏ Exchange sort

❏ Shell sort

In addition, the chapter looks at some methods for searching for data.

229

Sort Routines

There are two basic approaches to sorting a list. One method might be called "sort as you go." This method involves inserting each new element in its proper list location as soon as it is entered. The other method, "sort when needed," requires converting an entire unsorted list into a sorted list.

Sort as You Go

If each new list element is put in its proper location as soon as it is entered, the list never becomes unsorted, so it never needs to be sorted. In general terms, the procedure for this is

1. Find the list location where the new element is to be inserted.

2. Create a space for the new element by moving each list element between that location and the top of the list up one space.

3. Insert the new element.

That seems simple enough, but of course you need first to find the proper location to insert the new element. Because the existing list is already in order, you use a *binary search*. The binary search is a very efficient searching algorithm that eliminates half of the possibilities with each iteration. This is how it works:

1. Compare the new element with the element in the middle of the list.

2. If the new element is less than the existing element, the proper location must be in the first half of the existing list. Exclude the second half of the list from the search, and return to step 1.

3. If the new element is greater than the existing element, the proper location must be in the second half of the existing list. Exclude the first half of the list from the search, and return to step 1.

4. When the list has been pared down to a single element, you have found the desired location.

Binary searches are very efficient, requiring only $\log_2(n)$ loops to search an n element list. A binary search can be used to find an existing element in a list as well as to find the location for a new element.

The program in listing 7.1, INSERT.BAS, demonstrates the use of a binary search to keep a list sorted "as you go" by inserting each new entry in its proper location. The program starts by generating a sorted list of six words, which is displayed. The user then inputs new words one at a time; each word is immediately inserted in its proper location in this list, and the list is redisplayed.

Listing 7.1. *INSERT.BAS*

```
******************************************************************

DECLARE SUB insert (NewWord$)
DECLARE SUB printwords ()
' INSERT.BAS.

' "Sort as you go" demonstration.

DEFINT A-Z

CONST YES = 1, NO = 0

DIM SHARED words(100) AS STRING

CLS

' Enter 6 words into array.

words(1) = "apples"
words(2) = "dates"
words(3) = "grapes"
words(4) = "melons"
words(5) = "persimmons"
words(6) = "strawberries"

NumWords = 6

' Display the list.

CALL printwords
```

Listing 7.1 continues

***Listing 7.1** continued*

```
DO

    PRINT
    INPUT "Enter new word, a blank when done: ", NewWord$
    PRINT

    IF NewWord$ = "" THEN
        EXIT DO
    END IF

    CALL insert(NewWord$)

' Display the new list.

    CALL printwords

LOOP

END      'end of INSERT.BAS


SUB insert (NewWord$)
SHARED NumWords

high = NumWords
low = 1
inlist = NO

DO

center = (high + low) \ 2

    IF UCASE$(NewWord$) > UCASE$(words(center)) THEN
        low = center + 1
    ELSEIF UCASE$(NewWord$) = UCASE$(words(center)) THEN
        inlist = YES
        location = center
        EXIT DO
    ELSEIF UCASE$(NewWord$) < UCASE$(words(center)) THEN
        high = center - 1
    END IF
```

```
        IF low > high THEN EXIT DO
LOOP

IF inlist = NO THEN
    location = high + 1
END IF

' Now insert new word at location.

NumWords = NumWords + 1

' Move all words above location up one slot.

FOR i = NumWords TO location STEP -1
    words(i + 1) = words(i)
NEXT i

words(location) = NewWord$

END SUB      ' end of insert


SUB printwords

SHARED NumWords

FOR i = 1 TO NumWords
    PRINT STR$(i); ": "; words(i)
NEXT i
END SUB         ' end of printwords
```

****

Sorting When Needed

Keeping a list sorted by inserting new elements in their proper location is a useful technique, but it is not always possible or practical. Some situations that would preclude use of this technique include the following:

❏ You are adding entries to a large list and do not want to take time after each entry to perform the necessary search and insertion.

❏ You need to re-sort the list on different criteria at different times.

❏ You "inherit" an unsorted list from another application.

In these and other situations, you are faced with sorting an entire list. There are quite a few methods, or algorithms, available for sorting, and this chapter covers five of them. First, however, take a look at some general considerations.

Sorting Efficiency

There is really no trick to writing a program to sort a list. Conceptually it is a simple task. The trick comes in writing a sort routine that is efficient (read *fast*). Even with today's multimegahertz computers, sorting a long list with "brute-force" methods can be a time-consuming process. Improvements in algorithm efficiency can make a significant difference in program speed.

Any sorting algorithm depends almost exclusively on two operations: data comparison and data exchange. An algorithm's efficiency is primarily a function of how many times it must perform each of these operations to complete a sort. The fewer comparisons and exchanges required to sort a given size list, the more efficient an algorithm is. More emphasis is placed on minimizing exchanges, because a data exchange takes more computer time than a data comparison.

For illustration, look at the sorting method used in INDEX.BAS in Chapter 6. To sort the index arrays, the following brute-force method is used.

1. Go through the array comparing each element with the following element.

2. If the two elements are out of order, swap them.

3. Repeat steps 1 and 2 as many times as there are array elements.

This method works, resulting in a perfectly sorted list. It is extremely inefficient, however. For an n element list, this algorithm requires $(n)*(n-1)$ comparisons. For a 10-element list, 90 comparisons are needed; for 100 elements, 9900 comparisons; for 1000 elements, almost a million!

The number of exchanges required with this method depends on how disordered the list is to start with. Each exchange can move a data item only one position closer to its final position, so a large number of exchanges is required for a badly disordered list.

This suggests that the efficiency of a given algorithm depends not only on the algorithm itself, but also on the state of the list being sorted. This is quite true. As you will see later, the algorithm that is fastest in sorting an already-sorted list is slowest in sorting a badly disordered list.

The Bubble Sort

The bubble sort algorithm is, in fact, the one used in the brute-force method developed earlier. The name "bubble" comes from the fact that during the sort, smaller elements "float up" toward the top of the array like bubbles.

The original algorithm implemented in listing 7.1 is very inefficient. It can be significantly improved by using the fact that if a pass through the array terminates after making no swaps, the array is sorted. You can therefore modify the code so that the outer execution loop repeats only if one or more swaps were made in the inner loop. With an array that is already sorted or nearly sorted, this modification dramatically improves the performance of the bubble sort.

With this modification, the number of passes through the loop required by a bubble sort depends on the degree of "sortedness" of the list. Specifically, the number of loops is equal to the maximum number of positions that any element is away from its proper location.

The Exchange Sort

The exchange sort works by looking through the list for the smallest element and putting it in position 1, looking for the next smallest element and putting it in position 2, and so on. In more concrete terms,

1. Compare the first list element with the second through last elements. Whenever an element is smaller than the first element, swap them.

2. Compare the second list element with the third through last elements. Whenever an element is smaller than the second element, swap them.

3. Continue for the remainder of the list.

The exchange sort is unavoidably a brute-force method. On a list of n elements it always performs $(n - 1)!$ ($n - 1$ factorial) comparisons, no matter how soon the list becomes sorted. The number of exchanges depends on the list's initial degree of "sortedness," but in any case, the exchange sort is a poor performer.

The Shell Sort

The shell sort is similar to the bubble sort in that it compares pairs of array elements and swaps them if they are out of order. Unlike the bubble sort, which compares adjacent elements, the shell sort begins by comparing elements that are far apart. The procedure is

1. Divide the list into two partitions of equal size.

2. Compare each element in the first partition with the corresponding element in the second partition, swapping them if necessary. Thus, in a list of n elements:

   compare element(1) with element(1 + $n/2$); swap if needed

   compare element(2) with element(2 + $n/2$); swap if needed, and so on

3. Divide each partition into two partitions and repeat step 2 for each new pair of partitions.

4. When the partition size reaches zero, the sort is completed.

Note that during the last pass of a shell sort, when the partition size is one, the procedure is identical to a bubble sort.

The Quicksort

Many programmers consider the quicksort to be the best sorting algorithm available. And yes, *quicksort* is one word, the name assigned to this algorithm by its inventor, C. A. R. Hoare.

Like the shell sort, the quicksort repeatedly divides the list into smaller and smaller partitions. Quicksort first selects a pivot value, called the *comparand*. All list values greater than or equal to the comparand are placed in one partition, and all values less than the comparand are put in the other partition. For each resulting partition, a new comparand is selected, and the procedure is repeated. When partitions shrink to two elements, the two elements are swapped if necessary, and the sort is complete.

A necessary step in performing a quicksort is selecting a value for the comparand. The ideal value is the list's median value, that is, the value for which half the list's elements are larger and half are smaller. Finding a list's median is itself a time-consuming process, so other methods of selecting a comparand are usually used. One method is to randomly select a number of list elements and take their average. Another method, used in the example in this chapter, is to randomly select a single list element and use its value for the comparand. Fortunately, the performance of the quicksort is not seriously affected by the choice of comparand.

You may have noticed that the partitioning procedure used by the quicksort lends itself to use of a recursive procedure—one that repeatedly calls itself. This is how quicksorts are usually implemented, including this chapter's example. You may wish to refresh your memory on the problems that may arise with recursive procedures, as discussed in Chapter 2.

The Insertion Sort

The insertion sort procedure is essentially the same as illustrated in INSERT.BAS (listing 7.1) to insert a single item into an already sorted list. This algorithm can be used to sort an entire list as follows:

1. Compare the first two elements in the list and swap them if they are out of order. These first two elements now compose your temporary sorted list.

2. The insertion procedure is now used to insert the third element into this temporary sorted list. Compare it with each element in the sorted portion of the list until the proper location is found. Move elements up one position, if necessary, and insert the item. The sorted portion of this list is now three elements long.

3. Using the same procedure, insert the fourth element into the sorted portion containing the three elements. Continue inserting successive elements in this manner until the end of the list is reached.

The major problem with the insertion sort is that it requires moving a lot of data to make space for each insertion.

A Demonstration

The program in listing 7.2, SORTS.BAS, demonstrates all five sort algorithms. You select the type of array to be sorted: best case, in which the array is already sorted, average case, where the elements are somewhat out of order, and worst case, where the elements are in reverse order. At the end of each sort, a results table is displayed, showing the time, in seconds, for each sort algorithm and array type that has been tried.

As written, SORTS.BAS creates and sorts 500-element arrays. When run on an 8-megahertz PC/AT, this results in maximum sort times around 25 seconds. On a slower machine you might want to use smaller arrays to avoid spending too much time on the sorts. To use smaller arrays, change the value of the program constant ELEMENTS.

Listing *7.2. SORTS.BAS*

```
*******************************************************************

' SORTS.BAS-data sorting algorithms demonstration
'              and timing program.

DECLARE FUNCTION selectarraytype% ()
DECLARE FUNCTION selectsort% ()
DECLARE SUB exchange ()
DECLARE SUB quick ()
DECLARE SUB quicksort (min%, max%)
DECLARE SUB shellsort ()
DECLARE SUB insertionsort ()
DECLARE SUB fillarray ()
DECLARE SUB bubblesort ()

DEFINT A-Z

' Change value of ELEMENTS if desired for longer or shorter sorts.

CONST ELEMENTS = 500, TRUE = 1, FALSE = 0
' Labels for results table.

DIM labels(5) AS STRING * 16

labels(1) = "Quicksort"
labels(2) = "Shell sort"
labels(3) = "Exchange sort"
labels(4) = "Bubble sort"
labels(5) = "Insertion sort"

' Array for timing results.

DIM results!(1 TO 3, 1 TO 5)

' Arrays for data to be sorted.

DIM SHARED array(ELEMENTS) AS INTEGER
DIM SHARED best(ELEMENTS) AS INTEGER
DIM SHARED average(ELEMENTS) AS INTEGER
DIM SHARED worst(ELEMENTS) AS INTEGER
```

```
CLS

' Fill the arrays with data.

CALL fillarray

DO

' Select best, average, or worst array.

arraytype = selectarraytype

SELECT CASE arraytype
    CASE 1
        FOR i = 0 TO ELEMENTS
            array(i) = best(i)
        NEXT i
    CASE 2
        FOR i = 0 TO ELEMENTS
            array(i) = average(i)
        NEXT i
    CASE 3
        FOR i = 0 TO ELEMENTS
            array(i) = worst(i)
        NEXT i
END SELECT

' Select sort type.

sorttype = selectsort

' Start timing.

start! = TIMER

CLS
LOCATE 12, 35
PRINT "Working..."
```

Listing 7.2 *continues*

Listing 7.2 continued

```
SELECT CASE sorttype
    CASE 1
        CALL quick
    CASE 2
        CALL shellsort
    CASE 3
        CALL exchange
    CASE 4
        CALL bubblesort
    CASE 5
        CALL insertionsort
END SELECT

' End timing.

finish! = TIMER

' Place time in results array.

results!(arraytype, sorttype) = finish! - start!

' Display results table.

CLS

format$ = "##.####   ##.####   ##.####"

PRINT "Sort type         best      average     worst"
PRINT "========================================="
FOR i = 1 TO 5
    PRINT labels(i);
    PRINT USING format$; results!(1, i); results!(2, i); results!(3, i)
NEXT i

PRINT
PRINT

PRINT "Type X to exit, C to continue"
DO
    K$ = INKEY$
LOOP UNTIL K$ <> ""
```

```
IF UCASE$(K$) = "X" THEN EXIT DO

LOOP

CLS

END       ' end of SORTS.BAS


SUB bubblesort STATIC

' Bubble sort routine.

maximum = array(0)

DO

    index = 0
    FOR i = 1 TO (maximum - 1)

' If two adjacent elements are not in order, swap their values.

        IF array(i) > array(i + 1) THEN
            SWAP array(i), array(i + 1)
            index = i
        END IF

    NEXT i

' Set limit for next loop to location of last swap.

    maximum = index

LOOP WHILE index

END SUB       ' end of bubblesort


SUB exchange

' Exchange sort.
```

Listing **7.2** *continues*

Listing 7.2 *continued*

```
maximum = array(0)

FOR i = 1 TO maximum
   least = i

   FOR j = i + 1 TO maximum
      IF array(j) < array(least) THEN
         least = j
      END IF
   NEXT j

' If an item is smaller than the current item, swap the two.

   IF least > i THEN
      SWAP array(i), array(least)
   END IF

NEXT i

END SUB        'end of exchange


SUB fillarray STATIC

best(0) = ELEMENTS
average(0) = ELEMENTS
worst(0) = ELEMENTS

' Fills three arrays with integers as follows:

'    best() is filled in order
'    average() is partially ordered
'    worst() is in random order

CLS

LOCATE 12, 35
PRINT "Creating arrays..."
```

```
FOR i = 1 TO ELEMENTS
    worst(i) = INT(ELEMENTS * RND)
    best(i) = i
    average(i) = i
NEXT i

' average() starts out completely ordered;
' now "disorder" some of its elements.

top = ELEMENTS
bottom = 1

DO
    SWAP average(top), average(bottom)
    top = top - 4
    bottom = bottom + 4
    IF top < bottom THEN
        EXIT DO
    END IF
LOOP

END SUB      'end of fillarray


SUB insertionsort

' Insertion sort routine.

maximum = ELEMENTS

FOR i = 2 TO maximum

   temp1 = array(i)
   temp2 = temp1

   FOR j = i TO 2 STEP -1

      IF array(j - 1) > temp2 THEN
         array(j) = array(j - 1)
      ELSE
         EXIT FOR
      END IF
```

Listing 7.2 *continues*

Listing 7.2 continued

```
   NEXT j

   array(j) = temp1

NEXT i

END SUB       ' end of insertionsort


SUB quick

' First level of quicksort routines.

CALL quicksort(1, ELEMENTS)

END SUB       ' end of quick


SUB quicksort (min, max)

 ' Bottom level of quicksort routine.

IF min < max THEN

' If only two elements, swap them if they are out of order.

   IF max - min = 1 THEN

      IF array(min) > array(max) THEN
         SWAP array(min), array(max)
      END IF

   ELSE

' Pick a random "pivot element" and move it to the end.

      pivot = INT(RND * (max - min + 1)) + min
      SWAP array(max), array(pivot)
      border = array(max)

' Now "move in" from both directions toward the pivot element.
```

```
          DO
              i = min
              j = max

              DO WHILE (i < j) AND (array(i) <= border)
                 i = i + 1
              LOOP

              DO WHILE (j > i) AND (array(j) >= border)
                  j = j - 1
              LOOP

' If pivot element not reached, the two elements should
' be swapped.

              IF i < j THEN
                  SWAP array(i), array(j)
              END IF

          LOOP WHILE i < j

' Return pivot element to its proper location.

          SWAP array(i), array(max)

' Pass the two subdivisions to this routine (recursive call).

              IF (i - min) < (max - i) THEN
                  CALL quicksort(min, i - 1)
                  CALL quicksort(i + 1, max)
              ELSE
                  CALL quicksort(i + 1, max)
                  CALL quicksort(min, i - 1)
              END IF

      END IF
END IF

END SUB      'end of quicksort
```

Listing 7.2 *continues*

Listing 7.2 *continued*

```
FUNCTION selectarraytype

' Asks user to select type of array to sort.

CLS

PRINT "Select type of array to sort:"
PRINT
PRINT "    1 -> Best (already sorted)"
PRINT "    2 -> Average (partially sorted)"
PRINT "    3 -> Worst (random order)"

DO
    K$ = INKEY$
LOOP UNTIL K$ = "1" OR K$ = "2" OR K$ = "3"

selectarraytype = VAL(K$)

END FUNCTION          'end of selectarraytype


FUNCTION selectsort

' Asks user to select type or sort algorithm to use.

CLS

PRINT "Select type of sort:"
PRINT
PRINT "    1 -> Quicksort"
PRINT "    2 -> Shell sort"
PRINT "    3 -> Exchange sort"
PRINT "    4 -> Bubble sort"
PRINT "    5 -> Insertion sort"

DO
    K$ = INKEY$
LOOP UNTIL VAL(K$) < 6 AND VAL(K$) > 0

selectsort = VAL(K$)
```

```
END FUNCTION        'end selectsort


SUB shellsort

' Shell sort routine.

maximum = ELEMENTS

center = maximum \ 2

DO WHILE center > 0

    boundary = maximum - center

    DO
       flag = FALSE


       FOR i = 1 TO boundary

          IF array(i) > array(i + center) THEN
             SWAP array(i), array(i + center)
             flag = i
          END IF

       NEXT i

       boundary = flag - center

    LOOP WHILE flag

    center = center \ 2

LOOP

END SUB      'end of shellsort
```

****

The sort times in table 7.1 were obtained running SORTS.BAS from within the QB environment, using 500-element arrays. If you create SORTS.EXE and run it from DOS, the times are a lot faster, but their relationships do not change.

Table 7.1. *Memory-Based Sort Times*

Sort type	Best	Average	Worst
Quicksort	0.6523	1.6992	2.6289
Shell sort	0.2135	1.1602	0.8203
Exchange sort	7.9102	7.9102	9.1719
Bubble sort	0.0625	14.2773	25.1016
Insertion sort	0.1133	3.7891	14.6680

Some features of these results deserve mention.

❑ The bubble sort is the fastest algorithm when the array is already sorted, but it is by far the slowest for the other array types.

❑ The speed of the exchange sort is least affected by the array type, but its performance is uniformly poor.

❑ The speed of the insertion sort is most affected by the array type; it is quite good for an already-sorted array, but it is poor for a worst-case array.

❑ The quicksort is consistently quite fast for all three array types.

❑ The shell sort turns in the fastest times on average and worst-case arrays. Interestingly, it is actually faster on a worst-case array than on an average array!

As interesting as these results are, some caveats are in order. The arrays used in this demonstration program are highly artificial. In the real world of messy data, you rarely—if ever—sort a list that is already sorted (if it is already sorted, you probably know it). You also never have to deal with a worst-case list in which the elements are in reverse order. Even the average-case array used for these timings is artificial, in that it contains ordered disorder, meaning that the way in which the list elements are out of order has a definite structure. This may influence the timing results.

The sort routines in listing 7.2 can be incorporated with minor modifications into your own program. You could also incorporate them into a flexible sorting procedure that would use one of the file-sorting algorithms depending on a parameter passed by the calling program.

As you may already know, QB includes a program called SORTDEMO.BAS that demonstrates these five sort algorithms, accompanied by sound effects and a graphical display of sort progress. Although it is fun to watch, SORTDEMO suffers from two shortcomings. First, it does not offer a choice of how disordered the original array is. Second, the code necessary for the sound effects and visual display slows down the sorts significantly, so the sort times reported are not particularly meaningful.

Sorting Data in Files

Sometimes the data you need to sort is in a disk file rather than in an array in memory. Because reading and writing disk data are much slower than reading and writing RAM, disk-based sorts are unavoidably much slower than memory-based sorts. The ideal way to sort disk data is to read the data into an array, sort the array, then write it back to disk. If the disk file is too large to fit in an array, however, you are forced to perform a disk-based sort.

Disk data that needs to be sorted is almost always stored in a random access file. The structure of QB random-access files enables them to be sorted with the same algorithms used to sort arrays. Because each entry in the file has a record number, the individual records can be treated conceptually like array elements. The major difference is that, unlike array elements, file records are not directly available for comparison and SWAP statements. Each pair of records must be read into two variables with GET, compared and/or swapped, then PUT back into the file.

Listing 7.3 presents SORTFILE.BAS, a version of SORTS.BAS (listing 7.2) modified to perform disk-based sorts. SORTFILE.BAS creates best-case, average-case, and worst-case files with the same structures used for arrays in SORTS.BAS. The user selects the type of file to sort and the sort algorithm to use. Sort times are saved and displayed in a table. Because disk-based sorts are much slower than memory based sorts, I reduced ELEMENTS to 100 to obtain reasonable times.

When the program terminates, it erases the four disk files it uses. Should the program not terminate normally, perhaps due to an error, be sure to erase those files yourself before restarting the program. If the files already exist when the program starts, you receive unexpected results.

Listing *7.3. SORTFILE.BAS*

```
*******************************************************************

' SORTFILE.BAS-disk file data sorting demonstration program.

DECLARE FUNCTION selectfiletype% ()
DECLARE FUNCTION selectsort% ()
DECLARE SUB exchange ()
DECLARE SUB quick ()
DECLARE SUB quicksort (min%, max%)
DECLARE SUB shellsort ()
DECLARE SUB insertionsort ()
DECLARE SUB fillfiles ()
DECLARE SUB bubblesort ()

DEFINT A-Z

' Change value of ELEMENTS if desired for longer or shorter sorts.

CONST ELEMENTS = 100, TRUE = 1, FALSE = 0

 ' Labels for results table.

DIM labels(5) AS STRING * 16

labels(1) = "Quick sort"
labels(2) = "Shell sort"
labels(3) = "Exchange sort"
labels(4) = "Bubble sort"
labels(5) = "Insertion sort"

' Array for timing results.

DIM results!(1 TO 3, 1 TO 5)

' Establish data type.

TYPE recordtype
    number AS INTEGER
END TYPE
```

```
DIM SHARED value1 AS recordtype
DIM SHARED value2 AS recordtype

' Arrays for initial list creation.

DIM SHARED best(ELEMENTS) AS recordtype
DIM SHARED average(ELEMENTS) AS recordtype
DIM SHARED worst(ELEMENTS) AS recordtype

CLS

' Fill the files with data.

CALL fillfiles

DO

' Select best, average, or worst file.

filetype = selectfiletype

SELECT CASE filetype
    CASE 1
        SHELL "copy best.dat sort.dat"
    CASE 2
        SHELL "copy average.dat sort.dat"
    CASE 3
        SHELL "copy worst.dat sort.dat"
END SELECT

' Select sort type.

sorttype = selectsort

OPEN "sort.dat" FOR RANDOM AS #1 LEN = LEN(value1)

' Start timing.

start! = TIMER
```

*Listing **7.3** continues*

Listing 7.3 continued

```
CLS
LOCATE 12, 35
PRINT "Working..."

SELECT CASE sorttype
    CASE 1
        CALL quick
    CASE 2
        CALL shellsort
    CASE 3
        CALL exchange
    CASE 4
        CALL bubblesort
    CASE 5
        CALL insertionsort
END SELECT

' End timing.

finish! = TIMER

CLOSE #1

' Place time in results array.

results!(filetype, sorttype) = finish! - start!

' Display results table.

CLS

format$ = "###.###   ###.###   ###.###"

PRINT "Sort type        best     average     worst"
PRINT "=========================================="
FOR i = 1 TO 5
    PRINT labels(i);
    PRINT USING format$; results!(1, i); results!(2, i); results!(3, i)
NEXT i
PRINT
PRINT
```

```
PRINT "Type X to exit, C to continue"

DO
    K$ = INKEY$
LOOP UNTIL K$ <> ""

IF UCASE$(K$) = "X" THEN EXIT DO

LOOP

' Erase files.

KILL "best.dat"
KILL "average.dat"
KILL "worst.dat"
KILL "sort.dat"

CLS

END      ' end of SORTS.BAS


SUB bubblesort STATIC

' Bubble sort routine.

maximum = ELEMENTS

DO

   index = 0
   FOR i = 1 TO (maximum - 1)

' If two adjacent elements are not in order, swap their values.

   GET #1, i, value1
   GET #1, i + 1, value2

     IF value1.number > value2.number THEN
         PUT #1, i, value2
```

Listing 7.3 *continues*

Listing *7.3 continued*

```
          PUT #1, i + 1, value1
          index = i
      END IF

   NEXT i

 ' Set limit for next loop to location of last swap.

   maximum = index

LOOP WHILE index

END SUB       ' end of bubblesort


SUB exchange

' Exchange sort.

maximum = ELEMENTS

FOR i = 1 TO maximum

   least = i

   FOR j = i + 1 TO maximum
      GET #1, j, value1
      GET #1, least, value2
      IF value1.number < value2.number THEN
         least = j
      END IF
   NEXT j

 ' If item is smaller than the current item, swap them.

   IF least > i THEN
      GET #1, i, value1
      PUT #1, i, value2
      PUT #1, least, value1
   END IF
```

```
NEXT i

END SUB      'end of exchange


SUB fillfiles STATIC

' Fills three arrays with integers as follows:

'   best() is filled in order
'   average() is partially ordered
'   worst() is in reverse order

' Then writes each array to a random file.

CLS

LOCATE 12, 35
PRINT "Creating files..."

FOR i = 1 TO ELEMENTS
    worst(i).number = ELEMENTS - (i - 1)
    best(i).number = i
    average(i).number = i
NEXT i

' average() starts out completely ordered;
' now "disorder" some of its elements.

top = ELEMENTS
bottom = 1

DO
    SWAP average(top).number, average(bottom).number
    top = top - 4
    bottom = bottom + 4
    IF top < bottom THEN
        EXIT DO
    END IF
LOOP
```

Listing **7.3** *continues*

Listing 7.3 continued

```
' Now write each array to a random file.

OPEN "best.dat" FOR RANDOM AS #1 LEN = LEN(best(0))
OPEN "average.dat" FOR RANDOM AS #2 LEN = LEN(average(0))
OPEN "worst.dat" FOR RANDOM AS #3 LEN = LEN(worst(0))

FOR i = 1 TO ELEMENTS
    PUT #1, i, best(i)
    PUT #2, i, average(i)
    PUT #3, i, worst(i)
NEXT i

CLOSE

END SUB        'end of fillfiles


SUB insertionsort

' Insertion sort routine.

maximum = ELEMENTS

FOR i = 2 TO maximum
    GET #1, i, value1
    temp1 = value1.number
    temp2 = temp1

    FOR j = i TO 2 STEP -1

       GET #1, j - 1, value2
       IF value2.number > temp2 THEN
          GET #1, j, value1
          PUT #1, j, value2
          PUT #1, j - 1, value1
       ELSE
          EXIT FOR
       END IF

    NEXT j
```

```
        value1.number = temp1
        PUT #1, j, value1

NEXT i

END SUB      ' end of insertionsort


SUB quick

' First level of quicksort routines.

CALL quicksort(1, ELEMENTS)

END SUB       ' end of quick


SUB quicksort (min, max)

' Bottom level of quicksort routine.

IF min < max THEN
' If only two elements, swap  them if they are out of order.

   IF max - min = 1 THEN

      GET #1, min, value1
      GET #1, max, value2

      IF value1.number > value2.number THEN
         PUT #1, min, value2
         PUT #1, max, value1
      END IF

   ELSE

' Pick a random "pivot element" and move it to the end.

      pivot = INT(RND * (max - min + 1)) + min
```

Listing **7.3** *continues*

Listing **7.3** *continued*

```
        GET #1, max, value1
        GET #1, pivot, value2
        PUT #1, max, value2
        PUT #1, pivot, value1
        border = value2.number
```

' Now "move in" from both directions toward the pivot element.

```
        DO
            i = min
            j = max

            GET #1, i, value1

            DO WHILE (i < j) AND (value1.number <= border)
                i = i + 1
                GET #1, i, value1
            LOOP

            GET #1, j, value2

            DO WHILE (j > i) AND (value2.number >= border)
                j = j - 1
                GET #1, j, value2
            LOOP
```

' If pivot element not reached, swap the two elements.

```
            IF i < j THEN
                PUT #1, i, value2
                PUT #1, j, value1
            END IF

        LOOP WHILE i < j
```

' Return pivot element to its proper location.

```
        GET #1, max, value2
        PUT #1, max, value1
        PUT #1, i, value2
```

```
' Pass the two subdivisions to this routine (recursive call).

        IF (i - min) < (max - i) THEN
            CALL quicksort(min, i - 1)
            CALL quicksort(i + 1, max)
        ELSE
            CALL quicksort(i + 1, max)
            CALL quicksort(min, i - 1)
        END IF

    END IF
END IF

END SUB      'end of quicksort


FUNCTION selectfiletype

' Asks user to select type of file to sort.

CLS

PRINT "Select type of file to sort:"
PRINT
PRINT "   1 -> Best (already sorted)"
PRINT "   2 -> Average (partially sorted)"
PRINT "   3 -> Worst (reverse order)"

DO
    K$ = INKEY$
LOOP UNTIL K$ = "1" OR K$ = "2" OR K$ = "3"

selectfiletype = VAL(K$)

END FUNCTION        'end of selectfiletype


FUNCTION selectsort

' Asks user to select type or sort algorithm to use.
```

Listing 7.3 continues

***Listing** 7.3 continued*

```
CLS

PRINT "Select type of sort:"
PRINT
PRINT "    1 -> Quicksort"
PRINT "    2 -> Shell sort"
PRINT "    3 -> Exchange sort"
PRINT "    4 -> Bubble sort"
PRINT "    5 -> Insertion sort"

DO
    K$ = INKEY$
LOOP UNTIL VAL(K$) < 6 AND VAL(K$) > 0

selectsort = VAL(K$)

END FUNCTION          'end selectsort


SUB shellsort

' Shell sort routine.

maximum = ELEMENTS

center = maximum \ 2

DO WHILE center > 0

    boundary = maximum - center

    DO
        flag = FALSE

        FOR i = 1 TO boundary

          GET #1, i, value1
          GET #1, i + center, value2

            IF value1.number > value2.number THEN
                PUT #1, i, value2
```

```
          PUT #1, i + center, value1
          flag = i
        END IF
      NEXT i

    boundary = flag - center

  LOOP WHILE flag

  center = center \ 2

LOOP

END SUB      'end of shellsort
```

****

On an AT computer with a hard disk and no disk cache, the sort times in table 7.2 were obtained.

Table 7.2. *Disk-Based Sort Times*

Sort type	Best	Average	Worst
Quicksort	1.039	1.648	3.297
Shell sort	0.879	2.641	2.141
Exchange sort	8.449	8.461	8.621
Bubble sort	0.160	10.820	17.188
Insertion sort	0.281	4.777	17.301

Remember that for these times, ELEMENTS was reduced to 100. Files of that size could easily be read into an array and sorted there, with the resulting increase in speed. Files large enough to require a disk-based sort—files too large to fit in memory—take much longer to sort. When you need to sort a large database (one with several thousand records), many users schedule the sort for their lunch hour—such sorts can literally take an hour or longer!

One way to speed disk-based sorts is with a RAM disk. If you can set up a RAM disk large enough to hold the file, your disk-based sorts can be dramatically speeded up. Be sure to copy the file from the RAM disk back to a physical disk when the sort is done!

Even without a RAM disk you may find that the program does not access the disk during the actual sorting procedure (indicated when the disk activity lights do not come on). This is due to the disk buffers that DOS automatically sets up when the computer is booted. A disk buffer is a section of memory that is used to temporarily store data being read from or written to the disk. When a program repeatedly accesses the same small file, most of the data transfers will be with the buffer, resulting in much faster operation. See your DOS documentation for more information on disk buffers.

Search Routines

Now that you finally reached the chapter section on searching, notice that the material has, in essence, already been covered! The reason is that the methods used for searching are essentially the same as those used in data entry and sorting routines. To avoid redundancy, I refer you to earlier sections for details.

Linear Search

One search method that was not covered previously is the *linear search*. The linear search is a brute-force method used only when the data records being searched are not sorted in any way. It is a very simple algorithm; assuming *n* records to search:

1. Set $n = 1$.

2. Look at record *n*.

3. Does it match the search template?

4. If it matches, the search is done.

5. If it does not match, increment *n* and return to step 2.

Listing 7.4 demonstrates the linear search technique (although I expect you could code this yourself in a few minutes!). The searching is done by the function linsearch, which accepts as arguments the array to search and the template to search for. The function expects that the first (index 0) element of the array contains the number of array elements.

If the template is found, linsearch returns the array index at which the match occurred. If the template is not found, linsearch returns zero. Note that linsearch finds only the first instance of template. If you are searching an array that may contain multiple instances of a value and you must find them all, the search routine has to be modified. This is a good programming exercise.

Listing* 7.4. *LINEAR.BAS

```
*********************************************************************

' LINEAR.BAS

' Linear search demonstration.

DECLARE FUNCTION linsearch% (template%, array%())

DEFINT A-Z

DIM array(1000)

CONST ELEMENTS = 1000, NO = 0, YES = 1

FOR i = 1 TO ELEMENTS
    array(i) = i * 2
NEXT i
 array(0) = ELEMENTS

CLS

INPUT "Enter number to find: ", template

result = linsearch(template, array())

IF result THEN
    PRINT template; "found at index "; result
ELSE
    PRINT template; " not found."
END IF

END          ' end of LINEAR.BAS
```

***Listing* 7.4** *continues*

---

*Listing **7.4** continued*

```
FUNCTION linsearch (template, array())

' Searches an integer array for template.
' Expects size of array in array(0).
'
' Returns 0 if not found, array index number if found.

found = NO

FOR index = 1 TO array(0)
    IF array(index) = template THEN
        found = YES
        EXIT FOR
    END IF
NEXT index

IF found THEN
    linsearch = index
ELSE
    linsearch = 0
END IF

END FUNCTION         ' end of linsearch
```

****

Using a linear search on a random file is little different than using it on an array. Simply search by record number rather than by array index.

Binary Search

A linear search is the only choice when you search an unsorted list. When searching a sorted list, you will find that a binary search is much more efficient. The technique for a binary search was the first technique presented in this chapter. In that section, the binary search algorithm was used to insert individual items into their proper location is a sorted list. With minor modifications, the same technique can be used to find an existing element rather than to insert a new element:

1. Compare the template with the element in the middle of the list.

2. If the template and element match, the search is successful and you are finished.

3. If they do not match, and the template is less than the existing element, the search target must be in the first half of the list (if it is in the list at all). Exclude the second half of the list from the search, and return to step 1.

4. If the template is greater than the existing element, the search target must be in the second half of the list (if it is in the list at all). Exclude the first half of the list from the search, and return to step 1.

5. If the list has been pared down to a single element and the search target has still not been found, it is not in the list.

Searching a Binary Tree

Binary trees were covered in Chapter 6, where you should look for further information. In brief, the process of searching a binary tree is as follows:

1. Starting with the root node, compare the template with existing data records. Follow the left pointer if the template is less than the existing record; follow the right pointer if it is greater than or equal to the existing record.

2. If you find a match, the search is completed.

3. If you find a zero pointer before finding a match, the template is not in the tree.

As with binary searches, searching a binary tree is very efficient.

Summary

This chapter looked at five different methods for keeping data in arrays and random files in sorted order. It also showed how to search for data in both sorted and unsorted lists. Along with the information in Chapter 6, the methods presented in this chapter provide a solid foundation for the development of QB programs that manipulate large amounts of data.

Part III

Input and Output

Keyboard Input

Almost every PC program uses the keyboard as its main source of user control and data input. Obviously, then, an important part of most programs is the interface between the program and the keyboard. QuickBASIC's built-in facilities for accepting keyboard input, the INPUT and LINE INPUT functions, are adequate for simple tasks. Unfortunately, they leave a lot to be desired for more sophisticated tasks.

As you will see, it is not particularly difficult to write your own keyboard control and input routines. In this chapter, I will do the following:

❏ Explain how the IBM-PC receives information from the keyboard

❏ Describe QB's INKEY$ function

❏ Using INKEY$, develop several short but useful keyboard utility procedures

❏ Present a flexible procedure for data entry and editing

❏ Show how to program "keyboard macros" that permit a user-defined sequence of characters to be input with a single keystroke

By using the keyboard routines presented in this chapter or other routines you develop yourself, you can significantly enhance the ways in which your programs interact with the keyboard.

The PC Keyboard

The keyboard on your IBM-PC is not simply a collection of dumb switches connected to the computer. The keyboard is, in fact, rather smart. It contains its own processor and interacts with the computer in a flexible manner.

When a key is pressed, the keyboard sends a signal to the computer. This signal initiates a *hardware interrupt*, which causes the computer to suspend whatever it is doing at the moment and transfer execution to the *keyboard interrupt service routine* in the computer's ROM BIOS. The service routine reads the keystroke from the keyboard and then transfers execution back to where it came from. This sequence of events happens extremely quickly, so that even if the computer is engaged in some other task when a key is pressed, the brief "interruption" is not even noticed.

The identity of the key that was pressed is transmitted to the computer as a *scan code*. For most keys, the scan code is a single byte that, as you know, can code 256 different values. PC keyboards, however, have on the order of 80 to 101 keys, depending on the exact model. Each key can be pressed alone, or in combination with Shift, Ctrl, or Alt. Thus, there are more possible key combinations than can be coded by the 256 possible values of a single byte. This problem is solved by having certain keystrokes send an "extended scan code" that is two bytes long. The first byte of an extended scan code is always 0; the second byte identifies the key. The ASC function can be used to obtain the scan code. Note that a key's scan code may or may not be the same as the ASCII code of the character. A table of keyboard scan codes can be found in Appendix C.

The keystroke that was read from the keyboard is not sent directly to whatever program is running at the moment. Rather, it is placed in the *keyboard buffer*, sometimes called the *type-ahead* buffer. The keyboard buffer is a small area of memory that holds a maximum of 15 characters until they are requested (removed from the buffer) by a program. If you "type ahead" too far and fill the buffer, your computer stops accepting keystrokes and beeps every time you press a key.

Any program, therefore, must explicitly read characters from the keyboard buffer to obtain keyboard input. An INPUT statement, for example, reads characters from the buffer until it detects an Enter. The characters that were read are then strung together and passed back to the program as a numeric or string variable.

As you will see, it is relatively easy to program keyboard input routines that are vastly superior to INPUT and LINE INPUT. First, however, examine the QuickBASIC (QB) keyboard function that this chapter's routines employ.

The *INKEY$* Function

The most flexible of QB's keyboard functions is INKEY$. By itself, INKEY$ can do nothing but read a single character from the keyboard buffer. With a bit of programming, however, INKEY$ becomes very powerful. I will use INKEY$ exclusively in the keyboard routines presented later in this chapter.

The power and flexibility of INKEY$ derives from two characteristics:

❏ INKEY$ can read any and all keystrokes, including function keys, cursor movement keys, and keys in combination with Shift, Ctrl, and Alt.

❏ If there are no keystrokes waiting in the keyboard buffer, INKEY$ does not just hang around and wait until something is entered, but reports an empty buffer.

Recall that calling INKEY$ removes the next available character (if any) from the keyboard buffer. If you simply want to determine whether a key has been pressed, you can test INKEY$ directly. The following WHILE/WEND statement loops until a keystroke is available in the buffer:

```
WHILE INKEY$ = "" : WEND
```

To allow multiple tests, however, you should assign the value of INKEY$ to a variable. This is shown in listing 8.1, which illustrates the use of INKEY$ and enables you to experiment with keyboard input.

Now that you understand how INKEY$ works, move on to mastering some useful routines.

Keyboard Utility Routines

This section presents several keyboard utility routines that will be useful in a wide variety of programs. You may wish to modify them to meet your own needs better. A feature common to several of these routines is that they accept a parameter that determines whether the user is signaled (with a beep) if an inappropriate keystroke is entered.

These procedures make use of the QB CONST statement to define frequently used constants such as YES and ENTER. In the procedure listings

---

Listing 8.1. *Demonstration of* INKEY$

```
' Demonstration of INKEY$.

' Program waits for a keystroke and then displays
' the extended or nonextended scan code.

' Pressing ENTER terminates the program.

CLS

DO

    DO
        K$ = INKEY$
    LOOP WHILE K$ = ""

    IF LEN(K$) = 1 THEN
        PRINT "Nonextended scan code "; ASC(K$)
    ELSEIF LEN(K$) = 2 THEN
        PRINT "Extended scan code "; ASC(RIGHT$(K$, 1))
    END IF

LOOP UNTIL ASC(K$) = 13          ' scan code for ENTER

END
```

---

later in the chapter, each procedure includes the necessary CONST statement. When you use the procedures in a real program, however, it would
be preferable to define all the needed constants in the module-level code,
and remove the CONST statements from the procedure-level code.

Flushing the Keyboard Buffer

The PC's type-ahead buffer can be very convenient at times, but it can
also present a danger. A user can enter the answer to a question before
the question is even displayed! Likewise, an accidental elbow on the
keyboard can fill the keyboard buffer with garbage that can cause
disastrous results the next time your program asks for keyboard input.

To guard against "buffer garbage," a program should empty the
keyboard buffer just before prompting the user for critical input. The
FlushKBBuffer subprogram in listing 8.2 does the trick.

Listing 8.2. FlushKBBuffer

```
SUB FlushKBBuffer

    WHILE INKEY$ <> ""
    WEND

END SUB      ' end FlushKBBuffer
```

Waiting for a Keystroke

Programs often need to pause until the user responds in some way—usually by pressing a key. Such a pause is simple enough to program directly, requiring only a DO/LOOP or a WHILE/WEND structure that cycles until INKEY$ returns a character. Putting the code in an appropriately named subroutine can save programming keystrokes (if only a few), and improve source code readability.

By including a call to FlushKBBuffer (listing 8.2), you can ensure that the WaitKey routine in listing 8.3 does not respond to an earlier keystroke.

Listing 8.3. *WaitKey*

```
SUB WaitKey

' Displays a message then loops until any key is pressed.

' Call FlushKBBuffer here, if desired.

PRINT
PRINT "Press any key to continue ..."

DO
LOOP UNTIL INKEY$ <> ""

END SUB      ' end WaitKey
```

You can modify WaitKey to wait for a particular keypress (the space bar, for example) or to display its prompt at a specified screen location.

Accepting Cursor Key Input Only

Users frequently press the cursor movement keys to move some kind of pointer around the screen. One common example, used by QB itself, is to move the cursor or a highlight bar among various menu selections, then make a choice by pressing Enter. The function CursorKey in listing 8.4 waits for the user to press one of the cursor keys or Enter, then returns the corresponding scan code to the calling program.

Listing 8.4. CursorKey

```
FUNCTION CursorKey (TOOT)

' Accepts only cursor key input, plus Enter.
' If TOOT = 1 (YES), beeps on inappropriate keystroke.

DO

    keycode = 0

' Wait for a keystroke.

    DO
        k$ = INKEY$
    LOOP UNTIL k$ <> ""

' Set keycode equal to ASCII code of key.

IF LEN(k$) = 2 THEN
    keycode = ASC(RIGHT$(k$, 1))
ELSE
    keycode = ASC(k$)
END IF

' Assign return value if an appropriate key was pressed.
' Constants for the cursor key scan codes must be defined in
' the calling program as follows:

CONST YES = 1

CONST HOME = &H47, UP = &H48, PGUP = &H49, DOWN = &H50
CONST PGDN = &H51, ENDD = &H4F, RIGHT = &H4D, LEFT = &H4B, ENTER=&H0D
```

```
    SELECT CASE keycode
        CASE HOME, UP, PGUP, DOWN, PGDN, ENDD, RIGHT, LEFT, ENTER
            CursorKey = keycode
            EXIT FUNCTION
        CASE ELSE
            IF TOOT = YES THEN BEEP
    END SELECT

LOOP

END FUNCTION            ' end CursorKey
```

Accepting Function Key Input Only

The IBM PC's 10 function keys are convenient for various types of user input. The function FKeyOnly, given in Figure 8.5, accepts only a function keystroke, rejecting all others, and returns an integer between 1 and 10 to the calling program. The number indicates which function key was pressed.

Listing 8.5. FKeyOnly

```
FUNCTION FKeyOnly% (TOOT)

' Reads input from the keyboard, accepting only
' function keystrokes (F1-F10). Returns an integer to
' the calling program indicating which function key was
' pressed.

' Pressing a function key returns an extended scan code
' that is two characters long. The second character of
' the scan code has ASCII value 59 thru 68 for
' keys F1 thru F10.

' If TOOT = 1 (YES), the function beeps when any key
' except a function key is pressed.

CONST YES = 1

keycode = 0

DO
```

Listing 8.5 continues

Listing 8.5 *continued*

```
' loop until a key is pressed

    DO
        k$ = INKEY$
    LOOP UNTIL k$ <> ""

' If an extended scan code has been returned, set keycode
' equal to the ASCII code of the second character.

    IF LEN(k$) = 2 THEN keycode = ASC(RIGHT$(k$, 1))

' Beep if an inappropriate key.

    IF TOOT = YES THEN
        IF NOT (keycode > 58 AND keycode < 69) THEN BEEP
    END IF

' Repeat loop if any key except a function key was pressed.

LOOP UNTIL (keycode > 58 AND keycode < 69)

' Subtract 58 from keycode so the function returns
' 1 for key F1, 2 for key F2, and so on.

FKeyOnly% = keycode - 58

END FUNCTION            ' end FKeyOnly
```

Input an Integer

The usual way for a QB program to input an integer number from the keyboard is with the INPUT statement containing an integer variable:

```
INPUT X%
```

If you make a mistake, however, by entering a noninteger number or an alphanumeric string, you are not informed of the error until the entire entry is made and you press Enter. Then, you get the maddening and uninformative Redo from start message.

A better way to input an integer would be to check each individual character as the user enters it, accepting only those characters that could be part of an integer number and rejecting inappropriate keystrokes immediately.

The function GetInteger in listing 8.6 does just this, accepting only integer input and returning the input value to the calling program. If no entry is made, 0 is returned.

Listing 8.6. GetInteger

```
FUNCTION GetInteger% (TOOT)

CONST ENTER = &H0D, YES = 1

' Save current cursor location.

xcursor = POS(0)
ycursor = CSRLIN

' Set up an empty string to collect input characters.

num$ = ""

DO            ' main loop

' Loop until a key is pressed.

    DO
        k$ = INKEY$
    LOOP UNTIL k$ <> ""

' This IF block does the following:

'    (1) If Enter was pressed, advance cursor one line and exit loop.
'    (2) Accept "-" if it was entered as the first character.
'    (3) Accept any digit.
'    (4) Otherwise, beep if TOOT = 1 (YES).

    IF ASC(k$) = ENTER THEN
        PRINT
        EXIT DO
    ELSEIF k$ = "-" AND LEN(num$) = 0 THEN
        num$ = num$ + k$
    ELSEIF (ASC(k$) > 47 AND ASC(k$) < 58) THEN
        num$ = num$ + k$
```

Listing 8.6 *continues*

Listing 8.6 continued

```
    ELSE
        IF TOOT = YES THEN BEEP
    END IF

' Return cursor to original location and print
' the characters that have been input to this point.

LOCATE ycursor, xcursor
PRINT num$;

LOOP

' Convert input from a string to a value, then return.

GetInteger = VAL(num$)

END FUNCTION         ' end GetInteger
```

Accepting Any Number

The limitations of the INPUT statement also apply to keyboard input of floating-point numbers. The function GetNumber in listing 8.7 does for floating-point input what GetInteger does for integer input. The two functions are almost identical, differing only in that GetNumber accepts a decimal point.

Listing 8.7. GetNumber

```
FUNCTION GetNumber! (TOOT)

CONST ENTER = &H0D, YES = 1

' Get current cursor location.

xcursor = POS(0)
ycursor = CSRLIN

' Empty string to collect input.

num$ = ""
```

```
    DO

'   Loop until a key is pressed.

        DO
            k$ = INKEY$
        LOOP UNTIL k$ <> ""

'   This IF block does the following:

'       (1) If Enter was pressed, advance cursor one line and exit loop
'       (2) Accept "-" if it was entered as the first character.
'       (3) Accept a decimal point.
'       (4) Accept any digit.
'       (5) Otherwise, beep if TOOT = 1 (YES).

        IF ASC(k$) = Enter THEN
            PRINT
            EXIT DO
        ELSEIF k$ = "-" AND LEN(num$) = 0 THEN
            num$ = num$ + k$
        ELSEIF k$ = "." THEN
            num$ = num$ + k$
        ELSEIF (ASC(k$) > 47 AND ASC(k$) < 58) THEN
            num$ = num$ + k$
        ELSE
            IF TOOT = YES THEN BEEP
        END IF

'   Return cursor to original location and print input.

        LOCATE ycursor, xcursor
        PRINT num$;

    LOOP

'   Convert input from a string to a value, then return.

    GetNumber = VAL(num$)

    END FUNCTION          ' end GetNumber!
```

Demonstrating the Utility Routines

KBDEMO.BAS, in listing 8.8, demonstrates all the utility routines discussed so far and shows how they are used.

Listing 8.8. *KBDEMO.BAS*

```
DECLARE SUB FlushKBBuffer ()
DECLARE FUNCTION CursorKey (TOOT%)
DECLARE SUB WaitKey ()
DECLARE FUNCTION GetNumber! (TOOT%)
DECLARE FUNCTION GetInteger% (TOOT%)
DECLARE FUNCTION FKeyOnly% (TOOT%)

' Program KBDEMO, demonstrating keyboard utility functions.

DEFINT A-Z

' General constants.

CONST TOOT = 1, NOTOOT = 0, YES = 1, NO = 0, ENTER = &H0D

' Constants for cursor keys.

CONST HOME = &H47, UP = &H48, PGUP = &H49, DOWN = &H50
CONST PGDN = &H51, ENDD = &H4F, RIGHT = &H4D, LEFT = &H4B

CLS

PRINT "Demonstrating function FKEYONLY()."
PRINT
PRINT "Program will accept a function key (F1-F10) only,"
PRINT "and will beep if another key is pressed."
PRINT
keypress = FKeyOnly%(TOOT)
PRINT "You pressed function key"; keypress

WaitKey

CLS

PRINT "Demonstrating function GetInteger."
PRINT "Enter any integer number."
```

```
z = GetInteger%(TOOT)
PRINT "You entered "; z

WaitKey

CLS

PRINT "Demonstrating function GetNumber."
PRINT "Enter any floating-point number."

z! = GetNumber!(TOOT)
PRINT "You entered "; z!

WaitKey

CLS

LOCATE 12, 10
PRINT "Demonstrating CursorKey-use cursor movement keys to move"
LOCATE 13, 20
PRINT "the cursor, press Enter when done."

' Get cursor location.

xcursor = POS(0)
ycursor = CSRLIN

' Turn on large cursor.

LOCATE , , 1, 0, 7

DO
    SELECT CASE CursorKey(TOOT)
        CASE UP
            ycursor = ycursor - 1
            IF ycursor < 1 THEN ycursor = 24
        CASE DOWN
            ycursor = ycursor + 1
            IF ycursor > 24 THEN ycursor = 1
        CASE LEFT
            xcursor = xcursor - 1
            IF xcursor < 1 THEN xcursor = 80
```

Listing 8.8 continues

Listing 8.8 *continued*

```
        CASE RIGHT
            xcursor = xcursor + 1
            IF xcursor > 80 THEN xcursor = 1
        CASE PGDN
            ycursor = 24
        CASE PGUP
            ycursor = 1
        CASE ENDD
            xcursor = 80
        CASE HOME
            xcursor = 1
        CASE ENTER
            EXIT DO
        CASE ELSE
            IF TOOT = YES THEN BEEP
    END SELECT

    LOCATE ycursor, xcursor

LOOP

END     ' program KBDEMO
```

A Procedure for Data Entry and Editing

The shortcomings of QB's numeric input statements were discussed earlier. Its facilities for keyboard entry of string data are equally primitive. The INPUT and LINE INPUT statements can do nothing but accept a sequence of characters and assign them to a string variable. Most annoying, perhaps, is the lack of any ability to edit a string during input. If you are entering data in response to a LINE INPUT prompt and notice an error, you have no choice but to backspace (erase) back to the error and then reenter the data.

A more flexible keyboard data routine would allow the following:

❏ Input of new data or display of existing data for editing

❏ Complete flexibility for location of input on the screen

❏ Specification of maximum allowed input length, with longer inputs not accepted

❏ Optional display of a user-defined prompt message

❏ Display of a "template" showing maximum length of input

❏ Control of both foreground and background screen attributes

❏ Restoration of original screen attributes and cursor location upon exit

The subprogram GetString is shown in listing 8.9. GetString uses two functions named GetCurrentFGAttr and GetCurrentBGAttr. These functions use the QB SCREEN function to read the current foreground and background colors, enabling them to be reset if the data entry routine modifies them.

You may be wondering why I implemented GetString as a subprogram rather than as a function because it is intended to accept keyboard input and return it to the calling program. The reason is that the procedure should not only accept new input and return it but also be able to display an existing string variable for editing. By passing the variable as an argument, you can use it to both "send" and "receive" data.

GetString has certain limitations. It is intended to function in screen mode 0 only. The width of the input field is limited to 80 characters—the width of the screen. The input field width, which includes the input prompt, is calculated using the maximum specified input length, not the actual input length.

Data Entry Process

The calling program passes GetString the screen coordinates where data entry is to occur. GetString first checks these coordinates to insure that both the prompt and the data entry template will fit on a single screen line. If they will not, GetString beeps and returns to the calling program without accepting any data.

GetString next checks the arguments fattr% and battr%. If either one is negative, the current screen attributes are left unchanged. Otherwise, the current attributes are retrieved with GetCurrentFGAttr and GetCurrentBGAttr, and the new attributes are set with a COLOR statement.

The final step before the main loop of the procedure is to display the prompt string, input template, and data string.

Most of the main processing in `GetString` is done inside the main `DO` loop. The procedure accepts a keystroke, classifies it as regular or extended, and then enters a multiblock `IF` statement. Each individual `IF` block checks for one of the keystrokes that are of interest to the procedure (Right and Left Arrows, Del, and so on) and executes the appropriate statements. When an Enter is detected, the loop is exited, the original screen attributes are restored (if necessary), and the procedure terminates.

Control of the cursor position is quite straightforward. The procedure maintains two pointers—one to the end of the string and one to the current cursor position within the string. In response to cursor movement keys or the addition/removal of characters, the pointers are updated and the cursor moved with the `LOCATE` statement.

Editing Process

The method used for deleting a character from the string is as follows. The portion of the string from its beginning up to, but not including, the character to be deleted is copied to a temporary storage variable `TEMP1$`. The character to be deleted is either at the cursor location (if Del was pressed) or just to the left of the cursor position (if Backspace was pressed). The portion of the string to the right of the character is likewise copied to `TEMP2$`. At this point, either `TEMP1$` or `TEMP2$` is empty (null) if the deleted character was the first or last character in the string. Next, `TEMP1$` and `TEMP2$` are concatenated, forming a new string that is the same as the original string but minus the deleted character. Finally, the new string is displayed, and the cursor position and string length variables are updated.

The procedure for inserting a character is similar, except that a new character is inserted instead of removed during the concatenation.

Listing 8.9. `GetString`

```
SUB GetString (X$, prompt$, maxlen%, row%, col%, fattr%, battr%)

CONST YES = 1, NO = 0, ENTER = &H0D
' The parameters:

'    X$ is the variable where the input string will go. If X$ already
'    contains a string, it is displayed and can be edited.

'    prompt$ is the user-prompt string.
```

```
'    maxlen% is the maximum length, in characters, of the input.

'    row% and col% specify the screen location of the input, that
'        is where the first character of entered data, will be
'        displayed. If a prompt is specified, it will be displayed
'        to the left of col%, at column (col% - LEN(prompt$)).

'    fattr% and battr% specify the screen display attributes
'        to be used. If either is < 0, current display attributes are
'        used. If display attributes are changed, they are reset to
'        their original settings at the end of the procedure.

' ====================================================================

' The editing keys:

'   Left Arrow moves cursor one space left, but not past
'   the start of the string.

'   Right Arrow moves cursor one space right, but not past
'   the end of the string.

'   Home moves cursor to the start of the string.

'   End moves cursor to the end of the string.

'   Del deletes the character under the cursor.

'   Backspace deletes the character to the left of the cursor.

'   Ctrl-Backspace deletes the entire string.

'   Enter accepts string and return to calling program.

'   All ASCII keys add to string.

' ====================================================================

' The variables:

'   oldfattr% and oldbattr% hold the original foreground
'        and background screen attributes.
```

Listing 8.9 continues

Listing 8.9 continued

```
'    extnd% is a flag, set to 1 if a key with an extended scan
'        code was entered, 0 otherwise.

'    cpos% is the cursor position within the input string at any moment.

'    length% is the length of the input string at any moment.

' ====================================================================

' Start execution.

' First, verify that prompt$ will not extend off left edge of the
' screen and that input will not extend past right edge of screen.
' In either case, beep and exit procedure.

IF (col% - LEN(prompt$) < 0) OR (col% + maxlen% > 80) THEN
    BEEP
    EXIT SUB
END IF

' If screen attributes are to be changed, save the current
' attributes and then set the new ones.

IF fattr% >= 0 AND battr% >= 0 THEN
    LOCATE row%, col%
    PRINT " "
    oldfattr% = GetCurrentFGAttr%(row%, col%)
    oldbattr% = GetCurrentBGAttr%(row%, col%)
    COLOR fattr%, battr%
END IF

cpos% = LEN(X$)
length% = LEN(X$)

' Locate cursor at location for display of prompt$, turn cursor
' on, and set for full block cursor.

LOCATE row%, col% - LEN(prompt$), 1, 0, 7

' Display the prompt, the initial data string, and a row of spaces
' showing the maximum length allowed for input.
```

```
PRINT prompt$ + X$ + SPACE$(maxlen% - LEN(X$));

' Locate cursor at the location for input.

LOCATE row%, col% + cpos%

DO                    ' start of main procedure loop

' Wait for any keypress.

    DO
        K$ = INKEY$
    LOOP UNTIL K$ <> ""

' Determine whether it is an extended or normal scan code.

    IF LEN(K$) = 2 THEN
        extnd% = YES
        ky% = ASC(RIGHT$(K$, 1))
    ELSE
        extnd% = NO
        ky% = ASC(K$)
    END IF

' If Enter was pressed, exit the procedure.

    IF (extnd% = NO) AND (ky% = ENTER) THEN
        EXIT DO

' Look for Left Arrow.

    ELSEIF (extnd% = YES) AND (ky% = 75) AND (cpos% > 0) THEN
        cpos% = cpos% - 1
        LOCATE row%, col% + cpos%

' Look for Right Arrow.

    ELSEIF (extnd% = YES) AND (ky% = 77) AND (cpos% < length%) THEN
        cpos% = cpos% + 1
        LOCATE row%, col% + cpos%
```

Listing 8.9 continues

Listing 8.9 *continued*

```
' Look for End key.

    ELSEIF (extnd% = YES) AND (ky% = 79) THEN
        cpos% = length%
        LOCATE row%, col% + cpos%

' Look for Home key.

    ELSEIF (extnd% = YES) AND (ky% = 71) THEN
        cpos% = 0
        LOCATE row%, col% + cpos%

' Look for Ctrl-Backspace.

    ELSEIF (extnd% = NO) AND (ky% = 127) THEN
        X$ = ""
        cpos% = 0
        LOCATE row%, col%
        PRINT SPACE$(length%)
        length% = 0
        LOCATE row%, col%

' Look for Del key.

    ELSEIF (extnd% = YES) AND (ky% = 83) AND (length% > 0)
            AND (cpos% < length%) THEN
        temp1$ = LEFT$(X$, cpos%)
        temp2$ = RIGHT$(X$, length% - cpos% - 1)
        X$ = temp1$ + temp2$
        length% = length% - 1
        LOCATE row%, col%
        PRINT X$ + " "
        LOCATE row%, col% + cpos%

' Look for Backspace key.

    ELSEIF (extnd% = NO) AND (ky% = 8) AND (length% > 0) AND (cpos% > 0) THEN
        temp1$ = LEFT$(X$, cpos% - 1)
        temp2$ = RIGHT$(X$, length% - cpos%)
        X$ = temp1$ + temp2$
```

```
                length% = length% - 1
                cpos% = cpos% - 1
                LOCATE row%, col%
                PRINT X$ + " "
                LOCATE row%, col% + cpos%

' Look for actual input characters.

        ELSEIF (extnd% = NO) AND (ky% > 31) AND (ky% < 127)
                AND (length% < maxlen%) THEN
            temp1$ = LEFT$(X$, cpos%)
            temp2$ = RIGHT$(X$, length% - cpos%)
            X$ = temp1$ + CHR$(ky%) + temp2$
            length% = length% + 1
            cpos% = cpos% + 1
            LOCATE row%, col%
            PRINT X$
            LOCATE row%, col% + cpos%
        END IF

LOOP           ' end of main procedure loop

' If screen attributes changed, return them to original settings.

IF fattr% >= 0 AND battr% >= 0 THEN
    COLOR oldfattr%, oldbattr%
END IF

' Restore underline style cursor.

LOCATE , , , 6, 7

END SUB         ' end of GetString
```

Demonstrating the Use of *GetString*

The program in listing 8.10 demonstrates the use of GetString.

Listing 8.10. *Demonstration of* GetString

```
DECLARE SUB WaitKey ()
DECLARE FUNCTION GetCurrentBGAttr% (row%, col%)
DECLARE FUNCTION GetCurrentFGAttr% (row%, col%)
DECLARE SUB GetString (X$, prompt$, maxlen%, row%, col%, fattr%, battr%)

' Demonstration of procedure GetString.

CONST NO = 0, YES = 1, BLUE = 1, WHITE = 7

CLS

LOCATE 1, 1
PRINT "Entering data from scratch:"

X$ = ""
maxlen% = 40
prompt$ = "Your name? "

CALL GetString(X$, prompt$, maxlen%, 4, 12, WHITE, BLUE)

LOCATE 6, 1
PRINT "You entered: "; X$

LOCATE 12, 1
PRINT "Editing existing data:"

X$ = "Daffy Duck"
prompt$ = "Your friend's name? "

CALL GetString(X$, prompt$, maxlen%, 14, 21, BLUE, WHITE)

LOCATE 16, 1
PRINT "You entered: "; X$

WaitKey
CLS
```

```
END


FUNCTION GetCurrentBGAttr% (row%, col%)

    attr% = SCREEN(row%, col%, 1)
    GetCurrentBGAttr% = (attr% \ 16) AND &H7

END FUNCTION


FUNCTION GetCurrentFGAttr% (row%, col%)

    attr% = SCREEN(row%, col%, 1)
    GetCurrentFGAttr% = (attr% AND &HF) + (attr% AND &H80) \ 8

END FUNCTION
```

Keyboard Macros

Use of the procedure GetString (or something similar) can simplify the task of programming user input. It does not, however, simplify the user's task! Each data string must be typed in, a character at a time. In many situations, this is unavoidable. There are times, however, when data entry can be somewhat repetitive in nature. And after all, repetitive tasks are what computers are supposed to do so well.

Consider a program that maintains a mailing list for the Albuquerque Symphony Orchestra. For most of the new entries, the "City" entry will be "Albuquerque"—quite a handful of keystrokes! If you could enable the program to automatically enter this and other frequent, long entries with a single keystroke, data entry efficiency would be increased (and misspellings decreased as well).

The code in listing 8.11 enables the user to assign a data string to each of the 26 Alt-letterkey combinations, then to "replay" the strings during data entry. The data string assigned to each key can be modified or deleted as needed. There is no provision for saving the key definitions to a disk file, although this would be easy to add.

The DefineMacroKeys procedure accepts new key definitions and enables you to edit/delete old ones. The definitions are stored in the string array macrodefs().

Listing 8.11. `DefineMacroKey`

```
SUB DefineMacroKeys

' Assigns user-defined strings to Alt-letterkey combinations.
' Stores the designated string in array macrodefs(), element ky%,
' where ky% is the scan code returned by the corresponding
' Alt-key combination.

' Note that the scan code for an Alt-letterkey is not the
' same as the letter key's ASCII code. The string defined for
' Alt-Q is stored in macrodefs(16), and so on. Some array
' elements are not used because there is no corresponding
' Alt-letterkey scan code (specifically, elements 26-29 and
' 39-43 are not used).

' The program using the keyboard macros is responsible for
' detecting Alt-letterkey combinations and then
' doing whatever it wishes with the macro string stored
' in the array macrodefs().

' If the array keys() has been initialized with the
' procedure InitKeysArray, it will hold the letters
' corresponding to the scan code index. Thus,

'    keys(16) = "Q"
'    keys(17) = "W"
'    and so on.

SHARED macrodefs() AS STRING, keys() AS STRING * 1

DO

    CLS
    LOCATE 8, 1
    PRINT "Press Alt-letterkey combination to define or change."
    PRINT "Press Enter when you are finished."

' Get an Alt-letterkey combination (or Enter).

    ky% = GetAltLetterKey%
```

```
    IF ky% = Enter THEN
        EXIT DO
    END IF

    LOCATE 12, 1

    IF macrodefs(ky%) = "" THEN
        PRINT "Alt-"; keys(ky%); " is not currently defined."
    ELSE
        PRINT "Current definition of Alt-"; keys(ky%);
            " is: "; macrodefs(ky%)
    END IF

    CALL GetString(macrodefs(ky%), "New definition: ", 40, 14, 17, -1, -1)

LOOP

END SUB          ' end of DefineMacroKeys


SUB InitKeysArray

' This procedure initializes each element of the array keys()
' to the letter whose keyboard scan code is the same as
' the array element index.

SHARED keys() AS STRING * 1

keys(16) = "Q"
keys(17) = "W"
keys(18) = "E"
keys(19) = "R"
keys(20) = "T"
keys(21) = "Y"
keys(22) = "U"
keys(23) = "I"
keys(24) = "O"
keys(25) = "P"
keys(30) = "A"
keys(31) = "S"
keys(32) = "D"
keys(33) = "F"
```

Listing 8.11 continues

Listing 8.11 *continued*

```
keys(34) = "G"
keys(35) = "H"
keys(36) = "J"
keys(37) = "K"
keys(38) = "L"
keys(44) = "Z"
keys(45) = "X"
keys(46) = "C"
keys(47) = "V"
keys(48) = "B"
keys(49) = "N"
keys(50) = "M"


END SUB            ' end of InitKeysArray
```

When it accepts key definitions, the program needs a way to accept only Alt-letterkey combinations plus Enter. The function `GetAltLetterKey` does this, returning the scan code to the calling program (see listing 8.12).

Listing 8.12. GetAltLetterKey

```
FUNCTION GetAltLetterKey%

' Accepts only an Alt-letterkey combination or Enter.
' Returns an integer giving the scan code of the
' key (NOT the ASCII code!!) or 13 for Enter.

CONST ENTER = &H0D

DO

    DO
        K$ = INKEY$
    LOOP UNTIL K$ <> ""

    IF LEN(K$) = 1 THEN
        IF ASC(K$) = ENTER THEN
            GetAltLetterKey% = ENTER
            EXIT DO
        END IF
```

```
        ELSEIF LEN(K$) = 2 THEN
            ky% = ASC(RIGHT$(K$, 1))
        END IF

' Check for top row of letters (Q-P).

    IF ky% > 15 AND ky% < 26 THEN
        GetAltLetterKey% = ky%
        EXIT DO
    END IF

' Check for A-L.

    IF ky% > 29 AND ky% < 39 THEN
        GetAltLetterKey% = ky%
        EXIT DO
    END IF

' Check for Z-M.

    IF ky% > 43 AND ky% < 51 THEN
        GetAltLetterKey% = ky%
        EXIT DO
    END IF

LOOP

END FUNCTION          ' end of GetAltLetterKey
```

The procedure GetString must be modified so that it can use the keyboard macros. First, GetString must be able to access the macro definitions stored in the array macrodefs(). This can be done by declaring the array that holds the definitions, macrodefs(), to be SHARED. Second, GetString must be able to detect the input of Alt-letterkey combinations and then copy the designated macro string into the input data string. Because most of GetString does not change, I will not duplicate its listing here. Simply modify the code as follows:

1. Include the following line before the first executable statement in GetString:

    ```
    SHARED macrodefs() AS STRING
    ```

2. Add the following ELSEIF block to the main multiblock IF statement in GetString:

```
' Look for Alt-letterkey combinations (keyboard macros).
ELSEIF (extnd% = YES) AND (ky% > 15) AND (ky% < 51) AND (length% = 0) THEN
        X$ = macrodefs(ky%)
        length% = LEN(X$)
        cpos% = length%
        LOCATE row%, col%
        PRINT X$
        LOCATE row%, col% + cpos%
```

As implemented here, GetString accepts a keyboard macro only if the data string is empty. A useful programming exercise would be to modify the code so that a macro could also be used to add to an existing data string.

Finally you can put it all together. The program in listing 8.13, Getstr1, is a bare-bones data entry program that demonstrates defining and using keyboard macros.

Listing 8.13. GETSTR1.BAS

```
DECLARE SUB GetData ()
DECLARE SUB DefineMacroKeys ()
DECLARE FUNCTION GetAltLetterKey% ()
DECLARE SUB InitKeysArray ()
DECLARE FUNCTION GetCurrentBGAttr% (row%, col%)
DECLARE FUNCTION GetCurrentFGAttr% (row%, col%)
DECLARE SUB GetString (X$, prompt$, maxlen%, row%, col%, fattr%, battr%)
DECLARE FUNCTION FKeyOnly% (TOOT%)
DECLARE SUB WaitKey ()

' Demonstration of:

'   DefineMacroKeys, GetAltLetterKey%, and InitKeysArray-three
'   procedures that are used to define keyboard macros.

'   GetString modified to use keyboard macros.

'================================================================

DIM macrodefs(16 TO 50) AS STRING, keys(16 TO 50) AS STRING * 1
```

```
CONST NO = 0, YES = 1, BLUE = 1, WHITE  = 7, ENTER = &H0D

CALL InitKeysArray

DO

' Display the menu.

    CLS
    LOCATE 5, 25
    PRINT "F1: Define macro keys."
    LOCATE 7, 25
    PRINT "F2: Enter data."
    LOCATE 9, 24
    PRINT "F10: Exit program."

' Branch depending on input.

    SELECT CASE FKeyOnly%(YES)
        CASE 1
            DefineMacroKeys
        CASE 2
            GetData
        CASE 10
            EXIT DO
    END SELECT

LOOP

CLS
END                 ' of program GETSTR1.BAS


SUB GetData

' Procedure to demonstrate GetString.

DO
    CLS
    name$ = ""
    address$ = ""
    city$ = ""
```

Listing 8.13 continues

Listing 8.13 *continued*

```
    LOCATE 5, 5
    PRINT "Enter a blank for 'Name' to exit."

    CALL GetString(name$, "Name: ", 25, 10, 15, WHITE, BLUE)

    IF name$ = "" THEN
        EXIT DO
    END IF

    CALL GetString(address$, "Address: ", 40, 12, 15, WHITE, BLUE)
    CALL GetString(city$, "City: ", 20, 14, 15, WHITE, BLUE)

LOOP

END SUB          ' end of GetData
```

Summary

This chapter explored the way in which the PC interacts with the keyboard, and examined INKEY$, QB's most flexible keyboard input function. Using INKEY$, you learned about several useful keyboard utility routines. Finally, the chapter showed a sophisticated data entry and editing procedure and code allowing the definition of keyboard "macros." Using the procedures and information in this chapter, your QB programs can make the best possible use of the keyboard.

Programming for a Mouse

Mice seem to bring out strong feelings in most computer users. Some people love them, using their mouse whenever possible. Others dislike mice and cannot think of a single situation in which they would use a mouse instead of the keyboard. Whatever your own feelings happen to be, there is no denying that mice are becoming more and more important and accepted in the PC world. They have, of course, always been an integral part of the Macintosh world.

True, many programs function perfectly well without a mouse. But can you imagine a freehand "paint" program or a CADD (computer-aided drafting and design) program without a mouse? To give yourself maximum flexibility in your programming, you should have the option of including mouse support in your programs. Whereas the QuickBASIC (QB) environment makes excellent use of a mouse, there is no support for using a mouse in your QB programs. With the information in this chapter, you can provide that support yourself. This chapter

❏ explains how your program can interact with a mouse by making calls to the *mouse driver*.

❏ develops routines for interfacing a QB program to the Microsoft mouse driver in both text and graphics modes.

Mouse Background

To the uninitiated, programming for a mouse may seem like a formidable task. Fortunately, this is not the case. The programming task is greatly simplified by the mouse driver software supplied with the mouse. The driver is a small memory-resident program that sits unobtrusively in memory and continually monitors the activity of the mouse. This monitoring goes on in the background, so it does not interfere with program execution. When your program needs to make use of the mouse, all it has to do is "ask" the mouse driver a question to obtain the needed information. I will show how this is done in a minute.

The Microsoft mouse was the original IBM PC mouse and is still the most popular. This is a two-button mouse, so the Microsoft mouse driver, which has become an industry standard, supports two buttons. Several other companies manufacture mice, some with three buttons. However, all mice come with Microsoft-compatible driver software, so they can be used by programs that support only the Microsoft standard. The mouse routines in this book are for the Microsoft driver, so if you are using another mouse, be sure to use the Microsoft-compatible driver. Note: Some non-Microsoft mice provide features not available with the Microsoft mouse, such as extra buttons or higher resolution. These features will not, however, be available if you use the mouse's Microsoft-compatible driver.

Applications programs communicate with the mouse driver by means of a software interrupt and the processor registers. A *software interrupt* is a programming technique that allows an applications program to access procedures that are external to the program itself. A *processor register* is a data storage location that is part of the computer's central processing unit. More information on software interrupts and processor registers appears in Chapter 5.

To be more specific, communication with the mouse driver is done via software interrupt 33H. Before calling the interrupt, an applications program must put a code specifying the mouse service desired in register AX. Many mouse driver calls require additional parameters, which are placed in one or more of the registers BX through DX. Some mouse calls are control functions, which do not return any information to the program. Other calls are inquiry functions, which return information in registers BX-DX and, occasionally, AX. Table 9.1 lists the 16 function calls supported by the Microsoft mouse driver.

Table 9.1. *Microsoft Mouse Function Calls*

Function	Type	Task
0	control	initialize mouse
1	control	display mouse cursor
2	control	hide mouse cursor
3	inquire	get button and position status
4	control	set mouse cursor position
5	inquire	get button press information
6	inquire	get button release information
7	control	set horizontal cursor movement range
8	control	set vertical cursor movement range
9	control	define graphics-mode cursor shape
10	control	define text-mode cursor shape
11	inquire	get mouse movement information
12	control	define event handler
13	control	turn light pen emulation on
14	control	turn light pen emulation off
15	control	set ratio of mouse motion to screen pixels

Programming a mouse differs somewhat depending on whether your program is using text screen modes or graphics screen modes. There are two reasons for this.

The first difference concerns movement of the mouse cursor on the screen. In text mode, the screen is divided into discrete character cells. The precision with which the mouse can specify a screen location is limited by this matrix of cells. The mouse may be pointing to one character cell or to its neighbor, but there is no "in between." As the mouse is moved, the mouse cursor does not move smoothly across the screen but "hops" from cell to cell. When you use a mouse in the QB environment, the mouse is operating in text mode.

In graphics mode, mouse operation is quite different from operation in text mode. In graphics mode, mouse accuracy is not limited by a matrix of character cells, but only by the pixel resolution of the screen. The mouse can point to any individual screen pixel. When the mouse is moved, the cursor glides smoothly over the screen.

The second difference has to do with the mouse cursor itself. In text mode, the appearance of the mouse cursor is limited to the standard cursor shapes (blinking underline, box, and so on) or to one of the available characters. In graphics mode, you are free to design any cursor shape, such as an arrow or pointing hand.

Because of these differences, I cover text mode and graphics mode mouse programming separately. Do not jump ahead to the graphics section, however, because some of the mouse functions used in text mode are also used in graphics mode.

Mouse Programming in Text Mode

As mentioned earlier, movement of the mouse cursor in text mode is limited to the screen matrix of character cells. On all PC video systems, the default text mode is 80 by 25 characters. Some video adapters also have enhanced text modes that display more characters on the screen, but those modes need not concern you here. Look instead now at the mouse function calls that are used in text mode.

Function 0: Initialize Mouse

This function checks whether a mouse driver is installed, and if so, resets all mouse driver parameters to their default state. The mouse cursor is moved to the center of the screen. Any program using the mouse should execute function 0 before any other mouse functions, or an unknown mouse status will be inherited.

If a mouse driver is installed, function 0 returns a nonzero value in register AX. If no mouse driver is detected, 0 is returned.

Function 1: Display Mouse Cursor

The mouse cursor may either be on (visible) or off (invisible). Even when off, the cursor "exists" and moves in response to movement of the mouse. Mouse initialization (function 0) leaves the cursor off, so you must call function 1 to see what is happening.

Function 2: Hide Mouse Cursor

This function turns the cursor off. When writing code to control the on/off state of the mouse cursor, you should be aware of the details of how the cursor is controlled. The mouse driver has an internal variable called the *cursor flag*. If this flag is 0 or greater, the cursor is on; if the flag is less than 0, the cursor is off. Function 0 (initialize) sets the flag to -1; calls to function 1 (display cursor) increment the flag by 1, whereas calls to function 2 (hide cursor) decrement the flag by 1. If your program alternates calls to function 1 and function 2, the flag value will alternate between -1 and 0, and there will be no problem.

If, however, a program makes two consecutive calls to either function 1 or 2, the flag is incremented or decremented twice and will have the value -2 or +1. It then takes two calls to the alternate function to change the cursor's status. Unfortunately, there is no way to ask the mouse driver about the value of the cursor flag, so your program must maintain its own flag. The process for how this is done becomes clear when I develop the code for mouse function calls.

Function 3: Get Button and Position Status

Function 3 returns information about the mouse cursor's position and the status of the buttons. The information returned describes the mouse's status at one particular moment in time—the time the function was called.

The button status is returned in register BX as follows:

❏ No button down: BX = 0

❏ Left button down: BX = 1

❏ Right button down: BX = 2

❏ Both buttons down: BX = 3

The position is returned in registers CX (column) and DX (row). The mouse driver reports the cursor position based on screen pixels and not based on character position, as you might expect for a text-mode screen. Regardless of the video adapter in use, the mouse driver sees the screen as 640 pixels wide and 200 pixels high. Because a text-mode screen is 80 characters wide by 25 characters high, each character "cell" measures 8 by 8 pixels. The position of a character cell is given by the coordinates of the pixel in the top left corner of the cell. Thus, the character cell in the top left corner of the screen (row 1, column 1) has pixel coordinates 0,0; the cell immediately below has coordinates 0,8; and so on. To transform the mouse cursor position as reported by function 3 into character position, apply the following transformations:

character column = ((value in CX) / 8) + 1

character row = ((value in DX) / 8) + 1

Function 4: Set Mouse Cursor Position

This function moves the mouse cursor to the specified screen location. As with function 3, screen location is given in terms of the pixel address of the upper left corner of the character cell. The column and row coordinates must be placed in registers CX and DX, respectively. If you pass a pixel coordinate that is not at the upper left corner of a character cell (that is, it is not an exact multiple of 8), the driver "rounds down" and places the cursor accordingly. If you pass a pixel coordinate that is out of range (off the screen), no error results; the cursor is simply placed at the edge of the screen.

Function 5: Get Button Press Information

Function 5 returns a count of how many times the specified mouse button has been pressed. When the function is called, the value in register BX indicates which button is being queried: 0 for the left button and 1 for the right button. Upon return of control to the main program, the value in BX is the number of times the specified button has been pressed since the last call to this function (or since the mouse was initialized). Thus, function 5 retrieves information about the mouse's history. While your program is busy with other tasks, the mouse driver automatically detects button presses and records them in an internal variable. Function 5 reads that variable and resets it to zero.

Function 5 also returns information about the cursor position and button status. The current button status is returned in register AX, using the same codes as function 3. Row and column positions are returned in DX and CX, respectively. If the button specified in the function call is currently down, the current row and column position is reported. If the button is not down, the row and column give the cursor's position the last time the button was pressed.

Function 6: Get Button Release Information

This function works exactly like function 5, except that function 6 reports releases of the specified button rather than presses.

Functions 7 and 8: Set Horizontal and Vertical Cursor Movement Range

These functions restrict the movement of the mouse cursor to a rectangular region of the screen. This can be quite useful, for example, when you want to restrict the cursor to movement within a pop-up menu. Once the boundaries are set, the cursor simply will not move beyond them no matter how madly you push your mouse around the desktop.

Both functions require the minimum and maximum boundaries to be passed in registers CX and DX. Because the function sorts the arguments, it does not matter which register gets which argument (min or max). Recall that the mouse driver sees the screen as a 640 by 200 array of pixels, so you must multiply character row and column positions by 8. Thus, to restrict the cursor to an area 20 columns wide by 10 rows high in the center of the screen, you would do the following:

1. Call function 7 with arguments 240 and 400.

2. Call function 8 with arguments 64 and 144.

If the cursor is outside the bounded area when the functions are called, it automatically moves inside. To restore full-screen movement, you can call the functions with full-screen arguments or call the initialization function.

Function 10: Define Text-Mode Cursor Shape

When using a mouse in text mode, you have a choice of two cursors. One is a software cursor, which is totally under the control of the mouse driver and independent of the hardware cursor that is controlled by the video adapter. If you use a mouse in the QB environment, you have seen both of these cursors. The large block cursor that moves in response to mouse motion is the *software mouse cursor*. The underline cursor that marks the location where editing operations occur is the *video adapter hardware cursor*.

The mouse can also control the hardware cursor, which means that only one cursor is visible on the screen. Moving the hardware cursor with the mouse does not, however, move the text display position. If you have moved the hardware cursor with the mouse and execute a PRINT statement, the output appears at the location of the cursor when the mouse driver first took control of it. To select the text display position with the mouse, your program must perform the following steps:

1. Move the mouse cursor (either hardware or software) to the desired screen location.

2. Read the cursor position with mouse function call 3, 5, or 6.

3. Use the LOCATE statement to move the text display location to the cursor location.

With function 10, you can specify the type of mouse cursor and its appearance. The value passed to the function in BX determines the cursor type: 0 for a software cursor (the default upon mouse initialization) and 1 for a hardware cursor. Arguments passed in CX and DX determine the cursor's appearance. The way in which these arguments work depends on the type of cursor being selected.

You have relatively little control over the appearance of a hardware cursor. The arguments passed in CX and DX give the start and stop scan lines for the cursor (this is similar to the way in which the LOCATE statement can set cursor size). The top scan line in a character cell is always 0. The bottom scan line is 7 for all graphics adapters and 12 for monochrome text-only adapters. Thus, to set a hardware cursor that is a block occupying the entire character cell, call function 10 with the following arguments:

```
BX = 1
CX = 0
DX = 7
```

For an underline hardware cursor instead of a full box, change CX to 6.

Defining a software cursor is a bit more involved. The argument passed in CX is the *screen mask*, which determines how existing screen characters are displayed when the mouse cursor is overlying them. The argument passed in DX is the *cursor mask*, which determines the appearance of the mouse cursor itself.

Each screen character is represented by two bytes of information: an *attribute byte* that controls the appearance of the character (color, intensity, and so on) and a *character byte* that specifies the character itself. The screen and cursor masks also are two bytes each. The mouse driver sets the actual appearance of the mouse cursor on the screen by the following steps:

1. The existing screen character/attribute bytes are logically ANDed with the screen mask.

2. The cursor mask is XORed with the result of step 1.

This arrangement gives you essentially unlimited control over the appearance of the software mouse cursor. In practice, however, the following two types of software cursor are used most often (both are illustrated in the demonstration program—listing 9.1):

❏ A "see-through" rectangle that inverts the underlying screen character. For this type of cursor, call mouse function 10 with CX = &H77FF and DX = &H7700.

❏ A user-specified character that completely overwrites its current screen location. For this, call function 10 with CX = &H0000 and DX = &H07xx, where xx is the ASCII value of the desired character (for example, DX = &H0718 for an upward-pointing arrow).

Function 11: Get Mouse Movement Information

Like function 5, function 11 provides information about the mouse's history. Specifically, it returns information about the net mouse cursor movement since the last call to this function (or since mouse initialization). The unit of mouse movement is called, appropriately enough, the "mickey." With the Microsoft mouse, one mickey equals 1/200 of an inch, which is the limit of the mouse's resolution. Horizontal movement is returned in CX, and vertical movement in DX. The mickey count is always within the range -32768 to +32767; positive counts reflect movement up or to the right, and negative counts reflect movement down or to the left. Note that mickeys refer to actual mouse movement, not to cursor movement.

Functions 13 and 14: Turn Light Pen Emulation On/Off

The default condition, as set by mouse initialization, is for light-pen emulation to be on. The position of the mouse cursor is then interpreted as the light pen's position by software that expects light pen input.

If a program uses both a mouse and an actual light pen, turn emulation off so that the program does not receive dual light-pen signals.

The Remaining Functions: 9, 12, and 15

What about functions 9, 12, and 15? Functions 9 and 15 are used exclusively in graphics mode and are discussed in the next section. Function 12, unfortunately, brings up one of the few limitations of BASIC. Function 12 enables you to specify a procedure, or *event handler*, that will be automatically executed every time a specified mouse event occurs. When calling function 12, you must pass it the address of the event handler. This cannot be done in BASIC. Fortunately, function 12 is not necessary for the purpose of the demonstration program in listing 9.1.

Listing 9.1. *Text Mode Mouse Subroutines*

```
SUB M.GetBtnPress (button)

SHARED Mous AS mouseinfo

    CALL Mouse(5, button, 0, 0)

    Mous.BtnStatus = a
    Mous.BtnClicks = b
    Mous.Column = c
    Mous.Row = d

END SUB      ' end of M.GetBtnPress


SUB M.GetBtnRelease (button)

SHARED Mous AS mouseinfo

    a = 6
    b = button
    c = 0
    d = 0

    CALL Mouse(a, b, c, d)

    Mous.BtnStatus = a
    Mous.BtnClicks = b
    Mous.Column = c
    Mous.Row = d
```

```
END SUB          ' end of M.GetBtnRelease


SUB M.GetPos

' Returns mouse status at the time of the call.
' Mous.Column, Mous.Row give mouse cursor position.
' Mous.BtnStatus = 0 if no mouse button pressed
'                = 1 if left mouse button pressed
'                = 2 if right mouse button pressed
'                = 3 if both mouse buttons pressed

SHARED Mous AS mouseinfo

    a = 3

    CALL Mouse(a, b, c, d)

    Mous.BtnStatus = b
    Mous.Column = c
    Mous.Row = d

END SUB          ' end of M.GetPos


SUB M.HideCursor

' Turns off the mouse cursor if it is on.

SHARED Mous AS mouseinfo

    IF Mous.CursorOn = YES THEN

        CALL Mouse(2, 0, 0, 0)
        Mous.CursorOn = NO

    END IF

END SUB          ' end of M.HideCursor
```

Listing 9.1 continues

Listing 9.1 continued

```
SUB M.HorizRange (leftcol, rightcol)

' Restricts horizontal mouse cursor movement to the screen
' region between leftcol and rightcol. If the cursor is
' outside this range, it is moved inside.

    CALL Mouse(7, 0, leftcol, rightcol)

END SUB      ' end of M.HorizRange


SUB M.Initialize

' If a mouse is installed, initializes mouse and
' returns a = 1. If no mouse, a = 0.

SHARED Mous AS mouseinfo

    a = 0
    CALL Mouse(a, 0, 0, 0)
    Mous.Exists = a

END SUB      ' end of M.Initialize


SUB M.MoveCursor (Row, Col)

' Moves the mouse cursor to the screen position specified
' by col and row.

    CALL Mouse(4, 0, Col, Row)

END SUB      ' end of M.MoveCursor


SUB M.Movement

SHARED Mous AS mouseinfo

' Reports the net movement of the mouse cursor since
' the last call to this function.
```

```
        CALL Mouse(11, b, c, d)
        Mous.HMovement = c
        Mous.VMovement = d

END SUB      ' end of M.Movement


SUB M.PenOff

' Turns light-pen emulation off.

        CALL Mouse(14, 0, 0, 0)

END SUB      ' end of M.PenOff


SUB M.PenOn

' Turns light-pen emulation on (the default upon
' mouse initialization).

        CALL Mouse(13, 0, 0, 0)

END SUB      ' end of M.PenOn


SUB M.ShowCursor

SHARED Mous AS mouseinfo

        IF Mous.CursorOn = NO THEN

                CALL Mouse(1, 0, 0, 0)
                Mous.CursorOn = YES

        END IF

END SUB      ' end of M.Showcursor


SUB M.TextCursor (cursortype, scan1, scan2)
```

Listing 9.1 continues

Listing 9.1 continued

```
' Sets the text cursor type.
' If cursortype = 0, the software cursor is set, and scan1 and
' scan2 specify the screen and cursor masks.

' If cursortype = 1, the hardware cursor is set, and scan1 and
' scan2 specify start/stop scan lines for the cursor.

CALL Mouse(10, cursortype, scan1, scan2)

END SUB



SUB M.VertRange (upperrow, lowerrow)

' Restricts vertical mouse cursor movement to the screen
' region between upperrow and lowerrow. If the cursor is
' outside this range, it is moved inside.

    CALL Mouse(8, 0, upperrow, lowerrow)

END SUB      ' end of M.VertRange



SUB Mouse (a, b, c, d)

DIM InRegs AS RegTypeX, OutRegs AS RegTypeX

InRegs.ax = a
InRegs.bx = b
InRegs.cx = c
InRegs.dx = d

CALL INTERRUPTX(&H33, InRegs, OutRegs)

a = OutRegs.ax
b = OutRegs.bx
c = OutRegs.cx
d = OutRegs.dx

END SUB       ' end of Mouse
```

Mouse Utility Routines

Listing 9.2 presents two mouse utility routines you may find useful. FlushButtons is analogous to the keyboard utility routine FlushKBBuffer presented in the previous chapter. It zeros the mouse driver's internal button press counters. Use FlushButtons to ensure that your program is not responding to an "old" button press.

WaitClick is also analogous to one of Chapter 8's keyboard routines, WaitKey. WaitClick displays a message on the screen and then pauses until a mouse button is clicked and released. The button and message are specified by the argument passed to WaitClick: 0 for the left button, 1 for right, 2 for both, 3 for either. As implemented here, the constants LEFT, RIGHT, BOTH, and EITHER are used to improve program readability.

Listing 9.2. FlushButtons *and* WaitClick *Subroutines*

```
SUB FlushButtons

' Resets the mouse driver's internal "press" and "release"
' counters to 0 for both buttons.

    CALL Mouse(5, LEFT, 0, 0)
    CALL Mouse(5, RIGHT, 0, 0)
    CALL Mouse(6, LEFT, 0, 0)
    CALL Mouse(6, RIGHT, 0, 0)

END SUB      ' end of FlushButtons



SUB WaitClick (button)

' Pauses until the specified mouse button is clicked and released.

' if button = LEFT (0), left button
' if button = RIGHT (1), right button
' if button = BOTH (2), both buttons
' if button = EITHER (3), any button(s)

' Uses constants defined in the calling program as follows:
```

Listing 9.2 *continues*

Listing 9.2 continued

```
CONST LEFT = 0, RIGHT = 1, BOTH = 2, EITHER = 3

SHARED Mous AS mouseinfo

DIM whichbtn(3) AS STRING

whichbtn(LEFT) = "left button"
whichbtn(RIGHT) = "right button"
whichbtn(BOTH) = "both buttons"
whichbtn(EITHER) = "any button"

Mous.BtnStatus = 0

PRINT "Click "; whichbtn(button); " to continue ..."

DO

     M.GetPos

LOOP UNTIL Mous.BtnStatus = 0

IF button < EITHER THEN

     DO

          M.GetPos

     LOOP UNTIL Mous.BtnStatus = (button + 1)

ELSE

     DO

          M.GetPos

     LOOP UNTIL Mous.BtnStatus > 0

END IF

' Now wait for button release.
```

```
DO

    M.GetPos

LOOP UNTIL Mous.BtnStatus = 0

END SUB      ' end of WaitClick
```

The program in listing 9.3 demonstrates most of the mouse function calls developed to this point.

Listing 9.3. *Text-Mode Mouse Demonstration Program*

```
DECLARE SUB FlushButtons ()
DECLARE SUB M.PenOn ()
DECLARE SUB M.PenOff ()
DECLARE SUB M.Movement ()
DECLARE SUB M.GetBtnPress (button%)
DECLARE SUB M.GetBtnRelease (button%)
DECLARE SUB M.TextCursor (cursortype%, scan1%, scan2%)
DECLARE SUB WaitClick (button%)
DECLARE SUB M.HorizRange (leftcol%, rightcol%)
DECLARE SUB M.VertRange (upperrow%, lowerrow%)
DECLARE SUB M.GetPos ()
DECLARE SUB M.ShowCursor ()
DECLARE SUB M.HideCursor ()
DECLARE SUB M.Initialize ()
DECLARE SUB M.MoveCursor (Row%, Col%)
DECLARE SUB Mouse (a%, b%, c%, d%)

' $INCLUDE: 'QB.BI'

DEFINT A-Z

CONST TRUE = 1, FALSE = 0, YES = 1, NO = 0, LEFT = 0, RIGHT = 1
CONST BOTH = 2, EITHER = 3, HARDCURSOR = 1, SOFTCURSOR = 0

' Define a data type to hold information returned and used
' by the mouse procedures.
```

Listing 9.3 *continues*

Listing 9.3 continued

```
TYPE mouseinfo
     Exists AS INTEGER          ' > 0 if mouse exists
     CursorOn AS INTEGER        ' 1 if cursor on, 0 if off
     BtnStatus AS INTEGER       ' current button status (up/down)
     BtnClicks AS INTEGER       ' times button has been clicked
     Column AS INTEGER          ' mouse cursor column position
     Row AS INTEGER             ' mouse cursor row position
     HMovement AS INTEGER       ' horizontal mouse movement
     VMovement AS INTEGER       ' vertical mouse movement
END TYPE

DIM Mous AS mouseinfo

' Execution begins here.

CLS

' See whether mouse is installed.

M.Initialize

IF Mous.Exists THEN
     PRINT "Mouse detected"
     PRINT
     CALL WaitClick(LEFT)
     CLS
ELSE
     PRINT "No mouse detected."
     PRINT "You must have a mouse and a Microsoft-compatible"
     PRINT "mouse driver installed to run this program."
     PRINT
     PRINT "Press any key to exit."
     WHILE INKEY$ = "": WEND
     END
END IF

' Move cursor to center of screen and turn it on.

CALL M.MoveCursor(12 * 8, 40 * 8)
M.ShowCursor
```

```
LOCATE 1, 1
PRINT "Cursor movement demonstration."
PRINT "Left button turns cursor off."
PRINT "Right button turns it back on."
PRINT "Click both buttons to continue"

DO

M.GetPos

' Display the current row and column position of the mouse cursor.

LOCATE 6, 1
PRINT "Column ="; (Mous.Column / 8) + 1, "Row ="; (Mous.Row / 8) + 1

' Mous.BtnStatus = 0 if no mouse button was pressed
'                = 1 if the left button was pressed
'                = 2 if the right button was pressed
'                = 3 if both buttons were pressed

SELECT CASE Mous.BtnStatus
     CASE 1
          M.HideCursor
     CASE 2
          M.ShowCursor
     CASE 3
          EXIT DO
END SELECT

LOOP

' Hide the software cursor.

M.HideCursor

CLS
PRINT "Demonstrating hardware cursor (scan lines 6 and 7)."

' Now switch to hardware cursor and be sure it is on.
```

Listing 9.3 continues

Listing 9.3 continued

```
CALL M.TextCursor(HARDCURSOR, 6, 7)
M.ShowCursor
CALL WaitClick(EITHER)

' Now back to software cursor with program-defined cursor.
' These masks give an up-arrow on a black background.

CLS

PRINT "Demonstrating user-defined software cursor."
CALL M.TextCursor(SOFTCURSOR, 0, &H718)
CALL WaitClick(EITHER)

' Return to rectangular cursor.

CALL M.TextCursor(SOFTCURSOR, &H77FF, &H7700)

' Now demonstrate restricting cursor movement to a defined
' region of the screen.

CLS

PRINT "Cursor movement is now restricted to a rectangular"
PRINT "region in the center of the screen."
PRINT
PRINT "Click left button to continue ..."

FlushButtons
CALL M.HorizRange(20 * 8, 60 * 8)
CALL M.VertRange(8 * 8, 17 * 8)

DO

    CALL M.GetBtnRelease(LEFT)
    M.GetPos

' Display the current row and column position of the mouse cursor.

    LOCATE 6, 1
    PRINT "Column ="; (Mous.Column / 8) + 1, "Row ="; (Mous.Row / 8) + 1
```

```
LOOP UNTIL Mous.BtnClicks > 0

' Now demonstrate text entry.

CLS
PRINT "Move cursor to desired text-entry location and"
PRINT "click left button, then make entry followed by <RETURN>"
PRINT
PRINT "Click right button to continue."

' Reset mouse, show cursor,

M.ShowCursor
FlushButtons

' Restrict cursor movement to lower 20 rows and left 60
' columns so that input will not overwrite information
' on screen and will not try to extend past right edge.

CALL M.VertRange(4 * 8, 24 * 8)
CALL M.HorizRange(0, 60 * 8)

DO

    CALL M.GetBtnRelease(LEFT)

    IF Mous.BtnClicks > 0 THEN
        Col = Mous.Column / 8
        Row = Mous.Row / 8
        LOCATE Row + 1, Col + 2
        INPUT ": ", junk$
        M.ShowCursor
        FlushButtons
    END IF

    CALL M.GetBtnRelease(RIGHT)

LOOP UNTIL Mous.BtnClicks > 0

' Reset mouse to default state.
```

Listing 9.3 continues

Listing 9.3 continued

```
M.Initialize
CLS
PRINT "End of text-mode mouse demonstration."

END      ' end of MOUSDEMO.BAS

SUB FlushButtons

' Resets the mouse driver's internal "press" and "release"
' counters to 0 for both buttons.

     CALL Mouse(5, LEFT, 0, 0)
     CALL Mouse(5, RIGHT, 0, 0)
     CALL Mouse(6, LEFT, 0, 0)
     CALL Mouse(6, RIGHT, 0, 0)

END SUB      ' end of FlushButtons


SUB M.GetBtnPress (button)

SHARED Mous AS mouseinfo

     CALL Mouse(5, button, 0, 0)
     Mous.BtnStatus = a
     Mous.BtnClicks = b
     Mous.Column = c
     Mous.Row = d

END SUB      ' end of M.GetBtnPress


SUB M.GetBtnRelease (button)

SHARED Mous AS mouseinfo

     a = 6
     b = button
     c = 0
     d = 0
```

```
        CALL Mouse(a, b, c, d)

        Mous.BtnStatus = a
        Mous.BtnClicks = b
        Mous.Column = c
        Mous.Row = d

END SUB          ' end of M.GetBtnRelease


SUB M.GetPos

' Returns mouse status at the time of the call.
' Mous.Column, Mous.Row give mouse cursor position.
' Mous.BtnStatus = 0 if no mouse button pressed
'              = 1 if left mouse button pressed
'              = 2 if right mouse button pressed
'              = 3 if both mouse buttons pressed

SHARED Mous AS mouseinfo

        a = 3
        CALL Mouse(a, b, c, d)
        Mous.BtnStatus = b
       ·Mous.Column = c
        Mous.Row = d

END SUB       ' end of M.GetPos


SUB M.HideCursor

' Turns off the mouse cursor if it is on.

SHARED Mous AS mouseinfo

        IF Mous.CursorOn = YES THEN
            CALL Mouse(2, 0, 0, 0)
            Mous.CursorOn = NO
        END IF
```

Listing 9.3 continues

Listing 9.3 continued

```
END SUB      ' end of M.HideCursor


SUB M.HorizRange (leftcol, rightcol)

' Restricts horizontal mouse cursor movement to the screen
' region between leftcol and rightcol. If the cursor is
' outside this range, it is moved inside.

    CALL Mouse(7, 0, leftcol, rightcol)

END SUB      ' end of M.HorizRange


SUB M.Initialize

' If a mouse is installed, initializes mouse and
' returns a = 1.  If no mouse, a = 0.

SHARED Mous AS mouseinfo

    a = 0
    CALL Mouse(a, 0, 0, 0)
    Mous.Exists = a

END SUB      ' end of M.Initialize


SUB M.MoveCursor (Row, Col)

' Moves the mouse cursor to the screen position specified
' by col and row.

    CALL Mouse(4, 0, Col, Row)

END SUB      ' end of M.MoveCursor


SUB M.Movement

SHARED Mous AS mouseinfo
```

```
' Reports the net movement of the mouse cursor since
' the last call to this function.

    CALL Mouse(11, b, c, d)
    Mous.HMovement = c
    Mous.VMovement = d

END SUB     ' end of M.Movement


SUB M.PenOff

' Turns light-pen emulation off.

    CALL Mouse(14, 0, 0, 0)

END SUB     ' end of M.PenOff


SUB M.PenOn

' Turns light-pen emulation on (the default upon
' mouse initialization).

    CALL Mouse(13, 0, 0, 0)

END SUB     ' end of M.PenOn


SUB M.ShowCursor

SHARED Mous AS mouseinfo

    IF Mous.CursorOn = NO THEN
        CALL Mouse(1, 0, 0, 0)
        Mous.CursorOn = YES
    END IF

END SUB     ' end of M.Showcursor
```

Listing 9.3 continues

Listing 9.3 continued

```
SUB M.TextCursor (cursortype, scan1, scan2)

' Sets the text cursor type.
' If cursortype = 0, the software cursor is set, and scan1 and
' scan2 specify the screen and cursor masks.

' If cursortype = 1, the hardware cursor is set, and scan1 and
' scan2 specify specify start/stop scan lines for the cursor.

CALL Mouse(10, cursortype, scan1, scan2)

END SUB



SUB M.VertRange (upperrow, lowerrow)

' Restricts vertical mouse cursor movement to the screen
' region between upperrow and lowerrow. If the cursor is
' outside this range, it is moved inside.

    CALL Mouse(8, 0, upperrow, lowerrow)

END SUB      ' end of M.VertRange



SUB Mouse (a, b, c, d)

DIM InRegs AS RegTypeX, OutRegs AS RegTypeX

InRegs.ax = a
InRegs.bx = b
InRegs.cx = c
InRegs.dx = d

CALL INTERRUPTX(&H33, InRegs, OutRegs)

a = OutRegs.ax
b = OutRegs.bx
c = OutRegs.cx
d = OutRegs.dx
```

```
END SUB      ' end of Mouse


SUB WaitClick (button)

' Pauses until
 the specified mouse button is clicked and released.

' If button = 0, left button
' If button = 1, right button
' If button = 2, both buttons
' If button = 3, any button(s)

SHARED Mous AS mouseinfo

DIM whichbtn(3) AS STRING
whichbtn(0) = "left button"
whichbtn(1) = "right button"
whichbtn(2) = "both buttons"
whichbtn(3) = "any button"

Mous.BtnStatus = 0

PRINT "Click "; whichbtn(button); " to continue ..."

DO
     M.GetPos
LOOP UNTIL Mous.BtnStatus = 0

IF button < 3 THEN

     DO
          M.GetPos
     LOOP UNTIL Mous.BtnStatus = (button + 1)

ELSE

     DO
          M.GetPos
     LOOP UNTIL Mous.BtnStatus > 0

END IF
```

Listing 9.3 continues

Listing 9.3 *continued*

```
' Now wait for button release.

DO

    M.GetPos

LOOP UNTIL Mous.BtnStatus = 0

END SUB     ' end of WaitClick
```

Mouse Programming in Graphics Mode

As mentioned earlier, mouse programming in graphics mode is quite different from programming in text mode. Not only is the resolution of cursor movement much finer, but you have more control over the appearance of the cursor.

The Graphics Mode Mouse Cursor

The mouse driver includes a default graphics cursor, an upward-and-left pointing arrow that is fine for many applications. When the screen is in graphics mode, the default cursor is used unless a different one has been defined. In graphics mode, you can use mouse function 9 to define any cursor you like.

A graphics mouse cursor occupies a 16 by 16 pixel area on the screen. Its appearance is defined, as you might expect, by a 16 by 16 array of bits known as the *cursor mask*. The cursor mask works in conjunction with another 16 by 16 bit array called the *screen mask*. The screen mask determines how the underlying screen image is displayed when the mouse cursor moves over it.

Why do you need a screen mask? The mouse cursor must be visible no matter what the screen image over which it lies. A white arrow on a black background is fine; but if the arrow is moved onto a white region of the screen, it will be invisible. By defining an appropriate screen mask, you ensure that the cursor always has a border, so it remains visible no matter what the background. The relationship between screen and cursor mask bits and the resulting screen pixel is given in table 9.2

Table 9.2. *Relationship between Cursor and Screen Mask Bits and Actual Display*

Cursor Mask Bit	Screen Mask Bit	Display Bit
0	0	0
0	1	1
1	0	Not changed
1	1	Inverted

Now that you understand the ways in which graphics cursors are defined and mouse movement is measured, take a look at the two mouse functions that are specific to graphics screen modes.

Function 9: Define Graphics Cursor Shape

Function 9 allows a program to specify a customized graphics cursor shape. The cursor and screen masks are passed to mouse function 9 in a 32-element integer array. The first 16 array elements contain the screen mask, and the last 16 elements contain the cursor mask. The ideal way to define the mask array elements would be with binary constants, because the pattern of 0s and 1s shows the screen appearance of the cursor. Unfortunately, QB does not support binary constants. The best alternative is to design your cursor and screen masks using bit patterns, then convert the bit patterns into hexadecimal constants to initialize the mask array. This is demonstrated in the procedure `M.SetGrCursorMask` in the next program, listing 9.4.

Mouse function 9 also allows specification of the so-called hot spot. The hot spot is the mouse cursor pixel that defines the exact screen location that the cursor is pointing to. The hot spot is defined in terms of pixels relative to the top left corner of the screen mask's 16 by 16 pixel area. For example, a hot spot of 0,0 is the top left pixel in the cursor. The default graphics cursor's hot spot is 1,1. The vertical range for the hot spot is 0 through 15, whereas the horizontal range is 0 through 15 in all graphics modes except for the CGA 320 by 200 four-color mode (SCREEN 1), when it is 0 through 7.

Function 9 requires the following arguments:

❑ BX   Horizontal hot spot pixel (0 through 16).

❑ CX   Vertical hot spot pixel (0 through 16).

❑ DX   Address of the mask array (obtained with `VARPTR`).

Function 9 also requires that register ES contains the same value as register DS.

Function 15: Set Mickey/Pixel Ratios

This function sets the mickey-to-pixel ratio for both vertical and horizontal mouse movement. The values are passed in registers CX and DX, as follows:

CX   horizontal ratio.

DX   vertical ratio.

Each ratio should give the number of mickeys per 8 pixels of cursor movement. Smaller ratios result in greater cursor motion for a given mouse movement. The default ratios are 16 vertically and 8 horizontally. With the default ratios, the mouse must move 6.4 inches horizontally or 4 inches vertically to move the cursor across the entire screen.

More on Defining the Graphics Mode Cursor

There are at least two approaches to graphics mode cursor definition (assuming that you will not be using only the default cursor). One method is to initialize several different mask arrays, each holding the cursor and screen masks for a particular cursor design. When you call function 9, the address of the desired array is passed as an argument.

The second method is to dimension a single mask array that is always passed to function 9. To obtain different cursors, the mask array is reinitialized with different cursor and screen masks before each call to function 9. This method is used here. The integer array `MouseGrCursorMask` is always passed to function 9 by the procedure `M.SetGrCursor`. The procedure `M.SetGrCursorMask` must be called before the call to `M.SetGrCursor` to initialize the mask array with the desired patterns. If you call `M.SetGrCursor` without first calling `M.SetGrCursorMask` at least once, you will get a blank cursor (a ''black box''), because the uninitialized mask array is filled with 0s.

Listing 9.4 gives the code for the graphics mode mouse procedures `M.SetGrCursor` (function 9) and `M.SetRatio` (function 15), and for `M.SetGrCursorMask`, which is used to define the screen and cursor mask array. Listing 9.4 also gives a modified version of Mouse that incorporates the code to make register ES equal to register DS, necessary for function 9.

Listing 9.4. *Graphics Mode Mouse Procedures*

```
SUB M.SetGrCursor(xhot%,yhot%)

SHARED MouseGrCursorMask() AS INTEGER

CALL mouse(9, xhot%, yhot%, VARPTR(MouseGrCursorMask(1)))

END SUB          ' end of M.SetGrCursor


SUB M.SetGrCursorMask (pattern%)

SHARED MouseGrCursorMask() AS INTEGER

' Initializes the mouse graphics cursor mask array for the
' cursor shape specified by pattern%. Constants such as HAND
' must be defined in the calling program, as done in listing 9.5.

SELECT CASE pattern%

    CASE HAND

' Pointing-hand cursor.

' Screen mask.

        MouseGrCursorMask(1) = &HE1FF      '  1110000111111111
        MouseGrCursorMask(2) = &HE1FF      '  1110000111111111
        MouseGrCursorMask(3) = &HE1FF      '  1110000111111111
        MouseGrCursorMask(4) = &HE1FF      '  1110000111111111
        MouseGrCursorMask(5) = &HE1FF      '  1110000111111111
        MouseGrCursorMask(6) = &HE000      '  1110000000000000
        MouseGrCursorMask(7) = &HE000      '  1110000000000000
        MouseGrCursorMask(8) = &HE000      '  1110000000000000
        MouseGrCursorMask(9) = &H0         '  0000000000000000
        MouseGrCursorMask(10) = &H0        '  0000000000000000
        MouseGrCursorMask(11) = &H0        '  0000000000000000
```

Listing 9.4 *continues*

Listing 9.4 continued

```
        MouseGrCursorMask(12) = &H0        '  0000000000000000
        MouseGrCursorMask(13) = &H0        '  0000000000000000
        MouseGrCursorMask(14) = &H0        '  0000000000000000
        MouseGrCursorMask(15) = &H0        '  0000000000000000
        MouseGrCursorMask(16) = &H0        '  0000000000000000

' Cursor mask.

        MouseGrCursorMask(17) = &H1E00     '  0001111000000000
        MouseGrCursorMask(18) = &H1200     '  0001001000000000
        MouseGrCursorMask(19) = &H1200     '  0001001000000000
        MouseGrCursorMask(20) = &H1200     '  0001001000000000
        MouseGrCursorMask(21) = &H1200     '  0001001000000000
        MouseGrCursorMask(22) = &H13FF     '  0001001111111111
        MouseGrCursorMask(23) = &H1249     '  0001001001001001
        MouseGrCursorMask(24) = &H1249     '  0001001001001001
        MouseGrCursorMask(25) = &H1249     '  0001001001001001
        MouseGrCursorMask(26) = &H9001     '  1001000000000001
        MouseGrCursorMask(27) = &H9001     '  1001000000000001
        MouseGrCursorMask(28) = &H9001     '  1001000000000001
        MouseGrCursorMask(29) = &H8001     '  1000000000000001
        MouseGrCursorMask(30) = &H8001     '  1000000000000001
        MouseGrCursorMask(31) = &H8001     '  1000000000000001
        MouseGrCursorMask(32) = &HFFFF     '  1111111111111111


    CASE CHECK

    ' Check mark cursor.

    ' Screen mask.

        MouseGrCursorMask(1)  = &HFFF0
        MouseGrCursorMask(2)  = &HFFE0
        MouseGrCursorMask(3)  = &HFFC0
        MouseGrCursorMask(4)  = &HFF81
        MouseGrCursorMask(5)  = &HFF03
        MouseGrCursorMask(6)  = &H607
        MouseGrCursorMask(7)  = &HF
        MouseGrCursorMask(8)  = &H1F
        MouseGrCursorMask(9)  = &HC03F
        MouseGrCursorMask(10) = &HF07F
        MouseGrCursorMask(11) = &HFFFF
```

```
        MouseGrCursorMask(12) = &HFFFF
        MouseGrCursorMask(13) = &HFFFF
        MouseGrCursorMask(14) = &HFFFF
        MouseGrCursorMask(15) = &HFFFF
        MouseGrCursorMask(16) = &HFFFF

' Cursor mask.

        MouseGrCursorMask(17) = &H0
        MouseGrCursorMask(18) = &H6
        MouseGrCursorMask(19) = &HC
        MouseGrCursorMask(20) = &H18
        MouseGrCursorMask(21) = &H30
        MouseGrCursorMask(22) = &H60
        MouseGrCursorMask(23) = &H70C0
        MouseGrCursorMask(24) = &H1080
        MouseGrCursorMask(25) = &H700
        MouseGrCursorMask(26) = &H0
        MouseGrCursorMask(27) = &H0
        MouseGrCursorMask(28) = &H0
        MouseGrCursorMask(29) = &H0
        MouseGrCursorMask(30) = &H0
        MouseGrCursorMask(31) = &H0
        MouseGrCursorMask(32) = &H0

            CASE LEFTARROW

' Left Arrow cursor.

' Screen mask.

        MouseGrCursorMask(1) = &HFE1F
        MouseGrCursorMask(2) = &HF01F
        MouseGrCursorMask(3) = &H0
        MouseGrCursorMask(4) = &H0
        MouseGrCursorMask(5) = &H0
        MouseGrCursorMask(6) = &HF01F
        MouseGrCursorMask(7) = &HFE1F
        MouseGrCursorMask(8) = &HFFFF
        MouseGrCursorMask(9) = &HFFFF
        MouseGrCursorMask(10) = &HFFFF
```

Listing 9.4 continues

Listing 9.4 *continued*

```
        MouseGrCursorMask(11) = &HFFFF
        MouseGrCursorMask(12) = &HFFFF
        MouseGrCursorMask(13) = &HFFFF
        MouseGrCursorMask(14) = &HFFFF
        MouseGrCursorMask(15) = &HFFFF
        MouseGrCursorMask(16) = &HFFFF

' Cursor mask.

        MouseGrCursorMask(17) = &H0
        MouseGrCursorMask(18) = &HC0
        MouseGrCursorMask(19) = &H7C0
        MouseGrCursorMask(20) = &H7FFE
        MouseGrCursorMask(21) = &H7C0
        MouseGrCursorMask(22) = &HC0
        MouseGrCursorMask(23) = &H0
        MouseGrCursorMask(24) = &H0
        MouseGrCursorMask(25) = &H0
        MouseGrCursorMask(26) = &H0
        MouseGrCursorMask(27) = &H0
        MouseGrCursorMask(28) = &H0
        MouseGrCursorMask(29) = &H0
        MouseGrCursorMask(30) = &H0
        MouseGrCursorMask(31) = &H0
        MouseGrCursorMask(32) = &H0

      CASE CROSS

' Cross cursor.

' Screen mask.

        MouseGrCursorMask(1) = &HFC3F
        MouseGrCursorMask(2) = &HFC3F
        MouseGrCursorMask(3) = &HFC3F
        MouseGrCursorMask(4) = &H0
        MouseGrCursorMask(5) = &H0
        MouseGrCursorMask(6) = &H0
        MouseGrCursorMask(7) = &HFC3F
        MouseGrCursorMask(8) = &HFC3F
        MouseGrCursorMask(9) = &HFC3F
        MouseGrCursorMask(10) = &HFFFF
        MouseGrCursorMask(11) = &HFFFF
```

```
        MouseGrCursorMask(12) = &HFFFF
        MouseGrCursorMask(13) = &HFFFF
        MouseGrCursorMask(14) = &HFFFF
        MouseGrCursorMask(15) = &HFFFF
        MouseGrCursorMask(16) = &HFFFF

' Cursor mask.

        MouseGrCursorMask(17) = &H0
        MouseGrCursorMask(18) = &H180
        MouseGrCursorMask(19) = &H180
        MouseGrCursorMask(20) = &H180
        MouseGrCursorMask(21) = &H7FFE
        MouseGrCursorMask(22) = &H180
        MouseGrCursorMask(23) = &H180
        MouseGrCursorMask(24) = &H180
        MouseGrCursorMask(25) = &H0
        MouseGrCursorMask(26) = &H0
        MouseGrCursorMask(27) = &H0
        MouseGrCursorMask(28) = &H0
        MouseGrCursorMask(29) = &H0
        MouseGrCursorMask(30) = &H0
        MouseGrCursorMask(31) = &H0
        MouseGrCursorMask(32) = &H0

            CASE IBEAM

' I-beam cursor.

' Screen mask.

        MouseGrCursorMask(1) = &HFFFF
        MouseGrCursorMask(2) = &HFFFF
        MouseGrCursorMask(3) = &HFFFF
        MouseGrCursorMask(4) = &HFFFF
        MouseGrCursorMask(5) = &HFFFF
        MouseGrCursorMask(6) = &HFFFF
        MouseGrCursorMask(7) = &HFFFF
        MouseGrCursorMask(8) = &HFFFF
        MouseGrCursorMask(9) = &HFFFF
        MouseGrCursorMask(10) = &HFFFF
```

Listing 9.4 continues

Listing 9.4 continued

```
        MouseGrCursorMask(11) = &HFFFF
        MouseGrCursorMask(12) = &HFFFF
        MouseGrCursorMask(13) = &HFFFF
        MouseGrCursorMask(14) = &HFFFF
        MouseGrCursorMask(15) = &HFFFF
        MouseGrCursorMask(16) = &HFFFF

' Cursor mask.

        MouseGrCursorMask(17) = &HF00F
        MouseGrCursorMask(18) = &HC30
        MouseGrCursorMask(19) = &H240
        MouseGrCursorMask(20) = &H240
        MouseGrCursorMask(21) = &H180
        MouseGrCursorMask(22) = &H180
        MouseGrCursorMask(23) = &H180
        MouseGrCursorMask(24) = &H180
        MouseGrCursorMask(25) = &H180
        MouseGrCursorMask(26) = &H180
        MouseGrCursorMask(27) = &H180
        MouseGrCursorMask(28) = &H180
        MouseGrCursorMask(29) = &H240
        MouseGrCursorMask(30) = &H240
        MouseGrCursorMask(31) = &HC30
        MouseGrCursorMask(32) = &HF00F

END SELECT

END SUB          ' end of M.SetGrCursorMask


DEFINT A-Z
SUB M.SetRatio (horizontal, vertical)

    CALL mouse(15, 0, horizontal, vertical)

END SUB          ' end of M.SetRatio


SUB mouse (a, b, c, d) STATIC
```

```
DIM InRegs AS RegTypeX, OutRegs AS RegTypeX

SHARED MouseGrCursorMask() AS INTEGER

' For mouse function call 9, register ES must equal
' register DS. Because DS is the default data segment,
' you can get the value of DS with a call to VARSEG.

IF a = 9 THEN
     InRegs.es = VARSEG(MouseGrCursorMask(1))
END IF

InRegs.ax = a
InRegs.bx = b
InRegs.cx = c
InRegs.dx = d

CALL Interruptx(&H33, InRegs, OutRegs)

a = OutRegs.ax
b = OutRegs.bx
c = OutRegs.cx
d = OutRegs.dx

END SUB           ' end of Mouse
```

The program in listing 9.5 demonstrates graphics mode mouse cursors. It operates in screen mode 2, so you need a CGA, EGA, or VGA board to run it. The program first cycles through the different cursor shapes defined with M.SetGrCursorMask. A white rectangle is displayed on the screen so that you can see what the cursors look like against both black and white backgrounds. The program next cycles through several combinations of vertical and horizontal movement ratios. Note that this listing contains only module-level code. To compile and run it, include the procedure-level code for the procedures listing in DECLARE statements. This code is in listings 9.1, 9.2, and 9.4.

Listing 9.5. *Graphics Mouse Demonstration Program*

```
DECLARE SUB M.SetRatio (horizontal%, vertical%)
DECLARE SUB M.SetGrCursor (xhot% ,yhot%)
DECLARE SUB M.SetGrCursorMask (pattern%)
DECLARE SUB WaitClick (button%)
DECLARE SUB M.ShowCursor ()
DECLARE SUB M.Initialize ()
DECLARE SUB mouse (a%, b%, c%, d%)
DECLARE SUB M.GetPos()


' $INCLUDE: 'QB.BI'

DEFINT A-Z

' Array for graphics cursor and screen masks.

DIM MouseGrCursorMask(32) AS INTEGER

' Constants for logical values and for button specification.

CONST TRUE = 1, FALSE = 0, YES = 1, NO = 0, LEFT = 0, RIGHT = 1
CONST BOTH = 2, EITHER = 3, HARDCURSOR = 1, SOFTCURSOR = 0

' Constants for graphics cursor shapes.

CONST HAND = 1, CHECK = 2, LEFTARROW = 3, CROSS = 4, IBEAM = 5

' Define a data type to hold information returned and
' used by the mouse procedures.

TYPE mouseinfo
     Exists AS INTEGER        ' > 0 if mouse exists
     CursorOn AS INTEGER      ' 1 if cursor on, 0 if off
     BtnStatus AS INTEGER     ' current button status (up/down)
     BtnClicks AS INTEGER     ' times button has been clicked
     Column AS INTEGER        ' mouse cursor column position
     Row AS INTEGER           ' mouse cursor row position
     HMovement AS INTEGER     ' horizontal mouse movement
     VMovement AS INTEGER     ' vertical mouse movement
END TYPE

DIM Mous AS mouseinfo
```

```
' Execution begins here.

CLS

' See whether mouse is installed.

M.Initialize

IF Mous.Exists THEN
    PRINT "Mouse detected"
    PRINT
    CALL WaitClick(LEFT)
    CLS
ELSE
    PRINT "No mouse detected."
    PRINT "You must have a mouse and a Microsoft-compatible"
    PRINT "mouse driver installed to run this program."
    PRINT
    PRINT "Press any key to exit."
    WHILE INKEY$ = "": WEND
    END
END IF

SCREEN 2

' Display filled box in center of screen.

LINE (200, 100)-(440, 180), 1, BF

LOCATE 1, 1
PRINT "Left mouse button cycles through cursor shapes."

' Show the default arrow cursor.

M.ShowCursor

LOCATE 3, 1
PRINT "Default arrow cursor."
PRINT

WaitClick (LEFT)
```

Listing 9.5 continues

Listing 9.5 continued

```
' Show the checkmark cursor.

CALL M.SetGrCursorMask (CHECK)
CALL M.SetGrCursor (1, 1)
M.ShowCursor

LOCATE 3, 1
PRINT "Checkmark cursor.     "
PRINT

WaitClick (LEFT)

' Show the left-pointing arrow cursor.

CALL M.SetGrCursorMask (LEFTARROW)
CALL M.SetGrCursor (1, 1)
M.ShowCursor

LOCATE 3, 1
PRINT "Left-pointing arrow cursor."
PRINT

WaitClick (LEFT)

' Show the cross cursor.

CALL M.SetGrCursorMask (CROSS)
CALL M.SetGrCursor (1, 1)
M.ShowCursor

LOCATE 3, 1
PRINT "Cross cursor.               "
PRINT

WaitClick (LEFT)

' Show the I-beam cursor.

CALL M.SetGrCursorMask (IBEAM)
CALL M.SetGrCursor (1, 1)
M.ShowCursor
```

```
LOCATE 3, 1
PRINT "I-beam cursor."
PRINT

WaitClick (LEFT)

' Show the pointing-hand cursor.

CALL M.SetGrCursorMask (HAND)
CALL M.SetGrCursor (1, 1)
M.ShowCursor

LOCATE 3, 1
PRINT "Pointing-hand cursor."
PRINT

WaitClick (LEFT)

LOCATE 1, 1

PRINT "Demonstrating different mickey-to-pixel ratios."

LOCATE 3, 1
PRINT "Horizontal 8, vertical 16 (the default)."
PRINT

WaitClick (LEFT)

CALL M.SetRatio(3, 3)

LOCATE 3, 1
PRINT "Horizontal = 3, vertical = 3.          "
PRINT

WaitClick (LEFT)

CALL M.SetRatio(20, 4)

LOCATE 3, 1
PRINT "Horizontal = 20, vertical = 4."
PRINT
```

Listing 9.5 continues

Listing 9.5 *continued*

```
WaitClick (LEFT)

CALL M.SetRatio(4, 20)

LOCATE 3, 1
PRINT "Horizontal = 4, vertical = 20."
PRINT

WaitClick (LEFT)

CALL M.SetRatio(30, 30)

LOCATE 3, 1
PRINT "Horizontal = 30, vertical = 30."
PRINT

WaitClick (LEFT)

SCREEN 0

LOCATE 10, 22
PRINT "End of graphics cursor demonstration."

END
```

Summary

This chapter has explained the details of how application programs interact with a mouse. The chapter developed routines that enable you to include mouse support in your QB programs. The mouse driver software supplied with each mouse makes mouse programming relatively simple. In both text and graphics modes, mouse support can add a great deal of utility and sophistication to your programs.

The next chapter uses these mouse routines to develop a freehand drawing program. Later, Chapter 12 develops code for mouse-controlled pull-down menus.

CHAPTER 10

Screen Output—Graphics

M any of the most impressive PC programs use graphics in some or all of their screen displays. Programs for business or technical graphics, computer-aided drafting and design (CADD), freehand "painting," and entertainment all rely heavily on graphics. To make the most of your own programs, you need to generate graphics displays. Of course, graphics programming is far too broad a topic to be covered in detail in a single book chapter, and I make no attempt to do so here. Rather, I present some technical information and programming examples that I think will be particularly useful to QuickBASIC (QB) programmers. Specifically, I will do the following:

❑ Explain some technical details about graphics programming and about the various video adapters available for PCs

❑ Develop a software routine that allows a program to determine automatically the kind of video hardware that is installed

❑ Using the mouse programming routines presented in Chapter 9, develop a freehand "paint" program that uses the video hardware detection routine to take maximum benefit of the available video hardware

Graphics Mode Screen Displays

The screen display of graphics information is fundamentally different from the display of text. As the last chapter showed, the dot patterns that make up text characters are stored in memory on the video adapter. The program needs only to specify the character to display and its attributes (such as color and intensity). A screenful of text—2000 characters—can be specified with only 4000 bytes of information—one character byte and one attribute byte for each character.

In contrast, a program must specify every detail of a graphics image. With some graphics adapters, a full-screen image requires 256,000 bytes of information. This information must not only be generated by your program, but the data must also be transferred to the graphics adapter. This is why graphics displays are so much slower than text displays.

Bit-Mapped Graphics

To understand how graphics images are generated, you need to know something about how the hardware works. With few exceptions, PC graphics adapters all use bit-mapped graphics. This means that there is a direct correspondence between individual dots, or *pixels*, on the screen and bits stored in memory on the graphics adapter. The program writes information to video memory, and hardware on the graphics adapter reads the contents of that memory and converts the information to the signals required to drive the monitor.

In the simplest situation, monochrome graphics, each screen pixel can have one of only two values—on or off—and is controlled by one bit of video memory that can also have one of two values—0 or 1. If the bit has a value of 1, the pixel is on; if its value is 0, the pixel is off. The amount of memory required to hold a full screen of graphics information, in bytes, is

(horizontal resolution x vertical resolution) / 8

The simplest nonmonochrome configuration is where each screen pixel is controlled by 2 bits of video memory. Two bits can have 2^2, or 4, values and this mode can display 3 colors plus black (off).

More advanced modes devote 4 or 8 bits to each screen pixel, permitting 2^4 or 2^8 (16 or 256, respectively) colors to be displayed. Of course, the amount of video memory required is proportionately increased. In the Virtual Graphics Array's 16-color, 640 by 480 pixel mode, for example, each graphics screen requires 153,600 bytes of video memory.

Automatic Video Hardware Detection

If you write programs only for your own use and will always run them on the same computer system, you will always know the video hardware that your program will have to deal with. On the other hand, if your programs will be used by other people on a variety of computer systems, there is no way you can know the video hardware in advance. To see why this is important, first examine the various video options that a program might encounter (see table 10.1).

Table 10.1. *Video Adapters and Their Graphics Display Parameters*

Adapter	*Resolution*	*Colors*
Monochrome display/ printer adapter (MDPA)	text only	2^1
Color graphics adapter (CGA)	320 x 200 640 x 200	4 2
Hercules graphics card	720 x 348	2
Enhanced graphics adapter (EGA)	640 x 350	16
Multicolor graphics array (MCGA)	640 x 480 320 x 200	2 256
Video graphics array (VGA)	640 x 480 320 x 200	16 256

[1]*2-color means monochrome (black and white).*

Each "higher" video adapter can emulate those below it. The VGA can emulate an MCGA, EGA, or CGA; an EGA can emulate a CGA; and so on. (Hercules emulation is not included in the IBM EGA, MCGA, or VGA standards, but many third-party manufacturers have included it as an extra feature on their products.) All adapters can, of course, display text. Therefore, if you cannot predict what hardware your program will encounter, the safe thing to do is write for the lowest possible level, the CGA. If you do this, you are guaranteed that your program will work on any graphics adapter, but you sacrifice a great deal of resolution and/or color if the program runs on an EGA, MCGA, or VGA. Someone who has spent a lot of money on a VGA adapter and high-resolution monitor will not be thrilled if your program runs in two-color CGA mode! The solution? Have your program automatically detect the installed video hardware and then make maximum use of the available resolution and colors.

Using QuickBASIC's Resources

Perhaps the most obvious way to detect video hardware is by using QB's SCREEN statement. If you try to set a SCREEN mode not supported by the installed video hardware, QB generates a run-time error. By starting at SCREEN mode 12 and working down until no error is generated, therefore, a program can determine the video hardware it is running on.

There is a problem, however, with this approach. CGA, EGA, MCGA, and VGA boards can be connected to either monochrome or color monitors. The type in use obviously influences the range of options your program has for screen displays. Using the SCREEN statements as just described provides no information as to monitor type. Clearly, your application should detect both adapter type and monitor type.

Using Video BIOS Resources

This task is not as difficult as it may sound, because you can make use of hardware detection routines already contained in the computer's ROM BIOS. BIOS routines are accessed using the CALL INTERRUPT statement in conjunction with variables of type RegType (Chapter 5 contains detailed information on how to make BIOS calls). To understand the logic of video-hardware detection, you need to understand the three-layered hierarchy of IBM video BIOS, which is shown schematically in figure 10.1.

The innermost and oldest layer of the hierarchy consists of the MDPA and CGA video BIOS, as implemented on the original IBM PC. The next layer is the EGA BIOS, and the last and most recent layer is the MCGA/VGA BIOS. Each layer of the hierarchy is a superset of the one below, adding new functions while maintaining compatibility with the lower layers. The top-down approach described here, therefore, is to write a function named VideoHardware that returns a string indicating the type of hardware detected (ColorVGA, ColorEGA, and so on), as follows:

1. Call the MCGA/VGA BIOS hardware detection routine. If this BIOS is present, the BIOS call provides information about which adapter and monitor are installed. The function converts that information to the appropriate string and returns.

Fig. 10.1. *The three-layered hierarchy of IBM video BIOS.*

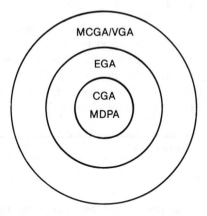

2. If a MCGA/VGA BIOS is not present, call the EGA BIOS hardware detection routine. If this BIOS is present, an EGA adapter is present, and the call determines whether a color or monochrome monitor is attached.

3. If an EGA BIOS is not present, call the CGA/MDPA BIOS, which determines whether a CGA or an MDPA is present. If neither a CGA nor MDPA is detected, the function returns Unknown.

There is one minor complication. The CGA adapter can drive a composite monitor that may be either color or monochrome. Unfortunately, there is no direct way of detecting which is in use, because the CGA and its BIOS are relatively stupid. If a CGA board is detected, you will just have to guess which type of monitor is in use. As an alternative, you could have the program accept a command-line argument indicating whether a monochrome monitor is attached.

Now, take a look at the BIOS call details. The Identify Adapter function in the VGA/MCGA BIOS is service 1AH, interrupt 10H. It is obtained by placing 1AH in register AH, placing 0 in register AL, and calling interrupt 10H. If the service exists (if a VGA/MCGA BIOS exists), the function returns 1AH in register AL and a code specifying the installed adapter/monitor in register BL. If the service does not exist, register AL does not contain 1AH.

The EGA BIOS function needed is also called via interrupt 10H, but with 12H in register AH and 10H in register BX. If the BIOS service exists, it changes the value in BX, which can be tested to see if an EGA is present; the type of monitor attached is indicated by the value in register BH. If the service does not exist, BX remains unchanged.

The final level, the MDPA/CGA BIOS, has an Equipment Determination Service that is called with interrupt 11H and returns adapter information in bits 4 and 5 of register AL.

Listing 10.1 implements the code as a function named VideoHardware$. You should remember that a function is an independent block of code that returns a value to the calling program. VideoHardware$ returns a string that describes the type of hardware detected. Listing 10.1 presents the code for the function itself. As you will see later in this chapter, some supporting code will be required in the calling program.

Listing 10.1. VideoHardware$

```
FUNCTION VideoHardware$

' Automatic video hardware detection. Function returns one of
' the following strings, depending on the video hardware detected:
'
'   MDPA        monochrome display and printer adapter
'   CGA         color graphics adapter
'   ColorEGA    enhanced graphics adapter with color monitor
'   MonoEGA     enhanced graphics adapter with monochrome monitor
'   ColorVGA    video graphics array with color monitor
'   MonoVGA     video graphics array with monochrome monitor
'   ColorMCGA   multicolor graphics array with color monitor
'   MonoMCGA    multicolor graphics array with monochrome monitor
'   Unknown     unknown adapter type
'
' Set up RegType variables for passing information
' to and from CALL INTERRUPT. Define constants for
' the two interrupts.

DIM InRegs AS RegType, OutRegs AS RegType

CONST VgaEgaBIOS = &H10, CgaBIOS = &H11

' Load AH with &H1A, AL with 0, and call VGA/EGA BIOS interrupt.

InRegs.AX = &H1A00
CALL INTERRUPT(VgaEgaBIOS, InRegs, OutRegs)

' The following two lines set AH and BH to 0 while leaving AL and
' BL unchanged. This ensures that you can test the values in AL
```

```
' and BL (where the interrupt returns its results) by looking
' at AX and BX.

OutRegs.AX = OutRegs.AX AND &HFF
OutRegs.BX = OutRegs.BX AND &HFF

' If AL contains &H1A, a VGA/MCGA BIOS was found. The value
' in BL tells the kind of hardware installed.

IF OutRegs.AX = &H1A THEN
    SELECT CASE OutRegs.BX
        CASE 1
            VideoHardware = "MDPA"
        CASE 2
            VideoHardware = "CGA"
        CASE 4
            VideoHardware = "ColorEGA"
        CASE 5
            VideoHardware = "MonoEGA"
        CASE 7
            VideoHardware = "MonoVGA"
        CASE 8
            VideoHardware = "ColorVGA"
        CASE &HB
            VideoHardware = "MonoMCGA"
        CASE &HA, &HC
            VideoHardware = "ColorMCGA"
        CASE ELSE
            VideoHardware = "CGA"
    END SELECT

    EXIT FUNCTION

END IF

' If execution reaches here, no VGA/MCGA BIOS was found.
' Now check for an EGA.

InRegs.AX = &H1200
InRegs.BX = &H10
CALL INTERRUPT(VgaEgaBIOS, InRegs, OutRegs)
```

Listing 10.1 continues

Listing 10.1 *continued*

```
' If BX has been changed, an EGA BIOS is present, and the value
' in BH tells whether a color or monochrome monitor is attached.

IF OutRegs.BX <> &H10 THEN

' Set BH to 0 so that BH = BX.

    OutRegs.BX = OutRegs.BX AND &HFF00

    IF OutRegs.BX = 0 THEN
        VideoHardware = "ColorEGA"
    ELSE
        VideoHardware = "MonoEGA"
    END IF

    EXIT FUNCTION
END IF

' If execution reaches here, there may be a CGA or MDPA installed.
' Call the CgaBIOS Interrupt, which returns the information
' in bits 4 and 5 of AL.

CALL INTERRUPT(CgaBIOS, InRegs, OutRegs)

' Isolate bits 4 and 5 of AL.

OutRegs.AX = OutRegs.AX AND &H30

SELECT CASE OutRegs.AX

    CASE &H10, &H20
        VideoHardware = "CGA"
    CASE &H30
        VideoHardware = "MDPA"
    CASE ELSE
        VideoHardware = "Unknown"

END SELECT

END FUNCTION          ' end of VideoHardware$
```

The Hercules Graphics Card

As it stands, VideoHardware$ detects all IBM standard video adapters (there are a few exceptions, such as the Professional Graphics Adapter, but they are encountered so rarely that you need not be concerned with them). The Hercules Graphics Card is, however, common enough—particularly in business settings—that your programs should be able to detect its presence. Because the HGC is not an IBM standard, there is no provision for it in any IBM PC video BIOS, and the hardware detection calls are totally oblivious to it. Fortunately, QB itself supports the HGC; screen mode 3 is specific to the HGC, and trying to execute SCREEN 3 generates a run-time error if there is no HGC present. Thus, by using SCREEN 3 in combination with an ON ERROR GOTO statement, the program can react appropriately to the presence or absence of an HGC. QB requires, however, that ON ERROR GOTO statements direct execution to a line in the main program module, not in a function or subprogram. Therefore, checking for an HGC must be done after program execution returns from the function that checks for other types of video adapters. To accommodate the Hercules, add the following step to the previous plan:

4. If VideoHardware$ returns Unknown, execute a SCREEN 3 statement. If no error results, a Hercules card is installed. If an error occurs, the adapter type remains Unknown.

Now you are ready to put everything together. Any program that calls VideoHardware$ must use QB's $INCLUDE metacommand to include the file QB.BI, which contains the definition of the RegType variable and the declaration of CALL INTERRUPT. The program proceeds as follows:

1. Create a user-defined variable type, VideoInfo, to hold information about the detected hardware.

2. Call VideoHardware$. If it returns Unknown, check for the presence of a Hercules Graphics Card.

3. Based on the hardware detected, put the appropriate values in the VideoInfo variable. A real-world application would then make use of this information as necessary. The demonstration program in listing 10.2 simply displays the data on the screen.

Listing 10.2. *VIDEO.BAS*

```
' Program VIDEO.BAS

' Demonstrates use of VideoHardware function to obtain
' information about the system's video hardware.

DECLARE FUNCTION VideoHardware$ ()

' The file QB.IN contains the definition of the RegType variable
' type and the declaration of CALL INTERRUPT.

' $INCLUDE: 'QB.BI'

' Define a variable structure to hold video information.

TYPE VideoInfo
     MaxMode AS INTEGER
     MaxColor AS INTEGER
     MaxX AS INTEGER
     MaxY AS INTEGER
     Adapter AS STRING * 9
END TYPE

DIM Video AS VideoInfo

' Call the hardware detection function.

Video.Adapter = VideoHardware$

' If function returns "Unknown", check for Hercules Graphics Card.

IF Video.Adapter = "Unknown  " THEN
     ON ERROR GOTO NoHerc
     SCREEN 3
     SCREEN 0
     Video.Adapter = "Hercules"
END IF

NoHerc:

     ON ERROR GOTO 0
```

```
' Now assign values to the variables in the Video structure.
' Note that the comparison strings in the CASE statements are
' padded on the right with spaces to a total length of 9.
' This is necessary to match the Video.Adapter variable, which
' is a fixed-length string of length 9.

' Video.MaxColor is made equal to highest color number that can
' be set. Because colors are numbered starting at 0, this is one
' less than the total number of colors available.

SELECT CASE Video.Adapter
    CASE "MDPA     "
        Video.MaxMode = 0
        Video.MaxX = 0
        Video.MaxY = 0
        Video.MaxColor = 1
    CASE "CGA      "
        Video.MaxMode = 2
        Video.MaxX = 639
        Video.MaxY = 199
        Video.MaxColor = 1
    CASE "Hercules "
        Video.MaxMode = 3
        Video.MaxX = 719
        Video.MaxY = 347
        Video.MaxColor = 1
    CASE "ColorEGA "
        Video.MaxMode = 9
        Video.MaxX = 639
        Video.MaxY = 349
        Video.MaxColor = 15
    CASE "MonoEGA  "
        Video.MaxMode = 10
        Video.MaxX = 639
        Video.MaxY = 349
        Video.MaxColor = 8
    CASE "ColorVGA "
        Video.MaxMode = 12
        Video.MaxX = 639
        Video.MaxY = 479
        Video.MaxColor = 15
```

Listing 10.2 continues

Listing 10.2 continued

```
    CASE "MonoVGA  ", "MonoMCGA "
        Video.MaxMode = 11
        Video.MaxX = 639
        Video.MaxY = 479
        Video.MaxColor = 2
    CASE "ColorMCGA"
        Video.MaxMode = 13
        Video.MaxX = 319
        Video.MaxY = 199
        Video.MaxColor = 255
END SELECT

' Display video information on the screen.

CLS

PRINT "Video adapter detected is "; Video.Adapter
PRINT "Maximum X coordinate ="; Video.MaxX
PRINT "Maximum Y coordinate ="; Video.MaxY
PRINT "Highest allowed SCREEN mode ="; Video.MaxMode
PRINT "Number of colors ="; Video.MaxColor + 1

END
```

Some of the code in VIDEO.BAS is essential; the file QB.BI must be $INCLUDEd for VideoHardware$ to work, and the statements that check for a Hercules card are essential if you want your program to detect most possible video adapters.

Other statements are optional. The exact use your program makes of the information about the video hardware depends on your specific application. You will see one example in the next section.

A Mouse-Based Paint Program

Now you can put some of what you have learned to use. Chapter 9 developed a collection of mouse routines. A mouse, of course, is ideally suited to "pointing" and often finds good use in programs that create and manipulate graphics screen images. By combining these routines with the video-hardware detection routine presented in this chapter, you can develop a mouse-based "paint" program that uses the mouse for freehand drawing on the screen while making maximum use of the colors and resolution of the installed video hardware.

The mouse routines from Chapter 9 and the procedure VideoHardware$ from this chapter are used by PAINT.BAS. You could, of course, simply include the code for these procedures in the main module of PAINT.BAS. It is better, however, to follow the precepts of modular programming and place the mouse and video routines in either a quick library or a secondary module.

If you opt for a quick library, be sure to have the default quick library QB.QLB loaded when you create the quick library containing the mouse and video routines. This is necessary because both the mouse and video procedures use CALL INTERRUPT, which requires QB.QLB.

Whichever method you use, remember that you will need to use COMMON statements to make the user-defined variables Video and Mous available where needed. The required main module COMMON statements are included in the listing. It is up to you to include them in the secondary module or quick library code as well.

PAINT.BAS divides the screen into two areas. The top inch or so is devoted to a five-part menu; the remainder of the screen is the drawing area. Program operations switch between menu mode and drawing mode. While the program is in menu mode, the cursor is restricted to the menu area. Clicking the left button on a menu box activates one of the three drawing procedures, changes the drawing color, or exits the program. While the program is in drawing mode, the cursor is restricted to the drawing area, and drawing is controlled with the left button. Clicking the right button switches back to menu mode.

There are three drawing procedures. Scribble is totally freehand, somewhat like drawing with a pencil. As the mouse cursor is moved, it draws a line if the left button is down. To be more precise, the cursor leaves a string of dots, or illuminated pixels. If the cursor is moved rapidly, the dots can be spread out quite a bit even though the left mouse button is held down continuously. This is an unavoidable consequence of the manner in which Scribble works, which is as follows:

1. Determine whether the left button is pressed.

2. If not, skip to step 6. If the button is pressed, proceed.

3. Hide the mouse cursor.

4. Illuminate the screen pixel at the current "hot-spot" location.

5. Redisplay the cursor.

6. Has the right button been pressed and released? If not, loop back to step 1. Otherwise, exit the loop.

Your computer can execute this loop very quickly, but the mouse cursor can move even faster. By the time the loop cycles once, the cursor may have moved several pixels away. The in-between pixels are not illuminated. The faster your computer, the less of a problem this will be. To obtain a solid line, draw slowly!

You may be wondering about steps 3 and 5—why does the program need to turn the mouse cursor off and on? While the cursor is displayed, the mouse driver has control over the 16 by 16 array of pixels under the cursor. To enable the program to change any of those pixels, the cursor must be off. Once the new image is in place, the cursor can be redisplayed. This off/on action is the reason the cursor may seem to flicker while you are drawing.

The DrawLine and Rectangle procedures work in a similar manner. The program loops, waiting for the left button to be pressed. As soon as the program detects that the button is down, it "anchors" the object (line or rectangle) at the current cursor location. As long as the button is kept down, the program tracks the cursor movement and redraws the line or box between the anchor position and the current cursor location. Each time a new item is drawn, the old one is erased. When the left button is released, drawing and erasing cease, and the last item is left on the screen.

PAINT.BAS is rather unsophisticated, providing no support for erasing, printing, other shapes, and so on (see listing 10.3). In addition, lines and rectangles being moved about the screen can erase small sections of objects they pass over.

Listing 10.3. *PAINT.BAS*

```
DECLARE SUB DrawColorBox ()
DECLARE FUNCTION GetMenuChoice$ ()
DECLARE SUB DisplayMenu ()
DECLARE SUB Rectangle ()
DECLARE SUB DrawLine ()
DECLARE SUB Scribble ()
DECLARE SUB AssignVideoInfo ()
DECLARE FUNCTION VideoHardware$ ()
```

```
' Program PAINT.BAS, a simple, mouse-based drawing program.

' Requires a Microsoft-compatible mouse and mouse driver.

' The file QB.BI contains the definition of the RegType variable
' type and the declaration of CALL INTERRUPT.

' The file MOUSDEFS.BI includes the definition of the MouseInfo
' variable type and declarations of the mouse procedures.

' $INCLUDE: 'QB.BI'
' $INCLUDE: 'MOUSDEFS.BI'

CONST TRUE = 1, FALSE = 0, YES = 1, NO = 0, LEFT = 0
CONST RIGHT = 1, BOTH = 2, EITHER = 3

' Define a variable structure to hold video information

TYPE VideoInfo
    MaxMode AS INTEGER
    MaxColor AS INTEGER
    MaxX AS INTEGER
    MaxY AS INTEGER
    Adapter AS STRING * 9
END TYPE

DIM SHARED Video AS VideoInfo

' The data structure MouseInfo is defined in MOUSDEFS.BI.

' COMMON statements share the mouse and video
' data between modules.

COMMON /mouseinformation/ Mous AS MouseInfo

CLS

' See whether mouse is installed.

M.Initialize
```

Listing 10.3 continues

Listing 10.3 *continued*

```
IF (Mous.Exists = NO) THEN

    PRINT "No mouse detected."
    PRINT "You must have a mouse and a Microsoft-compatible"
    PRINT "mouse driver installed to run this program."
    PRINT
    PRINT "Press any key to exit."
    WHILE INKEY$ = "": WEND
    END

END IF


' Call the video-hardware detection function.

Video.Adapter = VideoHardware$

' If function returns "Unknown," check for Hercules.

IF Video.Adapter = "Unknown  " THEN
    ON ERROR GOTO NoHerc
    SCREEN 3
    SCREEN 0
    Video.Adapter = "Hercules"
END IF

NoHerc:
    ON ERROR GOTO 0

' The procedure AssignVidoeInfo places video parameters in the
' Video data structure based on the value of Video.Adapter.

AssignVideoInfo

' Set screen mode to the highest possible value and display
' the default graphics mouse cursor.

SCREEN Video.MaxMode
M.ShowCursor

' Assign initial drawing color and display the menu.
```

```
drawcolor% = 1
DisplayMenu

' Restrict mouse cursor vertical movement to the area of the menu.

CALL M.VertRange(0, (Video.MaxY / 10) + 1)

' The following DO/LOOP is the heart of the program. It does the
' following:

' Calls the function GetMenuChoice$ (described later) and executes
' a CASE block based on the value returned by GetMenuChoice. If
' the choice is one of the three drawing options (Scribble,
' DrawLine, Rectangle),

'           (1) Cursor movement is restricted to the drawing
'               area on the screen.
'           (2) The appropriate drawing procedure is called.
'           (3) On return from the drawing procedure, the cursor
'               is returned to the menu area for another choice.

' If ChangeColor is selected,

'           (1) The variable drawcolor% is incremented, then set back to
'               one if it has exceeded the maximum allowable color.
'           (2) A patch of the new drawing color is displayed
'               in the menu.
'           (3) The cursor remains in the menu area.

' If Exit is selected, the loop is exited and program terminates.

DO

    SELECT CASE GetMenuChoice$
      CASE "Scribble"
        CALL M.VertRange((Video.MaxY / 9), Video.MaxY)
        Scribble
        CALL M.VertRange(0, (Video.MaxY / 10))
      CASE "Rectangle"
        CALL M.VertRange((Video.MaxY / 9), Video.MaxY)
```

Listing 10.3 continues

Listing 10.3 *continued*

```
        Rectangle
        CALL M.VertRange(0, (Video.MaxY / 10))
      CASE "Line"
        CALL M.VertRange((Video.MaxY / 9), Video.MaxY)
        DrawLine
        CALL M.VertRange(0, (Video.MaxY / 10))
      CASE "Exit"
        EXIT DO
      CASE "Changecolor"
        drawcolor% = drawcolor% + 1

        IF drawcolor% > Video.MaxColor THEN
           drawcolor% = 1
        END IF

        M.HideCursor
        DrawColorBox
        M.ShowCursor

  END SELECT

  LOOP

  ' Return to text mode.

  SCREEN 0

  END             ' end of PAINT.BAS


SUB AssignVideoInfo STATIC

' Assigns values to the variables in the Video structure.
' Note that the comparison strings in the CASE statements are
' padded on the right with spaces to a total length of 9.
' This is necessary to match the Video.Adapter variable,
' which is a fixed-length string of length 9.

SHARED Video AS VideoInfo
```

```
SELECT CASE Video.Adapter
    CASE "MDPA     "
        Video.MaxMode = 0
        Video.MaxX = 0
        Video.MaxY = 0
        Video.MaxColor = 1
    CASE "CGA      "
        Video.MaxMode = 2
        Video.MaxX = 639
        Video.MaxY = 199
        Video.MaxColor = 1
    CASE "Hercules "
        Video.MaxMode = 3
        Video.MaxX = 719
        Video.MaxY = 347
        Video.MaxColor = 1
    CASE "ColorEGA "
        Video.MaxMode = 9
        Video.MaxX = 639
        Video.MaxY = 349
        Video.MaxColor = 15
    CASE "MonoEGA  "
        Video.MaxMode = 10
        Video.MaxX = 639
        Video.MaxY = 349
        Video.MaxColor = 8
    CASE "ColorVGA "
        Video.MaxMode = 12
        Video.MaxX = 639
        Video.MaxY = 479
        Video.MaxColor = 15
    CASE "MonoVGA  ", "MonoMCGA "
        Video.MaxMode = 11
        Video.MaxX = 639
        Video.MaxY = 479
        Video.MaxColor = 2
    CASE "ColorMCGA"
        Video.MaxMode = 13
        Video.MaxX = 319
        Video.MaxY = 199
        Video.MaxColor = 255
END SELECT
```

Listing 10.3 continues

Listing 10.3 continued

```
END SUB        ' end of AssignVideoInfo


SUB DisplayMenu

' Displays a five-part menu at the top of the screen.

SHARED Video AS VideoInfo

' Draw a box encompassing the full width and
' the top 10% of the screen.

LINE (0, 0)-(Video.MaxX, (Video.MaxY / 10)), 1, B

' Divide the box into 5 smaller boxes of equal size.

deltax = Video.MaxX / 5

FOR I = 1 TO 4
    LINE (I * deltax, 0)-(I * deltax, (Video.MaxY / 10)), 1
NEXT I

' Display the five menu choices.

LOCATE 2, 2
PRINT "COLOR:"

LOCATE 2, 21
PRINT "SCRIBBLE"

LOCATE 2, 39
PRINT "LINE"

LOCATE 2, 52
PRINT "RECTANGLE"

LOCATE 2, 71
PRINT "EXIT"

' Display the current drawing color.
```

```
DrawColorBox

END SUB    ' end of DisplayMenu


SUB DrawColorBox

SHARED Video AS VideoInfo, drawcolor%

' Displays a small filled rectangle in the current drawing
' color in the menu.

   row = Video.MaxY
   col = Video.MaxX

   LINE (col / 9, row / 32)-(col / 6, row / 16), drawcolor%, BF

END SUB       ' end DrawColorBox


SUB DrawLine

SHARED Mous AS MouseInfo, drawcolor%

' Draw a line with the mouse. The start point is laid down
' when the left button is pressed. The line can be
' "dragged" around the screen with the mouse. The end point
' is laid down when the right left button is released.

' Multiple lines can be drawn. Clicking the right button
' exits the procedure.

FlushButtons

DO

   M.GetPos
   startx% = Mous.Column
   starty% = Mous.Row
   oldx% = startx%
   oldy% = starty%
```

Listing 10.3 continues

Listing 10.3 continued

```
    DO

        M.GetPos

        IF Mous.BtnStatus = 1 THEN
            M.HideCursor

' Erase old line, draw new one.

            LINE (startx%, starty%)-(oldx%, oldy%), 0
            LINE (startx%, starty%)-(Mous.Column, Mous.Row), drawcolor%
            M.ShowCursor
            oldx% = Mous.Column
            oldy% = Mous.Row
        END IF

' Continue looping until all buttons released.

    LOOP UNTIL Mous.BtnStatus = 0

' See whether right button has been clicked.

    CALL M.GetBtnRelease(RIGHT)

    IF Mous.BtnClicks > 0 THEN
        Mous.BtnClicks = 0
        EXIT DO
    END IF

LOOP

END SUB     ' end of DrawLine



FUNCTION GetMenuChoice$

' Accepts a user choice from the main PAINT menu.

SHARED Video AS VideoInfo, Mous AS MouseInfo
```

```
FlushButtons
Mous.BtnClicks = 0

' Wait until the left button has been pressed and released.

DO

   CALL M.GetBtnRelease(LEFT)

LOOP UNTIL Mous.BtnClicks > 0

' Now see where left button was clicked. You need only
' check the horizontal position, because cursor movement
' vertically is limited to the menu area.

SELECT CASE Mous.Column
   CASE 0 TO (Video.MaxX / 5)
      GetMenuChoice$ = "Changecolor"
   CASE ((VideoMaxX / 5) + 1) TO (2 * (Video.MaxX / 5))
      GetMenuChoice$ = "Scribble"
   CASE (2 * (VideoMaxX / 5) + 1) TO (3 * (Video.MaxX / 5))
      GetMenuChoice$ = "Line"
   CASE (3 * (VideoMaxX / 5) + 1) TO (4 * (Video.MaxX / 5))
      GetMenuChoice$ = "Rectangle"
   CASE IS > (4 * (Video.MaxX / 5))
      GetMenuChoice$ = "Exit"
END SELECT

END FUNCTION        ' end of GetMenuChoice$


SUB Rectangle

' Draw a rectangle with the mouse. First corner is laid down
' when left button is pressed. Mouse movement "rubber-bands"
' the rectangle. Diagonally opposite corner is laid down
' when left button is released.

SHARED Mous AS MouseInfo, drawcolor%

FlushButtons
```

Listing 10.3 continues

Listing 10.3 continued

```
DO

  M.GetPos

  startx% = Mous.Column
  starty% = Mous.Row
  oldx% = startx%
  oldy% = starty%

  DO

    M.GetPos
    IF Mous.BtnStatus = 1 THEN
      M.HideCursor
      LINE (startx%, starty%)-(oldx%, oldy%), 0, B
      LINE (startx%, starty%)-(Mous.Column, Mous.Row),drawcolor%,B
      M.ShowCursor
      oldx% = Mous.Column
      oldy% = Mous.Row
    END IF

    M.GetPos

  LOOP UNTIL Mous.BtnStatus = 0

  CALL M.GetBtnRelease(RIGHT)

  IF Mous.BtnClicks > 0 THEN
     Mous.BtnStatus = 0
     EXIT DO
  END IF

LOOP

END SUB          ' end of Rectangle


SUB Scribble

SHARED Mous AS MouseInfo, drawcolor%
```

```
' Freehand drawing on the screen while the left
' mouse button is held down.

FlushButtons

DO

    M.GetPos

    IF Mous.BtnStatus = 1 THEN
        M.HideCursor
        PSET (Mous.Column, Mous.Row), drawcolor%
        M.ShowCursor
    END IF

    CALL M.GetBtnRelease(RIGHT)

    IF Mous.BtnClicks > 0 THEN
        Mous.BtnClicks = 0
        EXIT DO
    END IF

LOOP

END SUB        ' end of Scribble
```

Summary

This chapter has explored some aspects of graphics programming on the PC. First a routine was developed to determine the type of video hardware installed on a PC. Using this routine, your QB programs can make maximum use of the resolution and colors available on a given system while remaining compatible with all PC graphics hardware. Then this hardware detection routine, along with mouse routines from Chapter 9, were used to develop a mouse-based freehand drawing program. The programming techniques used in the drawing program can be extended to other mouse-based graphics applications.

11

Screen Output—Text

Perhaps the most important element of the interaction between a computer and the user is the display screen. Almost all of the immediate information that a user receives from a program comes via the screen. A major difference between "good" and "bad" programs is the way they make use of the screen. A program that presents screen information clearly, logically, and in a visually pleasing manner has a great advantage over one that has cluttered and confusing screen displays.

PC display screens can operate in two distinct modes: text mode and graphics mode (a few early PC display systems were limited to text mode only). The graphics mode discussion appears in Chapter 10. Text mode is the subject of this chapter. Text mode screen displays are an extremely powerful and important tool, used extensively in almost every PC program. The QuickBASIC (QB) programming environment, for example, uses a text mode display.

Clearly, the ability to program effective text mode displays is an important aspect of overall programming skill. I make no attempt here to cover the subject exhaustively but rather present some programming examples that should be useful in many of your QB programs. This chapter does the following:

❏ Explains the fundamentals of how text mode screens operate

❏ Develops routines you use to incorporate "pop-up" windows in your QB programs

367

Text Mode Displays

In text mode, your display screen is divided into a discrete number of rows and columns. At the intersection of each row and column is a small rectangular region called a *character cell*. At any moment, a particular character cell may be blank, or it may be displaying a character. Only one character may be displayed per cell at any time.

The PC text screen is usually divided into 80 columns and 25 rows. Some video adapters offer, in addition to the standard 80 by 25 mode, other modes such as 40 columns by 25 rows, or 80 columns by 43 rows. The present discussion is confined to the standard 80 by 25 mode.

With 80 rows and 25 columns, there are 2000 character cells on the screen. Each cell can display one character from a predefined set of 256 characters. This set includes upper- and lowercase letters, numerals, punctuation marks, and other standard "typewriter" characters. It also contains a variety of special characters, such as foreign language characters, "happy faces," graphics and line-drawing characters, and mathematical symbols. A list of the entire character set can be found in Appendix B.

As you probably know, all computer video display screens actually consist of a matrix of small dots, or *pixels*. The display on the screen at any moment is formed by the pattern of pixels that are on (illuminated) and off (dark). The intensity (brightness) of individual pixels can also be controlled, and on color displays, their hues are changeable as well.

In text mode, therefore, each displayed character is defined by the pattern of on/off pixels in a character box. The pixel pattern that is used for each character is stored in read-only memory on the video adapter card. To display a given character, a program need only tell the video adapter card which character to display—it is *not* necessary to specify the pixel pattern for the character.

You may have noticed that the number of display characters corresponds exactly with the number of values that can be coded by a single byte—256. This is no coincidence. The result is that to display one character, a program need send only a single byte to the video adapter. In actuality, 2 bytes are needed, because for each character, PC video systems require an *attribute byte* that specifies how the character is displayed—its color, its intensity, and whether it is blinking.

On every PC video card is a bank of random-access memory (RAM). The hardware on the video card continually scans this memory, reading the character and attribute bytes stored there and converting this information to the video signals needed to create the display. The screen location of a character is specified by its address within video RAM. The first two bytes, or word, in video RAM specify the character/attribute for the top left character cell on the screen, the second word specifies the second character cell in the first row, and so on. To display all or part of a text screen, a program simply writes the necessary character/attribute byte pairs to the proper locations in video memory. A full screen of 2000 characters requires 4000 bytes of video memory.

The relationship between the contents of video memory and the screen display is shown in figure 11.1.

Fig. 11.1. *How the character and attribute bytes in video memory are mapped to the display screen.*

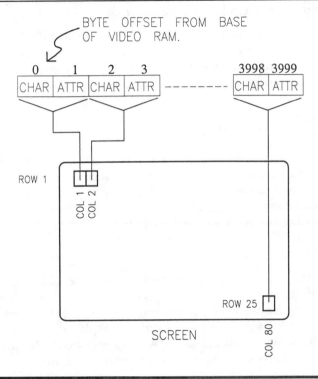

This has been an admittedly rudimentary introduction to text mode screen displays. There are plenty of more interesting details about topics such as multiple display pages, the structure of attribute bytes, and the video BIOS that you can investigate. For the present purpose, which is to develop some useful text mode routines for your QB programs, this introduction will be sufficient.

Pop-Up Screen Windows

A common action for screen displays is to display certain information briefly without disturbing the original contents of the screen. The most effective method for this sort of display is through the use of pop-up windows, rectangular display panels that can be displayed when needed and then removed, leaving the original display unchanged. A good example of pop-up windows is the dialog boxes used in the QB programming environment. Many QB menu choices, such as `Save As...`, cause a window to pop up to display additional information or prompt the user for a response. When the message has been communicated, the window disappears, restoring the original screen. If you have used the QB environment or any other program that uses windows, you probably agree that they are an extremely powerful screen display tool.

Unfortunately, the QB language does not include support for pop-up windows. You can, however, with a little bit of effort, devise routines that enable QB programs to use windows. First, look at the steps involved in displaying and removing a window.

Using Screen Windows

The first step is saving a copy of the original screen contents. As explained earlier in this chapter, a text mode screen display is defined by the contents of video memory. By making a copy of video memory, you create an exact copy of the screen display at the time the copy was made. For windows that occupy less than the whole screen, you need copy only that portion of video memory that corresponds to the section of the screen that the window overwrites.

The next step is displaying the window. To make the window contents distinct from the rest of the screen, it is common practice to surround the window with a border composed of the line-drawing characters. These characters, plus the window text itself, can be displayed using the `PRINT` statement. By using the `LOCATE` and `COLOR` statements, the location and color of the window components can be precisely controlled.

The third step is really independent of the window itself and depends on the needs of the calling program. The window can be displayed for a fixed time period, or the program can wait for a keystroke or a menu selection to be made.

The final step is removing the window and restoring the original screen display, which are actually the same process. By copying the saved contents of video memory back to its original location in video memory, the window is erased and the screen restored.

In summary, therefore, there are three steps: (1) Save the screen, (2) display the window, and (3) restore the screen. Step 2 is quite straight-forward, using QB statements that you should be familiar with. Steps 1 and 3 seem to present a challenge: How do you copy information to and from video memory?

Saving and Restoring Screens

Well, video memory is no different from any other memory once you know its address, and you could accomplish the screen save/restore operations using BASIC statements alone. For the purpose of this chapter, however, you are going to turn to assembly language. There are two reasons.

One reason is entirely practical. Although it is difficult to program in assembly language, it retains a speed advantage over high-level languages such as QB. Because you want windows to appear and disappear instantly even on relatively slow PCs, assembly language is preferred for this sort of operation.

The second reason is instructional. Chapter 2 dealt with mixed-language programming, but that chapter did not present an actual example. By seeing how this assembly language routine is incorporated into a QB program, you will have a better feel for mixed-language programming procedures.

SCREENS.ASM is an assembly language program that contains two procedures, SaveScreen and RestoreScrn. SaveScreen saves a rectangular screen region to an integer array, and RestoreScrn restores a rectangular screen region from an array saved with SaveScreen. The listing for SCREENS.ASM, plus an explanation of how it works and how to incorporate it into a QB program, appears in Appendix A.

SaveScreen and *RestoreScrn*

For now, suffice it to say that both SaveScreen and RestoreScrn take six arguments. Four of the arguments specify the top, bottom, left, and right edges of the window, expressed in screen rows (1 through 25) and columns (1 through 80). The fifth parameter specifies the type of video hardware in use; the need for this is explained in Appendix A. The final argument is the 0th element of the integer array that is used for storing the original screen.

The windows implementation presented here works as follows. For each window there is a separate procedure. The procedures are named Window1, Window2, and so on. Each Window SUB takes three integer arguments:

❑ TopEdge%: the screen row (1 through 24) where the top of the window is to be displayed.

❑ LeftEdge%: the screen column (1 through 79) where the left edge of this window is to be located.

❑ Action%: whether the window is to be displayed or removed.

The size, color, and contents of each window are completely defined within that window's procedure code. The procedure also DIMensions an array to hold the saved screen section and uses a variable called windisplayed whose value indicates whether the window is currently displayed. Because the array and other variables are local to the individual Window procedures, each procedure can use the same array and variable names. Because the Window procedures are defined as STATIC, all of the variables keep their values between calls to the procedure—an obvious necessity for the procedures to function correctly.

The Windows procedures make use of a BASIC procedure called DrawBox that, as you may have guessed, draws a rectangular box on the screen. DrawBox takes seven arguments. Four of them specify the top, left, right, and lower boundaries of the box; two specify the foreground and background colors to be used; and one specifies the type of line drawing characters to use: single-line or double-line. DrawBox checks the location arguments and, if any part of the box would be located off the screen, returns without drawing anything.

The Windows Procedures

Now try stepping through the functioning of a Windows procedure. The procedure first dimensions an integer array to hold the saved screen section. The required array size is equal to the row times column size of the window. Because each screen character position is defined by 2 bytes in video memory (a character byte and an attribute byte), and each element of an integer array consists of 2 bytes, this works out just right.

The code next checks the action% argument and the windisplayed flag. If action% = HIDE and windisplayed = YES, you need to remove an existing window. The procedure RestoreScrn is called to restore the original screen, and execution returns to the calling program. When a screen is being restored, the position arguments passed to the Window procedure are ignored.

The combination action% = HIDE and windisplayed = NO is not valid. The same is true of the combination action% = SHOW and windisplayed = YES. In either of these cases, the procedure returns to the calling program without taking any action.

The other valid combination is action% = SHOW and windisplayed = NO, which displays an undisplayed window. The procedure first checks the specified window location to see whether either the right or bottom edge (or both) extends past the edge of the screen. If so, the procedure adjusts the window location "upward" and/or "leftward" so the edge is brought just within the screen boundaries—to column 80 or row 25.

The next five steps are

1. Call SaveScreen to save the portion of the screen that will be overwritten by the window.

2. Set the flag windisplayed to YES.

3. Call DrawBox to place a box around the window.

4. Use the COLOR statement to set the desired foreground and background colors.

5. Use LOCATE and PRINT statements to display the window text in the box.

There is no limitation to the number of windows you can define, although eventually you run out of memory. You can display any number of windows on the screen at one time, and you can overlap windows as much or little as you like. The only restriction is that, when multiple windows are displayed, they should be removed in reverse order—last displayed, first removed. Thus, the following sequence is acceptable:

```
display window 1
display window 4
display window 3
remove window 3
display window 2
remove window 2
remove window 4
remove window 1
```

The following sequence, however, gives unpredictable results:

```
display window 1
display window 4
display window 3
remove window 4
display window 2
remove window 1
remove window 3
remove window 1
```

WINDOWS.BAS, in listing 11.1, demonstrates the screen Windows routines. Because the Windows routines need to know the type of video hardware installed, you use the automatic video hardware detection routine, VideoHardware$, developed in Chapter 10. See that chapter for details. Instructions for incorporating VideoHardware$ and SCREENS.ASM, also used by WINDOWS.BAS, are located in Appendix A.

The demonstration program fills the screen with text, then with each keypress displays one of three windows and then removes them one at a time.

Listing 11.1. *WINDOWS.BAS*

```
DECLARE SUB Window1 (TopEdge%, LeftEdge%, action%)
DECLARE SUB Window2 (TopEdge%, LeftEdge%, action%)
DECLARE SUB Window3 (TopEdge%, LeftEdge%, action%)
DECLARE SUB Waitkey ()
DECLARE SUB DrawBox (TopRow%, BotRow%, LeftCol%, RightCol%,
                     fgcolor%, bgcolor%, BorderType%)
DECLARE FUNCTION VideoHardware$ ()

' BASIC windows demonstration program.

DEFINT A-Z

CONST SHOW = 1, HIDE = 0, YES = 1, NO = 0, SNGLE = 0, DBLE = 1

' Call the video hardware detection function.

Adapter$ = VideoHardware$

' If function returns "Unknown," check for Hercules.
```

```
IF Adapter$ = "Unknown" THEN
     ON ERROR GOTO NoHerc
     SCREEN 3
     SCREEN 0
     Adapter$ = "Hercules"
END IF

NoHerc:
     ON ERROR GOTO 0

' Now assign value to Monitor% based on type of video
' adapter detected.

SELECT CASE Adapter$
     CASE "MDPA", "Hercules"
          Monitor% = -1
     CASE "CGA"
          Monitor% = 1
     CASE ELSE
          Monitor% = 0
END SELECT

CLS

' Fill the screen with text.
FOR i = 1 TO 200
     PRINT "abcdefghif";
NEXT i

' Each keystroke displays a window, then removes it
' in reverse order.

CALL Waitkey
CALL Window1(5, 10, SHOW)
CALL Waitkey
CALL Window2(8, 13, SHOW)
CALL Waitkey
CALL Window3(6, 14, SHOW)
CALL Waitkey
CALL Window3(0, 0, HIDE)
CALL Waitkey
```

Listing 11.1 continues

Listing 11.1 continued

```
CALL Window2(0, 0, HIDE)
CALL Waitkey
CALL Window1(0, 0, HIDE)
CALL Waitkey

COLOR 7, 0

CLS

END


SUB DrawBox (TopRow, BotRow, LeftCol, RightCol, fgcolor, bgcolor,
            BorderType)
'
' TopRow = 1-24
' BotRow = 2-25 AND > TopRow
' LeftCol = 1-79
' RightCol = 2-80 and > LeftCol

' If any of these conditions is violated, SUB returns without
' doing any drawing.
'
' BorderType = SNGLE or DBLE, indicating type of line to use

' First check arguments.
IF TopRow < 1 OR TopRow > 24 THEN
    EXIT SUB
ELSEIF BotRow < 2 OR BotRow > 25 OR BotRow <= TopRow THEN
    EXIT SUB
ELSEIF LeftCol < 1 OR LeftCol > 79 THEN
    EXIT SUB
ELSEIF RightCol < 2 OR RightCol > 80 OR RightCol <= LeftCol THEN
    EXIT SUB
END IF

' Now set drawing characters for SNGLE or DBLE.
IF BorderType = DBLE THEN
    tlcorner$ = CHR$(201)
    trcorner$ = CHR$(187)
    llcorner$ = CHR$(200)
```

```
        lrcorner$ = CHR$(188)
        line1$ = CHR$(205)
        line2$ = CHR$(186)
ELSE
        tlcorner$ = CHR$(218)
        trcorner$ = CHR$(191)
        llcorner$ = CHR$(192)
        lrcorner$ = CHR$(217)
        line1$ = CHR$(196)
        line2$ = CHR$(179)
END IF

COLOR fgcolor, bgcolor

LOCATE TopRow, LeftCol
temp$ = tlcorner$ + STRING$((RightCol - LeftCol - 1), line1$)
                  + trcorner$
PRINT temp$;

LOCATE BotRow, LeftCol
temp$ = llcorner$ + STRING$((RightCol - LeftCol - 1), line1$)
                  + lrcorner$
PRINT temp$;

FOR i = TopRow + 1 TO BotRow - 1
    LOCATE i, LeftCol
    PRINT line2$;
    LOCATE i, RightCol
    PRINT line2$;
NEXT i

COLOR 7, 0

END SUB      ' end of DrawBox


SUB Waitkey

DO
LOOP UNTIL INKEY$ <> ""

END SUB
```

Listing 11.1 continues

Listing 11.1 continued

```
SUB Window1(topedge%, leftedge%, action%) STATIC

SHARED Monitor%

DIM Windata( 420)

rows% =  10
cols% =  42
IF action% = HIDE AND windisplayed = YES THEN
    CALL RestoreScrn(TopRow, LeftCol, TopRow + rows% - 1,
                     LeftCol + cols% -1, Monitor%, SEG Windata(0))
    windisplayed = NO
    EXIT SUB
ELSEIF action% = SHOW AND windisplayed = NO THEN

IF (TopEdge% + rows%) > 25 THEN
    TopEdge% = 25 - rows%
ELSE
    TopRow = TopEdge%
END IF

IF (LeftEdge% + cols%) > 81 THEN
    LeftCol = 81 - cols%
ELSE
    LeftCol = LeftEdge%
END IF

CALL SaveScreen(TopRow, LeftCol, TopRow + rows% - 1,
                LeftCol + cols% - 1, Monitor%, SEG Windata(0))
windisplayed = YES

CALL DrawBox(TopRow, TopRow + rows% - 1, LeftCol,
             LeftCol + cols% - 1, 7, 1, DBLE)
COLOR  7, 1
LOCATE topedge% + 1,leftedge% + 1
PRINT "One common use for pop-up windows is to ";
COLOR  7, 1
LOCATE topedge% + 2,leftedge% + 1
PRINT "provide on-line help. By displaying dif-";
COLOR  7, 1
LOCATE topedge% + 3,leftedge% + 1
```

```
PRINT "ferent help windows at different points ";
COLOR  7, 1
LOCATE topedge% + 4,leftedge% + 1
PRINT "in program execution, a context-          ";
COLOR  7, 1
LOCATE topedge% + 5,leftedge% + 1
PRINT "sensitive help system can be             ";
COLOR  7, 1
LOCATE topedge% + 6,leftedge% + 1
PRINT "implemented.                            ";
COLOR  7, 1
LOCATE topedge% + 7,leftedge% + 1
PRINT "                                       ";
COLOR  7, 1
LOCATE topedge% + 8,leftedge% + 1
PRINT "                                           ";

END IF

END SUB


SUB Window2(topedge%, leftedge%, action%) STATIC

SHARED Monitor%

DIM Windata( 308)

rows% =  14
cols% =  22

IF action% = HIDE AND windisplayed = YES THEN
    CALL RestoreScrn(TopRow, LeftCol, TopRow + rows% - 1,
                     LeftCol + cols% -1, Monitor%, SEG Windata(0))
    windisplayed = NO
    EXIT SUB
ELSEIF action% = SHOW AND windisplayed = NO THEN

IF (TopEdge% + rows%) > 25 THEN
    TopEdge% = 25 - rows%
```

Listing 11.1 continues

Listing 11.1 continued

```
ELSE
    TopRow = TopEdge%
END IF

IF (LeftEdge% + cols%) > 81 THEN
    LeftCol = 81 - cols%
ELSE
    LeftCol = LeftEdge%
END IF

CALL SaveScreen(TopRow, LeftCol, TopRow + rows% - 1,
                LeftCol + cols% - 1, Monitor%, SEG Windata(0))
windisplayed = YES

CALL DrawBox(TopRow, TopRow + rows% - 1, LeftCol,
             LeftCol + cols% - 1,  1,
7, DBLE)

COLOR  1, 7
LOCATE topedge% + 1,leftedge% + 1
PRINT " Menus can also be  ";
COLOR  1, 7
LOCATE topedge% + 2,leftedge% + 1
PRINT "    implemented:    ";
COLOR  1, 7
LOCATE topedge% + 3,leftedge% + 1
PRINT "                    ";
COLOR  1, 7
LOCATE topedge% + 4,leftedge% + 1
PRINT "F1: Load data       ";
COLOR  1, 7
LOCATE topedge% + 5,leftedge% + 1
PRINT "F2: Sort records    ";
COLOR  1, 7
LOCATE topedge% + 6,leftedge% + 1
PRINT "F3: Print data      ";
COLOR  1, 7
LOCATE topedge% + 7,leftedge% + 1
PRINT "F4: Start new file ";
COLOR  1, 7
LOCATE topedge% + 8,leftedge% + 1
```

```
           PRINT "F5: Erase records    ";
           COLOR  1, 7
           LOCATE topedge% + 9,leftedge% + 1
           PRINT "F6: Enter data        ";
           COLOR  1, 7
           LOCATE topedge% + 10,leftedge% + 1
           PRINT "                       ";
           COLOR  1, 7
           LOCATE topedge% + 11,leftedge% + 1
           PRINT "F10: Exit program    ";
           COLOR  1, 7
           LOCATE topedge% + 12,leftedge% + 1
           PRINT "                       ";

       END IF

   END SUB


   SUB Window3(topedge%, leftedge%, action%) STATIC

   SHARED Monitor%

   DIM Windata( 132)

   rows% =  6
   cols% =  22

   IF action% = HIDE AND windisplayed = YES THEN
       CALL RestoreScrn(TopRow, LeftCol, TopRow + rows% - 1,
                        LeftCol + cols% - 1, Monitor%, SEG Windata(0))
       windisplayed = NO
       EXIT SUB
   ELSEIF action% = SHOW AND windisplayed = NO THEN

   IF (TopEdge% + rows%) > 25 THEN
       TopEdge% = 25 - rows%
   ELSE
       TopRow = TopEdge%
   END IF
```

Listing 11.1 continues

Listing 11.1 continued

```
IF (LeftEdge% + cols%) > 81 THEN
    LeftCol = 81 - cols%
ELSE
    LeftCol = LeftEdge%
END IF

CALL SaveScreen(TopRow, LeftCol, TopRow + rows% - 1,
                LeftCol + cols% - 1, Monitor%, SEG Windata(0))
windisplayed = YES

CALL DrawBox(TopRow, TopRow + rows% - 1, LeftCol,
             LeftCol + cols% - 1, 14, 0, DBLE)

COLOR  14, 0
LOCATE topedge% + 1,leftedge% + 1
PRINT "Error messages, too:";
COLOR  14, 0
LOCATE topedge% + 2,leftedge% + 1
PRINT "                       ";
COLOR  31, 4
LOCATE topedge% + 3,leftedge% + 1
PRINT "NOT THAT KEY, DUMMY!";
COLOR  14, 0
LOCATE topedge% + 4,leftedge% + 1
PRINT "                       ";

END IF

END SUB
```

Automated Code Generation

If you examine the source code in WINDOWS.BAS, you may notice that the code in each of the three Windows procedures is very similar. The differences lie only in the size of the window, the colors, and location of the window contents, and the window text itself. Tasks that are repetitive in nature often lend themselves to computer solutions. Why should you have to manually type in the code for each Windows procedure? For a program that uses a large number of windows, this can represent a lot of work (and a large number of opportunities for mistakes!). Let the computer write the procedures for you.

Hold on, you may say, computers run programs, rather than write them! Strictly speaking, of course, this is true. You can write a program, though, that can generate source code. Specifically, you can write a program that accepts as input the size, color, and contents of a screen window, then writes to disk an ASCII file containing the source code for the Windows procedure. When writing your main program, you need only use an $INCLUDE: statement or the QB Merge... menu command to incorporate the Windows routine into the source code.

GENERATE.BAS

GENERATE.BAS, in listing 11.2, generates include files containing Windows procedures source code. You can specify the height, width, colors, and text for each window.

As currently implemented, GENERATE.BAS has some limitations. It allows definition of only nine different Windows procedures, named Window1 through Window9. The box surrounding each window is, by default, drawn in double lines in the same foreground/background colors as the first text line in the window. Also, you cannot go back and edit a window definition; if you make a mistake, you can only cancel the definition and start over. If it is a minor mistake, it may be easier to edit the source code in the include file.

Once you start GENERATE, the first step is selecting foreground and background colors for the window text. The Change window colors menu selection brings up a display of current color settings and a sample of text displayed in those colors. Function keys enable you to change the foreground and background colors, with the effects of your changes immediately visible on the screen. If you are using a video system that cannot display the full range of colors, you should change the values of the constants MAXFGCOLOR and MAXBGCOLOR to reflect the capabilities of your hardware.

When you exit the color changing routine, the selected colors remain in effect for subsequently entered lines of window text. To enter text, select the Start/continue window definition menu choice. If you are starting a new window definition, you are prompted for window dimensions. These dimensions are for the text area of the window and do not include the surrounding box. The final window is two rows taller and two columns wider than the dimensions you enter here.

Enter each line of window text, using Backspace to correct mistakes. After entering each line, specify whether it is to be left-justified, right-justified, or centered in the window. You can interrupt window definition at any time by entering a backslash. Once back at the main menu, you can select Display current window to see the results of your entries to this point. You can also change the text colors. The new colors are then used for subsequent text that you enter.

If your window text does not fill the window top-to-bottom, be sure to enter blank lines for the unused lines. Otherwise, the specified colors are not used for the background in that part of the window.

When the window is defined, select Write include file to disk. You are prompted for a window number, *n*, and for a file name, and the program writes the source code to disk in a file with a .BI extension. The Window procedure in the file is named Window*n*, where *n* is the window number you specified.

Listing 11.2. GENERATE.BAS

```
DECLARE SUB Cancel ()
DECLARE FUNCTION Justify$ (strng$, code$, lngth%)
DECLARE SUB DefineWindow ()
DECLARE SUB DisplayWindow ()
DECLARE SUB WriteFile ()
DECLARE FUNCTION MainMenu% ()
DECLARE SUB WaitKey ()
DECLARE SUB DrawBox (TopRow%, BotRow%, LeftCol%, RightCol%,
                     fgcolor%, bgcolor%, BorderType%)
DECLARE FUNCTION FKeyOnly% (TOOT%)
DECLARE SUB ChangeColors (fgcolor%, bgcolor%, leftedge%, topedge%)
DECLARE SUB ShowColors (fgcolor%, bgcolor%, leftedge%, topedge%)

' INCLUDE file generator for WINDOWS.BAS.

CONST NO = 0, YES = 1
CONST SNGLE = 0, DBLE = 1

' Maximum and default foreground and background colors.

CONST MAXFGCOLOR = 31, MAXBGCOLOR = 7
CONST DEFAULTFGCOLOR = 7, DEFAULTBGCOLOR = 0

' Colors for boxes.

CONST BOXFGCOLOR = 7, BOXBGCOLOR = 0
```

```
DEFINT A-Z

CONST MAXLINES = 23, MAXROWS = 78

' lines$() will hold the window strings.

' colors() will hold colors:
'    colors(0,n) = foreground color for line n
'    colors(1,n) = background color for line n

' menu$() will hold the program's menu selections.

' position() will hold the justification for each line:
' C = centered in window
' R = right justified
' L = left justified

DIM SHARED lines$(MAXLINES)
DIM SHARED colors(1, MAXLINES)
DIM SHARED menu$(10)
DIM SHARED position(MAXLINES) AS STRING * 1

' winstatus = YES if a window is in the process of being defined,
' NO otherwise.

winstatus = NO
wincols = 0
winrows = 0

fgcolor = DEFAULTFGCOLOR
bgcolor = DEFAULTBGCOLOR

' Main menu choices.
menu$(0) = STR$(6)
menu$(1) = "Start/continue window definition"
menu$(2) = "Change window colors"
menu$(3) = "Display current window"
menu$(4) = "Write include file to disk"
menu$(5) = "Cancel window definition"
menu$(6) = "Exit program"
```

Listing 11.2 continues

Listing 11.2 *continued*

```
DO

    CLS

    SELECT CASE MainMenu
        CASE 1
            DefineWindow
        CASE 2
            CALL ChangeColors(fgcolor, bgcolor, 19, 8)
        CASE 3
            DisplayWindow
        CASE 4
            WriteFile
        CASE 5
            Cancel
        CASE 6
            EXIT DO
    END SELECT
LOOP

CLS

END     'end of GENERATE.BAS


SUB Cancel

' Cancels an ongoing window definition.

SHARED wincols, winrows, winstatus

CLS

ERASE lines$
wincols = 0
winrows = 0
winstatus = NO
LOCATE 10, 34
PRINT "CANCELED"
FOR i = 1 TO 25000: NEXT i
```

```
END SUB       ' end of Cancel


SUB ChangeColors (fgcolor, bgcolor, leftedge, topedge)
' Changes foreground and background color settings
' while displaying effects of changes.

CLS

' Draw a box around the display area.

CALL DrawBox(topedge - 2, topedge + 6, leftedge - 2, leftedge + 35,
             BOXFGCOLOR, BOXBGCOLOR, DBLE)

DO

    ' Display current color numbers.

    LOCATE topedge, leftedge
    PRINT "Current colors are foreground: "; fgcolor
    LOCATE topedge + 1, leftedge
    PRINT "                     background: "; bgcolor

    ' Show a sample of text with the current colors.

    CALL ShowColors(fgcolor, bgcolor, leftedge + 10, topedge + 4)

    ' Display menu in inverse text along screen bottom.

    LOCATE 24, 6
    COLOR 0, 7
    PRINT "  F1 fg+      F2 fg-      F3 bg+      F4 bg-
             F10 exit ";
    COLOR 7, 0

    ' Get user's choice and execute appropriate statements.

    SELECT CASE FKeyOnly(NO)
        CASE 1
            fgcolor = fgcolor + 1
```

Listing 11.2 continues

Listing 11.2 continued

```
            IF fgcolor > MAXFGCOLOR THEN
                fgcolor = 0
            END IF
        CASE 2
            fgcolor = fgcolor - 1
            IF fgcolor < 0 THEN
                fgcolor = MAXFGCOLOR
            END IF
        CASE 3
            bgcolor = bgcolor + 1
            IF bgcolor > MAXBGCOLOR THEN
                bgcolor = 0
            END IF
        CASE 4
            bgcolor = bgcolor - 1
            IF bgcolor < 0 THEN
                bgcolor = MAXBGCOLOR
            END IF
        CASE 10
            EXIT DO
    END SELECT

LOOP

END SUB      'end of ChangeColors


SUB DefineWindow STATIC

' Enters window text.

SHARED winstatus, winrows, wincols, fgcolor, bgcolor
STATIC rowcounter

CLS

IF winstatus = NO THEN

    DO
```

```
      INPUT "Number of window rows
              (1-22, not including borders): ", winrows
LOOP UNTIL winrows > 0 AND winrows < 23

DO

      INPUT "Number of window columns
              (1-78, not including borders): ", wincols
LOOP UNTIL wincols > 0 AND wincols < 79

winstatus = YES
rowcounter = 1

END IF

DO

    CLS
    PRINT "Enter each window line."
    PRINT "Blank lines are allowed."
    PRINT "To end entry, enter a single backslash (\)."

    LOCATE 5, 1
    PRINT "Line"; rowcounter; ":"
    LOCATE 6, 1
    PRINT SPACE$(80);

    charcounter = 0
    temp$ = ""

    DO
        DO
            K$ = INKEY$
        LOOP UNTIL K$ <> ""

        IF K$ = "\" THEN
            EXIT DO
        END IF
```

Listing 11.2 continues

Listing 11.2 *continued*

```
            IF ASC(K$) = 8 THEN
                IF charcounter > 0 THEN
                    charcounter = charcounter - 1
                    temp$ = LEFT$(temp$, charcounter)
                END IF
            ELSEIF ASC(K$) = 13 THEN
                EXIT DO
            ELSE
                charcounter = charcounter + 1
                temp$  = temp$ + K$
            END IF

            LOCATE 6, 1
            PRINT SPACE$(80);
            COLOR fgcolor, bgcolor
            LOCATE 6, 1
            PRINT temp$;
            COLOR DEFAULTFGCOLOR, DEFAULTBGCOLOR
        LOOP UNTIL charcounter = wincols

IF K$ = "\" THEN EXIT DO

lines$(rowcounter) = temp$

' Enter colors into colors() array.
colors(0, rowcounter) = fgcolor
colors(1, rowcounter) = bgcolor

' If line is not a blank, get its display position.
IF temp$ <> "" THEN

    LOCATE 10, 1
    PRINT "Left-right position of this line in window?"
    PRINT
    PRINT "Enter L for left-justified."
    PRINT "      R for right-justified."
    PRINT "      C for centered."

    DO
        K$ = UCASE$(INKEY$)
    LOOP UNTIL K$ = "C" OR K$ = "L" OR K$ = "R"
```

```
ELSE
    K$ = "C"
END IF

' Enter position in position() array.

position(rowcounter) = K$

rowcounter = rowcounter + 1

LOOP UNTIL rowcounter > winrows

winstatus = YES

END SUB        ' end of DefineWindow


SUB DisplayWindow

' Displays the currently defined window, centered on the
' screen with a double border. The border is displayed in
' the color of the first window line.

SHARED wincols, winrows, winstatus

CLS

IF winstatus = NO THEN
    LOCATE 10, 30
    PRINT "Nothing to display"
    LOCATE 12, 30
    PRINT "  Press any key"
    WaitKey
    EXIT SUB
END IF

' Draw a box around window in the colors of the first window line.

tr = (24 - winrows) \ 2
br = tr + winrows + 1
lc = (80 - wincols) \ 2 - 1
rc = lc + wincols + 1
```

Listing 11.2 continues

Listing 11.2 continued

```
CALL DrawBox(tr, br, lc, rc, colors(0, 1), colors(1, 1), DBLE)

FOR i = 1 TO winrows
    LOCATE ((24 - winrows) \ 2) + i, (80 - wincols) \ 2
    COLOR colors(0, i), colors(1, i)
    PRINT Justify$(lines$(i), position(i), wincols);
NEXT i

COLOR DEFAULTFGCOLOR, DEFAULTBGCOLOR

WaitKey

END SUB       ' end of DisplayWindow


SUB DrawBox (TopRow, BotRow, LeftCol, RightCol, fgcolor, bgcolor,
             BorderType

' Draws a box on the screen using either double or single lines.
' TopRow = 1-23
' BotRow = 2-24 AND > TopRow
' LeftCol = 1-79
' RightCol = 2-80 and > LeftCol

' If any of these conditions is violated, SUB returns without
' doing any drawing.
'
' BorderType = SNGLE or DBLE, indicating type of line to use

' First check arguments.

IF TopRow < 1 OR TopRow > 23 THEN
    EXIT SUB
ELSEIF BotRow < 2 OR BotRow > 24 OR BotRow <= TopRow THEN
    EXIT SUB
ELSEIF LeftCol < 1 OR LeftCol > 79 THEN
    EXIT SUB
ELSEIF RightCol < 2 OR RightCol > 80 OR RightCol <= LeftCol THEN
    EXIT SUB
END IF
```

```
' Now set drawing characters for SNGLE or DBLE.

IF BorderType = DBLE THEN
    tlcorner$ = CHR$(201)
    trcorner$ = CHR$(187)
    llcorner$ = CHR$(200)
    lrcorner$ = CHR$(188)
    line1$ = CHR$(205)
    line2$ = CHR$(186)
ELSE
    tlcorner$ = CHR$(218)
    trcorner$ = CHR$(191)
    llcorner$ = CHR$(192)
    lrcorner$ = CHR$(217)
    line1$ = CHR$(196)
    line2$ = CHR$(179)
END IF

COLOR fgcolor, bgcolor

' Draw top of box.

LOCATE TopRow, LeftCol
temp$ = tlcorner$ + STRING$((RightCol - LeftCol - 1), line1$)
                  + trcorner$
PRINT temp$

' Draw bottom of box.

LOCATE BotRow, LeftCol
temp$ = llcorner$ + STRING$((RightCol - LeftCol - 1), line1$)
                  + lrcorner$
PRINT temp$
' Draw sides of box.

FOR i = TopRow + 1 TO BotRow - 1
    LOCATE i, LeftCol
    PRINT line2$
    LOCATE i, RightCol
    PRINT line2$
NEXT i
```

Listing 11.2 continues

Listing 11.2 continued

```
' Reset colors.

COLOR DEFAULTFGCOLOR, DEFAULTBGCOLOR

END SUB      ' end of DrawBox


FUNCTION FKeyOnly (TOOT)

' Reads input from the keyboard, accepting only
' function key presses (F1-F10). Pressing a function key
' returns an extended scan code that is two characters long.
' The second character of the scan code has an ASCII value
' of from 59 through 68 for keys F1 thru F10.

' If TOOT = 1 (YES), the function beeps when
' an inappropriate key is pressed.

keycode = 0

DO

' Loop until a key is pressed.

    DO
        K$ = INKEY$
    LOOP UNTIL K$ <> ""

' If an extended scan code has been returned, set keycode
' equal to the ASCII code of the second character.

    IF LEN(K$) = 2 THEN keycode = ASC(RIGHT$(K$, 1))

' Beep if an inappropriate key.

    IF TOOT = YES THEN
        IF NOT (keycode > 58 AND keycode < 69) THEN BEEP
    END IF

' Repeat loop if a nonfunction key was pressed.
```

```
LOOP UNTIL (keycode% > 58 AND keycode% < 69)

' Subtract 58 from keycode so the function returns
'1 for key F1, 2 for key F2, and so on.

FKeyOnly = keycode - 58

END FUNCTION      ' end fkeyonly()


FUNCTION Justify$ (strng$, code$, lngth%)

' Returns a string of length lngth% with strng$ left-justified,
' right-justified, or centered in it. Pads with spaces as needed.

' code$ = "C" for centered, "L" for left-justified,
' "R" for right-justified. Left justifies as default (that is,
' if code$ does not match one of these choices.

SELECT CASE UCASE$(code$)
    CASE "L"
        temp$ = strng$ + SPACE$(lngth% - LEN(strng$))
    CASE "R"
        temp$ = SPACE$(lngth% - LEN(strng$)) + strng$
    CASE "C"
        num = lngth% - LEN(strng$)
        IF num MOD 2 = 0 THEN
            temp1$ = SPACE$(num \ 2)
            temp2$ = temp1$
        ELSE
            temp1$ = SPACE$((num - 1) \ 2)
            temp2$ = temp1$ + " "
        END IF
        temp$ = temp1$ + strng$ + temp2$
    CASE ELSE
        temp$ = strng$ + SPACE$(lngth% - LEN(strng$))
END SELECT

Justify$ = temp$

END FUNCTION     ' end of justify
```

Listing 11.2 continues

Listing 11.2 continued

```
FUNCTION MainMenu

' Displays the main menu in a box and returns a function keypress.

menuentries = VAL(menu$(0))
menuwidth = 0

FOR i = 1 TO menuentries
    IF LEN(menu$(i)) > menuwidth THEN
        menuwidth = LEN(menu$(i))
    END IF
NEXT i

menuwidth = menuwidth + 8
menulength = menuentries + 4

topedge = (24 - menulength) / 2
btmedge = topedge + menulength
leftedge = (80 - menuwidth) / 2
rtedge = leftedge + menuwidth

    CALL DrawBox(topedge, btmedge, leftedge, rtedge, 7, 0, DBLE)

    FOR i = 1 TO menuentries
        IF i = 10 THEN
            temp$ = "F10"
        ELSE
            temp$ = "F" + RIGHT$(STR$(i), 1)
        END IF
        LOCATE topedge + i, leftedge + 2
        temp$ = temp$ + "-> " + menu$(i)
        PRINT temp$;
    NEXT i

DO

    x = FKeyOnly(NO)

LOOP UNTIL x > 0 AND x <= menuentries

MainMenu = x
```

```
END FUNCTION          ' end of MainMenu


SUB ShowColors (fgcolor, bgcolor, leftedge, topedge)

' Displays a sample of text and a box in specified screen colors.

LOCATE topedge, leftedge
COLOR fgcolor, bgcolor
PRINT "    Sample Text    "

CALL DrawBox(topedge - 1, topedge + 1, leftedge - 1, leftedge + 16,
             fgcolor, bgcolor, SNGLE)

COLOR DEFAULTFGCOLOR, DEFAULTBGCOLOR

END SUB      ' end of ShowColors

SUB WaitKey

' Waits until any key is pressed.

WHILE INKEY$ = "": WEND
END SUB       ' end of WaitKey

SUB WriteFile

' Writes the currently defined window to disk as an ASCII file
' that can be $INCLUDEd in a BASIC source file. The include file
' contains full code for a subroutine Windowx (where x = 1-9) that
' displays the defined window text in a box or removes the window,
' restoring original screen.

SHARED wincols, winrows, winstatus

' If no window is defined.

IF winstatus = NO THEN
    CLS
    LOCATE 10, 30
    PRINT "Nothing to save now"
```

Listing 11.2 continues

Listing 11.2 continued

```
    LOCATE 12, 30
    PRINT "   Press any key"
    WaitKey
    EXIT SUB
END IF

DO

' Get a file name. File is saved to current disk/directory.

    CLS
    PRINT "Enter name for file (1-8 chars). Do not specify an
          extension;"
    PRINT "program automatically supplies .BI"
    PRINT
    PRINT "If file already exists, it is overwritten."

    INPUT filename$

    IF LEN(filename$) > 1 AND LEN(filename$) < 9 THEN
        filename$ = filename$ + ".BI"
        EXIT DO
    END IF

    BEEP

LOOP

INPUT "Enter window number (1-9)", winnumber$

winsubname$ = "Window" + winnumber$

OPEN filename$ FOR OUTPUT AS #1

' Print SUB name and parameters, DIM statement, window dimensions.
temp$ = "SUB " + winsubname$ + "(topedge%, leftedge%, action%)
         STATIC"
PRINT #1, temp$
PRINT #1
PRINT #1, "SHARED Monitor%"
PRINT #1,
```

```
temp$ = "DIM Windata(" + STR$((winrows + 2) * (wincols + 2)) + ")"
PRINT #1, temp$
PRINT #1,
temp$ = "rows% = " + STR$(winrows + 2)
PRINT #1, temp$
temp$ = "cols% = " + STR$(wincols + 2)
PRINT #1, temp$

' Is window to be removed?

PRINT #1,
PRINT #1, "IF action% = HIDE AND windisplayed = YES THEN"
PRINT #1, "    CALL RestoreScrn(TopRow, LeftCol,
            TopRow + rows% - 1, LeftCol + cols% - 1,
            Monitor%, SEG Windata(0))"
PRINT #1, "    windisplayed = NO"
PRINT #1, "    EXIT SUB"
PRINT #1, "ELSEIF action% = SHOW AND windisplayed = NO THEN"
PRINT #1,

' If window would extend past edge of screen, display it
' as far down or to the right as possible.

PRINT #1, "IF (TopEdge% + rows%) > 25 THEN"
PRINT #1, "    TopEdge% = 25 - rows%"
PRINT #1, "ELSE"
PRINT #1, "    TopRow = TopEdge%"
PRINT #1, "END IF"
PRINT #1,
PRINT #1, "IF (LeftEdge% + cols%) > 81 THEN"
PRINT #1, "    LeftCol = 81 - cols%"
PRINT #1, "ELSE"
PRINT #1, "    LeftCol = LeftEdge%"; ""
PRINT #1, "END IF"
PRINT #1,

' Call to routine that saves screen contents under window.

PRINT #1, "CALL SaveScreen(TopRow, LeftCol,
            TopRow + rows% - 1, LeftCol + cols% - 1,
            Monitor%, SEG Windata(0))"
```

Listing 11.2 continues

Listing 11.2 *continued*

```
PRINT #1, "windisplayed = YES"

e$ = STR$(colors(0, 1)) + "," + STR$(colors(1, 1)) + ", DBLE)"

' Call to box-drawing routine.

PRINT #1,
PRINT #1, "CALL DrawBox(TopRow, TopRow + rows% - 1,
                        LeftCol, LeftCol + cols% - 1, " + e$
PRINT #1,
' Print each line of window in proper color.

FOR i = 1 TO winrows
    temp$ = "COLOR " + STR$(colors(0, i)) + "," + STR$(colors(1, i))
    PRINT #1, temp$
    temp$ = "LOCATE topedge% +" + STR$(i) + ",leftedge% + 1"
    PRINT #1, temp$
    temp$ = "PRINT " + CHR$(34)
    temp$ = temp$ + Justify(lines$(i), position(i), wincols)
                  + CHR$(34) + ";"
    PRINT #1, temp$
NEXT i

PRINT #1,
PRINT #1, "END IF"
PRINT #1,
PRINT #1, "END SUB"

CLOSE #1
' Cancel window definition once file is written.

CALL Cancel

END SUB      ' end of WriteFile
```

Once you have designed your window(s) and generated the include file(s), the next steps depend on the method of program development you are using.

If you are using the stand-alone method, all that is needed to incorporate the windows routines into your program is to place one or more `$INCLUDE: 'filename.bi'` metacommands in the main program source code. Place the include statement(s) where you normally place procedure-level code, typically at the end of the source code after the `END` statement. During compilation, each include file is "pulled in" and compiled as if it were actually part of the main program file. Do not forget to add a `DECLARE` statement at the beginning of the program for each `Window` procedure.

If you are using the QB environment, you need to use another approach. The QB environment does not allow `SUB...END SUB` statements inside include files. Rather than using `$INCLUDE:` statements, therefore, you must use the `Merge` command (on the File menu) to read each include file from disk into the program module being edited. You need do this only once for each Window routine. Once merged, the procedure code becomes part of the main program and is saved to disk when you save the main program. The original include file(s) are no longer needed, although they remain, unchanged, on disk. QB automatically generates the needed `DECLARE` statements.

Whichever program development method you use for your windows program, remember the following:

1. The procedure `VideoHardware$` and the procedures in SCREENS.ASM must be incorporated into the program. Doing this is explained in Appendix A.

2. The procedure `DrawBox` must also be incorporated. Include the BASIC code for `DrawBox` as a procedure in your program.

3. Use the `CONST` statement to define `SHOW`, `HIDE`, `SNGLE`, `DBLE`, `YES`, and `NO` as shown in WINDOWS.BAS.

4. Using the program WINDOWS.BAS (Listing 11.1) as a model, determine the type of video hardware in use by calling `VideoHardware$` and then assign the variable `Monitor%` the value of −1, 0, or 1, depending on the result. Do not use the variable name `Monitor%` elsewhere in your program.

Summary

This chapter has explained the fundamentals of how text mode screens operate and has developed BASIC routines that, with the help of two assembly language procedures, enable you to use pop-up screen windows in your programs. You have also developed a code-generation program that greatly simplifies the programming involved in using windows. The tools presented here, as-is or enhanced with your own additions, should be useful in many of your QB programming projects.

CHAPTER 12

Pull-Down Mouse Menus

Most people who use QuickBASIC (QB) become quickly addicted to the pull-down menu system. These menus provide a fast and intuitive way of accessing many of QB's features. If you have a mouse, you can quickly navigate the various menu levels with only one hand. How great it would be to have the power of mouse-controlled pull-down menus in the QB programs you write!

Well, now you can. This book has already developed most of the tools you need: mouse programming routines in Chapter 9 and screen windows in Chapter 11. Whereas programming pull-down menus is not trivial, neither is it terribly difficult, particularly if you adhere to the principles of structured and modular programming described in Chapter 2. This chapter does the following:

❑ Explores some of the choices to be made when you design a pull-down menu system

❑ Develops QB code to implement mouse-controlled pull-down menus

To minimize complexity, the menu routines developed in this chapter use mouse input only; they do not respond to the keyboard. Because not all computer users have a mouse, a menu system for real-world applications would of course be controllable from the keyboard as well, as is the case with QB's menus. Later in the chapter, I discuss how to add keyboard support to the menu routines.

403

Designing a Menu System

Menu systems are almost always designed with a tree-like branching structure. The top level, or main menu, is the first one displayed. Any menu operation starts with a selection from the main menu. A main menu selection may perform a particular program action, or it may display a submenu. Once a submenu is displayed, its selections can also either perform a program action or display yet another submenu. In this way each submenu level gives you the option of making a selection or of leaving the menu without making a selection.

Perhaps the most important decisions to make when you design a menu system regard the placement of various program options within the menu structure. It goes without saying that related functions should be placed near each other on the tree. For example, in the QB menu system, all file functions are on one submenu, all editing functions are on another, and so on.

Another design decision is the number of submenu levels the application requires. For many applications, a single submenu level is sufficient. This is the structure used in the QB environment: each submenu selection performs a specific program function, sometimes involving a dialog box, but never involving another menu. There are times, however, particularly for complex programs, when a multilevel menu system is appropriate. If you have ever used one of Borland's Turbo language environments, you have seen a multilevel menu system. The example in this chapter uses a single level of submenus.

Other decisions affect the details of the menus' appearance and operation. Here are some examples; the comments in parentheses refer to the sample program developed later in this chapter.

❑ Is the main menu displayed and available all the time, or is it called up by a special command? (Always displayed)

❑ In addition to pointing with the mouse, can menu selections be made by highlighting a selection with the cursor movement keys and pressing Enter, by pressing a letter key, or both? (No to all)

❑ When a submenu is displayed, is the movement of the mouse cursor restricted to the menu? (Yes)

❑ Can individual menu selections be "deactivated" (made unselectable) under program control? (Yes)

❑ Is an "active" submenu selection that the mouse is pointing to displayed in a different color? (Yes)

These and other details of menu design are decided by your personal preferences and, in some cases, by the needs of your program.

MOUSMENU.BAS

The program MOUSMENU.BAS in listing 12.1 demonstrates a mouse-driven pull-down menu system. It incorporates an always-available main menu, one level of submenus, and the ability to ''deactivate'' selected submenu selections. As mentioned earlier, the program responds only to mouse input, so you can run it only if you have a mouse. The left mouse button is used to make a selection from either the main menu or a submenu. The right mouse button is used to exit a submenu without making a selection or, when no submenu is displayed, to exit the program.

MOUSMENU.BAS automatically detects the kind of video hardware in use and sets the menu colors appropriately for color or monochrome video adapters. If you are using a monochrome monitor attached to a color graphics adapter, the program assumes you have a color display. Use the /B switch on the command line when you start the program to force it into monochrome display mode:

C> mousmenu /B

The operation of the program is explained by the comments in the source code. As written, the program simply displays menus and reports the selection made. To use the menus in a real application, you add code to the section of the program labeled as the ''main execution loop.'' This code addresses two situations:

❏ Whenever a selection is made from a submenu, the program should branch to the code that executes the indicated action.

❏ When the menu system is not active, the code should respond to keystrokes and/or mouse input as needed.

To modify the program so that menu selections can be made with the cursor movement keys, do the following:

1. Find the locations in the code where the program checks the state of the mouse (position and/or button status) with a call to one of the mouse procedures. Add the necessary statement(s) to check for keyboard input. Use INKEY$ for this. Do *not* use a loop that waits for keyboard input; include a statement that simply accepts any waiting keystrokes.

2. Find the locations in the code where the program takes actions based on the state of the mouse. Add statements that branch to the same actions based on the keystrokes that have been input.

Listing 12.1. MOUSMENU.BAS

```
*********************************************************************
DECLARE SUB definemenu1 ()
DECLARE SUB definemenu2 ()
DECLARE SUB definemenu3 ()
DECLARE SUB definemainmenu ()
DECLARE SUB showmenu (menu%, choice%)
DECLARE SUB displaymenu (menunumber%)
DECLARE SUB waitkey ()
DECLARE SUB drawbox (TopRow%, BotRow%, LeftCol%, RightCol%,
                     fgcolor%, bgcolor%, BorderType%)
DECLARE FUNCTION VideoHardware$ ()

' BASIC mouse menu demonstration program.

DEFINT A-Z

CONST ACTIVE = "A", INACTIVE = "I"
CONST SNGLE = 1, DBLE = 2
CONST TRUE = 1, FALSE = 0, YES = 1, NO = 0
CONST LEFT = 0, RIGHT = 1

' MOUSDEFS.BI contains the declarations of the mouse procedures
' and the definition of the mousinfo data type.

' $INCLUDE: 'mousdefs.bi'

' Values in Mous variable must be SHARED and COMMON
' with the mouse routines.

COMMON SHARED /mouseinformation/ Mous AS MouseInfo

' Initialize the mouse and continue only if one is detected.

CALL M.Initialize

IF Mous.Exists = NO THEN
    BEEP
    PRINT "Mouse needed"
    CALL waitkey
    END
END IF
```

```
' This constant specifies how much wider (in spaces) than
' its widest entry each menu will be.

CONST EXTRAWIDTH = 4

' Total number of menus and maximum number of
' entries/columns per menu.

CONST NUMMENUS = 4, MAXENTRIES = 10, MAXCOLS = 30

' Maximum number of entries on main menu.

CONST MAXMAINENTRIES = 8

' Arrays for main menu text and the size, in spaces,
' of each entry's "space" on the menu bar.

DIM SHARED mainmenu$(MAXMAINENTRIES)
DIM SHARED mainmenulimit(MAXMAINENTRIES)

' Array for saving screen under menus.

DIM SHARED savearray((MAXENTRIES + 2) * (MAXCOLS + 2))

' Array for menu entries.

DIM SHARED menu$(NUMMENUS, MAXENTRIES)

' Entries is the action() array that determines whether the
' corresponding menu choice is active (available).

DIM SHARED action(NUMMENUS, MAXENTRIES) AS STRING * 1

' Set all to ACTIVE, the default condition.

FOR i = 1 TO NUMMENUS
    FOR j = 1 TO MAXENTRIES
        action(i, j) = ACTIVE
    NEXT j
NEXT i
```

Listing 12.1 continues

Listing 12.1 *continued*

```
' TYPE an array to hold size/location information
' about each menu.

TYPE menuinfo
     wide AS INTEGER
     high AS INTEGER
     toprow AS INTEGER
     leftcol AS INTEGER
END TYPE

DIM SHARED menudata(NUMMENUS) AS menuinfo

' Define the various menus.

CALL definemainmenu
CALL definemenu1
CALL definemenu2
CALL definemenu3

' Call the video hardware detection function.

Adapter$ = VideoHardware$

' If function returns "Unknown," check for Hercules adapter.

IF Adapter$ = "Unknown" THEN
     ON ERROR GOTO NoHerc
     SCREEN 3
     SCREEN 0
     Adapter$ = "Hercules"
END IF

NoHerc:
     ON ERROR GOTO 0

' Now assign value to Monitor% based on type of video
' adapter detected.

SELECT CASE Adapter$
    CASE "MDPA", "Hercules"
        Monitor% = -1
```

```
        CASE "CGA"
                Monitor% = 1
        CASE ELSE
                Monitor% = 0
END SELECT
CLS

' Now set colors for menu display depending on type
' of video adapter installed.

IF Monitor% = -1 OR INSTR(COMMAND$, "/B") > 0 THEN
        menufg1 = 7
        menubg1 = 0
        menufg2 = 0
        menubg2 = 7
ELSE
        menufg1 = 7
        menubg1 = 1
        menufg2 = 1
        menubg2 = 7
END IF

' Print a screen background.

FOR i = 1 TO 1000
        PRINT "-*";
NEXT i

' Set colors and display the main menu, instructions,
' and mouse cursor.

COLOR menufg1, menufg2

LOCATE 1, 2
FOR i = 1 TO VAL(mainmenu$(0))
        PRINT mainmenu$(i);
NEXT i

instructions$ = " left mouse button selects, right button exits"
x$ = SPACE$((78 - LEN(instructions$)) / 2)
LOCATE 24, 2
PRINT x$; instructions$; x$;
```

Listing 12.1 continues

Listing 12.1 continued

```
M.ShowCursor

 ' Here is the main execution loop.

DO

     choice = 0
     mainchoice = 0

     CALL M.GetBtnRelease(LEFT)

' If the left button was clicked in the first screen row,
' a selection was made from the main menu.

     IF Mous.BtnClicks > 0 AND Mous.Row = 0 THEN

' Determine which main menu selection was made, then display
' the appropriate submenu.

         SELECT CASE (Mous.Column / 8)
             CASE mainmenulimit(0) TO mainmenulimit(1) - 1
                 mainchoice = 1
                 CALL showmenu(1, choice)
             CASE mainmenulimit(1) TO mainmenulimit(2) - 1
                 mainchoice = 2
                 CALL showmenu(2, choice)
             CASE mainmenulimit(2) TO mainmenulimit(3) - 1
                 mainchoice = 3
                 CALL showmenu(3, choice)
         END SELECT

     END IF

' If a main menu choice was made.

     IF mainchoice <> 0 THEN

' If a submenu choice was made.
```

```
            IF choice <> 0 THEN
                 LOCATE 20, 25
                 PRINT "You selected choice"; choice;
                      "from menu"; mainchoice;
            ELSE
                 LOCATE 20, 25
                 PRINT "        No selection made            "
            END IF

            END IF

' If right button clicked here, exit loop and end program.

      M.GetBtnRelease (RIGHT)

  LOOP UNTIL Mous.BtnClicks > 0

M.HideCursor

COLOR 7, 0
CLS

END       ' end of MOUSMENU.BAS


SUB definemainmenu

' Put main menu text entries here. mainmenu$(0) holds # of
' entries as text.

mainmenu$(0) = "3"
mainmenu$(1) = " Main menu 1"
mainmenu$(2) = " Main menu 2"
mainmenu$(3) = " Main menu 3"

' Calculate total length of entries.

total = 0

FOR i = 1 TO VAL(mainmenu$(0))
    total = total + LEN(mainmenu$(i))
```

Listing 12.1 continues

Listing 12.1 continued

```
NEXT i

' Number of spaces to put before and after each menu entry.

spaces = (80 - total) \ (2 * VAL(mainmenu$(0)))
extra$ = SPACE$(spaces)

' Now pad menu strings with spaces fore and aft. Also fill in
' mainmenulimit() with values. Thus, "active" area for the first
' main menu choice starts at column mainmenulimit(0) and extends
' to column (mainmenulimit(1) - 1). The active area for the
' second main menu choice starts at column mainmenulimit(1) and
' extends to column (mainmenulimit(2) - 1), and so on.

mainmenulimit(0) = 1

FOR i = 1 TO VAL(mainmenu$(0))
    mainmenu$(i) = extra$ + mainmenu$(i) + extra$
    mainmenulimit(i) = mainmenulimit(i - 1) + LEN(mainmenu$(i))
NEXT i

END SUB          ' end of definemainmenu


SUB definemenu1

' Define submenu 1 text.
' A menu entry of "-" results in a horizontal dividing
' line at that menu position.

menu$(1, 1) = "choice 1"
menu$(1, 2) = "choice 2"
menu$(1, 3) = "-"
menu$(1, 4) = "choice 3"
menu$(1, 5) = "choice 4"
menu$(1, 6) = "the last choice"

' Now determine overall width and height of menu.

maxwidth = 0
counter = 1
```

```
DO

        x = LEN(menu$(1, counter))
        IF x = 0 THEN EXIT DO
        IF x > maxwidth THEN maxwidth = x
        counter = counter + 1

LOOP UNTIL counter = MAXENTRIES

' Now set height and width of this menu.

menudata(1).wide = maxwidth + EXTRAWIDTH
menudata(1).high = counter - 1

' Now fill out each entry to full width, padding with
' spaces if needed. Look also for dividing lines.

FOR counter = 1 TO menudata(1).high

    IF menu$(1, counter) = "-" THEN
        menu$(1, counter) = STRING$(menudata(1).wide, CHR$(196))
        action(1, counter) = INACTIVE
    ELSE
        x = menudata(1).wide - LEN(menu$(1, counter))
        menu$(1, counter) = menu$(1, counter) + SPACE$(x)
    END IF

NEXT counter

' Now specify location for top left corner of menu.

menudata(1).toprow = 3
menudata(1).leftcol = 6

END SUB      ' end of definemenu1


SUB definemenu2

' Same as definemenu1.
```

Listing 12.1 continues

Listing 12.1 *continued*

```
menu$(2, 1) = "first choice"
menu$(2, 2) = "second choice"
menu$(2, 3) = "third choice"
menu$(2, 4) = "fourth choice"
menu$(2, 5) = "-"
menu$(2, 6) = "another choice"
menu$(2, 7) = "and still another"

maxwidth = 0
counter = 1

DO

     x = LEN(menu$(2, counter))
     IF x = 0 THEN EXIT DO
     IF x > maxwidth THEN maxwidth = x
     counter = counter + 1

LOOP UNTIL counter = MAXENTRIES

menudata(2).wide = maxwidth + EXTRAWIDTH
menudata(2).high = counter - 1

FOR counter = 1 TO menudata(2).high

     IF menu$(2, counter) = "-" THEN
          menu$(2, counter) = STRING$(menudata(2).wide, CHR$(196))
          action(2, counter) = INACTIVE
     ELSE
          x = menudata(2).wide - LEN(menu$(2, counter))
          menu$(2, counter) = menu$(2, counter) + SPACE$(x)
     END IF
NEXT counter

menudata(2).toprow = 3
menudata(2).leftcol = 28

END SUB          ' end of definemenu2


SUB definemenu3
```

```
' Same as definemenu1.

menu$(3, 1) = "first choice"
menu$(3, 2) = "second choice"
menu$(3, 3) = "third choice" menu$(3, 4) = "fourth choice"
menu$(3, 5) = "-"
menu$(3, 6) = "another choice"
menu$(3, 7) = "and still another"
menu$(3, 8) = "-"
menu$(3, 9) = "and another"
menu$(3, 10) = "and the last"

maxwidth = 0
counter = 1

DO

      x = LEN(menu$(3, counter))
      IF x = 0 THEN EXIT DO
      IF x > maxwidth THEN maxwidth = x
      counter = counter + 1

LOOP UNTIL counter = MAXENTRIES

menudata(3).wide = maxwidth + EXTRAWIDTH
menudata(3).high = counter - 1

FOR counter = 1 TO menudata(3).high

      IF menu$(3, counter) = "-" THEN
          menu$(3, counter) = STRING$(menudata(3).wide, CHR$(196))
          action(3, counter) = INACTIVE
      ELSE
          x = menudata(3).wide - LEN(menu$(3, counter))
          menu$(3, counter) = menu$(3, counter) + SPACE$(x)
      END IF
NEXT counter

menudata(3).toprow = 3
menudata(3).leftcol = 55
```

Listing 12.1 continues

Listing 12.1 *continued*

```
END SUB          ' end of definemenu3


SUB displaymenu (menunumber) STATIC

' Displays menu menunumber, saving the screen that is overwritten.

' If another menu is currently displayed, it is removed first.

' If menunumber = 0, any currently displayed menu is removed, but
' no new menu is displayed.

SHARED menufg1, menufg2, menubg1, menubg2

' If a menu is currently displayed, hide it.

IF menudisplayed > 0 THEN

    a = menudata(menudisplayed).toprow - 1
    b = a + menudata(menudisplayed).high + 1
    c = menudata(menudisplayed).leftcol - 1
    d = c + menudata(menudisplayed).wide + 1

    CALL RestoreScrn(a, c, b, d, Monitor%, SEG savearray(0))
    menudisplayed = 0

END IF

' If a new menu is specified, display it.

IF menunumber > 0 THEN

    a = menudata(menunumber).toprow - 1
    b = a + menudata(menunumber).high + 1
    c = menudata(menunumber).leftcol - 1
    d = c + menudata(menunumber).wide + 1

    CALL SaveScreen(a, c, b, d, Monitor%, SEG savearray(0))

    CALL drawbox(a, b, c, d, menufg1, menufg2, SNGLE)
```

```
        FOR i = 1 TO menudata(menunumber).high
            LOCATE menudata(menunumber).toprow + i - 1,
                menudata(menunumber).leftcol
            PRINT menu$(menunumber, i)
        NEXT i

        menudisplayed = menunumber

    END IF

    END SUB              ' end of displaymenu


    SUB drawbox (toprow, BotRow, leftcol, RightCol, fgcolor, bgcolor,
            BorderType)

    ' TopRow = 1-24
    ' BotRow = 2-25 AND > TopRow
    ' LeftCol = 1-79
    ' RightCol = 2-80 and > LeftCol

    ' If any of these conditions is violated, SUB returns without
    ' doing any drawing.
    '
    ' BorderType = SNGLE or DBLE, indicating type of line to use.

    ' First check arguments.

    IF toprow < 1 OR toprow > 24 THEN
        EXIT SUB
    ELSEIF BotRow < 2 OR BotRow > 25 OR BotRow <= toprow THEN
        EXIT SUB
    ELSEIF leftcol < 1 OR leftcol > 79 THEN
        EXIT SUB
    ELSEIF RightCol < 2 OR RightCol > 80 OR RightCol <= leftcol THEN
        EXIT SUB
    END IF

    ' Now set drawing characters for SNGLE or DBLE.
```

Listing 12.1 continues

Listing 12.1 continued

```
IF BorderType = DBLE THEN
     tlcorner$ = CHR$(201)
     trcorner$ = CHR$(187)
     llcorner$ = CHR$(200)
     lrcorner$ = CHR$(188)
     line1$ = CHR$(205)
     line2$ = CHR$(186)
ELSE
     tlcorner$ = CHR$(218)
     trcorner$ = CHR$(191)
     llcorner$ = CHR$(192)
     lrcorner$ = CHR$(217)
     line1$ = CHR$(196)
     line2$ = CHR$(179)
END IF

COLOR fgcolor, bgcolor

LOCATE toprow, leftcol
temp$ = tlcorner$ + STRING$((RightCol - leftcol - 1),
        line1$) + trcorner$
PRINT temp$;

LOCATE BotRow, leftcol
temp$ = llcorner$ + STRING$((RightCol - leftcol - 1),
        line1$) + lrcorner$
PRINT temp$;

FOR i = toprow + 1 TO BotRow - 1
     LOCATE i, leftcol
     PRINT line2$;
     LOCATE i, RightCol
     PRINT line2$;
NEXT i

END SUB        ' end of drawbox


SUB showmenu (menu, choice) STATIC
```

```
' Displays a submenu, manages mouse cursor movement, and
' returns (in the choice argument) the number of the menu entry
' that was selected. If SUB returns with choice=0, no selection
' was made.

SHARED menufg1, menubg1, menufg2, menubg2

' Display the menu.

CALL displaymenu(menu)

' Restrict cursor movement to the displayed menu.

a = (menudata(menu).leftcol * 8) - 1
b = (menudata(menu).leftcol + menudata(menu).wide - 2) * 8

CALL M.HorizRange(a, b)

a = (menudata(menu).toprow * 8) - 1
b = (menudata(menu).toprow + menudata(menu).high - 2) * 8

CALL M.VertRange(a, b)

' Display the selected main menu choice in different colors.

COLOR menufg2, menubg2
LOCATE 1, mainmenulimit(menu - 1)
PRINT mainmenu$(menu)

' Display the first menu choice in different colors.

LOCATE menudata(menu).toprow, menudata(menu).leftcol
M.HideCursor
PRINT menu$(menu, 1);
M.ShowCursor

' Set oldrow to top row in menu.

oldrow = menudata(menu).toprow

' Position mouse cursor on first menu entry.
```

Listing 12.1 continues

Listing 12.1 continued

```
a = menudata(menu).toprow * 8 - 1
b = menudata(menu).leftcol * 8 - 1
CALL M.MoveCursor(a, b)

' Zero the mouse driver's "click" counters.

FlushButtons

' Nested DO loops used for main part of procedure.

DO
DO

' Get the current mouse cursor row. If the cursor has moved
' onto a different selection in the submenu:
'    1. Return the previous menu selection to the original colors.
'    2. If the newly pointed-to selection is active, display
'       it in alternate colors.

    M.GetPos
    newrow = (Mous.Row \ 8) + 1

    IF newrow <> oldrow THEN
        COLOR menufg1, menubg1
        LOCATE oldrow, menudata(menu).leftcol
        M.HideCursor
        PRINT menu$(menu, oldrow - menudata(menu).toprow + 1)
        M.ShowCursor
    END IF

    IF newrow <> oldrow AND action(menu, newrow
            - menudata(menu).toprow + 1) = "A" THEN
        LOCATE newrow, menudata(menu).leftcol
        COLOR menufg2, menubg2
        M.HideCursor
        PRINT menu$(menu, newrow - menudata(menu).toprow + 1)
        M.ShowCursor
        oldrow = newrow
    END IF

' Look for a left button click.
```

```
        CALL M.GetBtnRelease(LEFT)

    IF Mous.BtnClicks > 0 THEN
        selected = YES
        FlushButtons
        EXIT DO
    END IF

' Look for a right button click.

    CALL M.GetBtnRelease(RIGHT)

    IF Mous.BtnClicks > 0 THEN
        selected = NO
        FlushButtons
        EXIT DO
    END IF

LOOP


' If right button was clicked, no selection was made and you
' should exit the submenu with choice = 0.

IF selected = NO THEN
    choice = 0
    EXIT DO
END IF

' If left button was clicked on an active menu entry,
' set choice to indicate which selection was made, then
' exit loop.

choice = newrow - menudata(menu).toprow + 1

IF selected = YES AND action(menu, choice) = "A" THEN
    EXIT DO
END IF

LOOP
```

Listing 12.1 continues

Listing 12.1 continued

```
' You reach here when the submenu is exited, regardless of
' whether user makes a selection.

' First, hide the submenu.

M.HideCursor
CALL displaymenu(0)
M.ShowCursor

' Turn mouse cursor movement restrictions off.

CALL M.HorizRange(0, 640)
CALL M.VertRange(0, 200)

' Return the selected main menu choice to original colors.

COLOR menufg1, menubg1
LOCATE 1, mainmenulimit(menu - 1)
PRINT mainmenu$(menu)

END SUB       ' end of showmenu


SUB waitkey

DO
LOOP UNTIL INKEY$ <> ""

END SUB
```

****

Compiling and Linking MOUSMENU.BAS

MOUSMENU.BAS uses the video hardware detection routine developed in Chapter 10, plus the assembly language screen save/restore routines developed in Appendix A. The QB environment can load a single quick library at a time. As explained in Appendix A, this limitation makes it impossible to use the QB environment to compile programs that use both non-BASIC routines *and* the INTERRUPT routines defined in the default quick library. Thus, as was the case with the windows routines in Chapter 11, you use stand-alone program development for the mouse menus program.

If you have worked through the screen windows programming examples in Chapter 11, you have already seen how to create object files for the video hardware detection and screen save/restore routines. You should in fact have these object files on your disk. If you have not read Chapter 11 yet, refer to Appendix A for information on how to create SCREENS.OBJ and VIDEO.OBJ.

MOUSMENU.BAS also uses the mouse routines developed in Chapter 9. The procedure for creating an object file containing these routines is similar to that outlined in Appendix A for the video hardware detection routine. Here you also create an INCLUDE file named MOUSDEFS.BI that contains the mouse procedure declarations and the definition of the MousInfo data type. Here are the steps to follow:

First, use the DOS COPY command to make two copies of MOUSDEMO.BAS, one named MOUSPROC.BAS and one named MOUSDEFS.BI:

COPY MOUSDEMO.BAS MOUSPROC.BAS
COPY MOUSDEMO.BAS MOUSDEFS.BI

To create the INCLUDE file, load MOUSDEFS.BI in your editor and delete *all* of the procedure level code and *all* of the module-level code except for the procedure declarations and the definition of the MousInfo data type. Save the modified file to disk. If you are using the QB editor, use Save As... and select Text-Readable by Other Programs. The resulting include file is shown in listing 12.2.

To create the object file containing the mouse procedures:

1. Load the program MOUSPROC.BAS into the QB environment, then delete all of the module-level code *except* the function declarations, the $INCLUDE statement, and the END statement. Do *not* delete any of the procedure-level code.

2. Add the following statement before the END statement:

   COMMON /mouseinformation/ Mous AS MouseInfo

3. Select Make EXE File from the Run menu, then select Stand-Alone EXE File. QB creates both MOUSPROC.OBJ and MOUSPROC.EXE; you can delete the latter file, because you require only the .OBJ file.

Listing 12.2. MOUSDEFS.BI

```
******************************************************************
DECLARE SUB M.SetRatio (horizontal%, vertical%)
DECLARE SUB SetCursor ()
DECLARE SUB FlushButtons ()
DECLARE SUB M.PenOn ()
DECLARE SUB M.PenOff ()
DECLARE SUB M.Movement ()
DECLARE SUB M.GetBtnPress (button%)
DECLARE SUB M.GetBtnRelease (button%)
DECLARE SUB M.TextCursor (cursortype%, scan1%, scan2%)
DECLARE SUB WaitClick (button%)
DECLARE SUB M.HorizRange (leftcol%, rightcol%)
DECLARE SUB M.VertRange (upperrow%, lowerrow%)
DECLARE SUB M.GetPos ()
DECLARE SUB M.ShowCursor .()
DECLARE SUB M.HideCursor ()
DECLARE SUB M.Initialize ()
DECLARE SUB M.MoveCursor (Row%, Col%)
DECLARE SUB mouse (a%, b%, c%, d%)

' Define a data type to hold information returned and used
' by the mouse procedures.

TYPE MouseInfo
     Exists AS INTEGER        ' > 0 if mouse exists
     CursorOn AS INTEGER      ' 1 if cursor on, 0 if off
     BtnStatus AS INTEGER     ' current button status (up/down)
     BtnClicks AS INTEGER     ' times button has been clicked
     Column AS INTEGER        ' mouse cursor column position
     Row AS INTEGER           ' mouse cursor row position
     HMovement AS INTEGER     ' horizontal mouse movement
     VMovement AS INTEGER     ' vertical mouse movement
END TYPE

******************************************************************
```

You now have the three necessary object files, SCREENS.OBJ, VIDEO.OBJ, and MOUSPROC.OBJ. To compile and link MOUSMENU.BAS, follow these steps.

1. Compile the BASIC source program MOUSMENU.BAS with the command

   ```
   bc mousmenu/o/e;
   ```

2. Link the resulting object file MOUSMENU.OBJ with the other object files and the necessary libraries with the command

   ```
   link mousmenu+screens+video+mousproc,,,qb;
   ```

The result is MOUSMENU.EXE, which you can run from the DOS prompt. Remember to install your mouse driver first.

Summary

This chapter showed how to program mouse-driven pull-down menus similar to those used in the QB environment. These menus can provide a fast and easy-to-use interface between your programs and the user. They are a good example of the "slick" and sophisticated user interfaces that are becoming the norm for PC programs.

The programming example in this chapter also demonstrated the benefits of structured and modular programming, as discussed previously in Chapter 2. Using the mouse, screen, and video routines developed elsewhere in this book, the task of programming the mouse menus was greatly simplified.

Mixed-Language
Programming

Chapter 2 covered the procedures involved in mixed-language programming without actually providing a concrete example. This appendix presents a complete example that shows how to incorporate assembly language routines in your QuickBASIC programs.

SCREENS.ASM is used in the windowing program presented in Chapter 11. There are two routines in SCREENS.ASM; SaveScreen, which saves a rectangular region of the screen in a BASIC array, and RestoreScrn, which restores a rectangular region of the screen from a BASIC array.

Saving and restoring screens is conceptually quite simple. Remember from Chapter 11 that an 80 by 25 text screen is represented by 4000 bytes of video memory. Saving a screen region requires only that data be copied from video memory to another storage location. Restoring the screen requires that the data be copied back to the original addresses in video memory.

Three factors complicate the process of saving and restoring screen regions. One involves the addresses of video memory. On the original IBM monochrome display adapter (text only) and the Hercules graphics card, the base address of video memory is &H800; all other video cards have a base address of &HB800. The save/restore routines must, therefore, be aware of the type of video card installed and use the appropriate base address.

The second complication also concerns the type of video adapter in use. The IBM color graphics adapter (CGA) displays interference, or "snow," on the screen if a program accesses video memory while the CGA is actually writing to the screen. To avoid snow, you restrict video memory accesses to the so-called retrace periods. Retrace periods occur at the end of each row of screen pixels, when the cathode ray tube's electron beam is turned off and moved back to the start of the next row. By testing a register on the CGA, a program can detect when a retrace is in progress and limit video memory reads and writes to those periods. No other video adapters have this problem.

The final complication concerns video memory addressing. A rectangular region of the screen that is less than 80 characters wide is not represented by a contiguous section of video memory. Rather, it is held in a number of separate sections. Each section holds one row of characters/attributes, and there are as many sections as there are rows. When you are saving or restoring a screen window, therefore, the code must adjust addressing to read/write each window row properly.

The listing for SCREENS.ASM is presented here (see listing A.1). Each routine, SaveScreen and RestoreScrn, takes six arguments. Four of them specify the top, left, right, and bottom boundaries of the screen region to be saved or restored. These arguments must be within the ranges given in the program comments. The fifth argument gives the monitor type and is used to establish the video memory base address and to determine whether the routines must limit video memory access to retrace periods. The final argument is the address of the array used to store the video data. This should be a one-dimensional integer array, with a minimum dimension of n * m for an n row by m column screen region. The array address is passed using the QB SEG keyword, which passes both the array's segment and offset addresses. SCREENS.ASM does not perform any range checking. It is up to the calling program to ensure that the arguments are in the proper ranges.

Listing A.1. SCREENS.ASM

```
*******************************************************************

; SCREENS.ASM

; Saves and restores rectangular text screen regions to/from arrays.

; To save portion of screen:
; Call SaveScreen(TopRow%, LeftCol%, BottomRow%, RightCol%,
                  Monitor%, SEG
Array%(0))

; To restore portion of screen:
; Call RestoreScrn(TopRow%, LeftCol%, BottomRow%, RightCol%,
                  Monitor%, SEG
Array%(0))

; TopRow% must be in the range 1-25.
; BottomRow% must be in the same range and >= TopRow.

; LeftCol% must be in the range 1-80.
; RightCol% must be in the same range and >= LeftCol%.

; Monitor% = -1 for IBM monochrome or Hercules.
;             1 for CGA.
;             0 for all others.

.Model Medium

; Note: no DATA segment.

.Code

Include Mixed.Inc

HProc SaveScreen, <Uses DS>, TopRow:Ptr, LeftCol:Ptr, BottomRow:Ptr,
RightCol:Ptr, Monitor:Ptr, ArrayAddress:DWord
```

Listing A.1 continues

Listing A.1 continued

```
; First steps are to set up for monitor type, depending on value
;    passed in Monitor% argument.

    Mov   SI,Monitor
    Mov   AX,[SI]              ; get Monitor in AX
    Or    AX,AX
    Jg    Scga                 ; if value is positive, it is a CGA
    Jl    Smono                ; if value is negative, it is monochrome
    Mov   CS:Video_seg,0B800h  ; if value is neither, it is "other"
    Mov   CS:CGA_port,0        ; no CGA
    Jmp   S1

Scga:
    Mov   CS:Video_seg,0B800h  ; CGA base address
    Mov   CS:CGA_port,3DAh     ; CGA port for retrace info
    Jmp   S1

Smono:
    Mov   CS:Video_seg,800h    ; monochrome base address
    Mov   CS:CGA_port,0        ; no CGA

S1:
    Mov   SI,TopRow            ; address of TopRow% in SI
    Mov   AL,[SI]              ; value of TopRow% in AL
    Dec   AL                   ; decrement by 1
    Mov   AH,160               ; screen width (chars + attributes)
    Mul   AH                   ; the start address of the top row in
                              ;    video memory is obtained by
                              ;    multiplying by the row length
    Mov   SI,LeftCol           ; address of LeftCol% in SI
    Mov   BX,[SI]              ; value of LeftCol% in BX
    Dec   BX                   ; decrement by 1
    Add   AX,BX                ; add BX twice to determine the start
    Add   AX,BX                ; address of the screen rectangle to
                              ;    be saved
    Mov   SI,BottomRow         ; address of BottomRow% in SI
    Mov   CH,[SI]              ; value of BottomRow% in CH
    Mov   SI,TopRow            ; address for TopRow% in SI
    Sub   CH,[SI]              ; number of rows = BottomRow%-TopRow%+1
    Inc   CH
```

```
        Mov   SI,RightCol          ; address of RightCol% in SI
        Mov   CL,[SI]              ; value of RightCol% in CL
        Mov   SI,LeftCol           ; address for LeftCol% in SI
        Sub   CL,[SI]              ; subtract to get the number of columns
        Inc   CL                   ; #columns = RightCol% - LeftCol% + 1

        Les   DI,ArrayAddress      ; load address of Array%(0) into ES:DI
        Mov   DX,CS:CGA_port
        Mov   DS,CS:Video_seg      ; DS points at screen memory
        Mov   BP,AX                ; start address into BP
        Mov   BL,CL                ; column counter into BL
        Cld                        ; forward moves

S_Next_Row:
        Mov   CL,BL                ; column counter into CL
        Mov   SI,BP                ; point SI to current screen row

S_Next_Col:
        Or    DL,DL                ; check for CGA
        Jz    S_No_CGA             ; no, so skip retrace code

Loop1:
        In    AL,DX                ; loop until horizontal retrace done
        Test  AL,1
        Jnz   Loop1
        Cli

Loop2:
        In    AL,DX                ; loop until retrace starts
        Test  AL,1
        Jz    Loop2

S_No_CGA:
        Movsw                      ; move character:attribute word
                                   ;    from screen to array
        Sti
        Dec   CL                   ; decrement column counter
        Jnz   S_Next_Col           ; loop back if not done

        Mov   AX,160               ; row length (chars + attr)
        Add   BP,AX                ; adjust address to point to next row
```

Listing A.1 continues

Listing A.1 continued

```
      Dec  CH                      ; decrement row counter
      Jnz  S_Next_Row              ; loop if not done

      HRet                         ; return

HEndp


;======================================================================
; This is the restore screen routine.

; The procedure is the reverse of the SaveScrn routine, and the program
;    comments included there apply here as well. Where there are
;    differences, they are noted.

HProc RestoreScrn, <Uses DS>, TopRow:Ptr, LeftCol:Ptr, BottomRow:Ptr,
RightCol:Ptr, Monitor:Ptr, ArrayAddress:DWord

      Mov  SI,Monitor
      Mov  AL,[SI]
      Or   AL,AL
      Jg   Rcga
      Jl   Rmono
      Mov  CS:Video_seg,0B800h
      Mov  CS:CGA_port,0
      Jmp  Other

Rcga:
      Mov  CS:Video_seg,0B800h
      Mov  CS:CGA_port,3DAh
      Jmp  Other

Rmono:
      Mov  CS:Video_seg,800h
      Mov  CS:CGA_port,0

Other:
      Mov  SI,TopRow
      Mov  AX,[SI]
      Dec  AX
      Mov  BL,160
      Mul  BL
```

```
        Mov   SI,LeftCol
        Mov   BX,[SI]
        Dec   BX
        Shl   BX,1
        Add   BX,AX

        Mov   DX,CS:CGA_port

        Mov   SI,BottomRow
        Mov   CH,[SI]
        Mov   SI,TopRow
        Sub   CH,[SI]
        Inc   CH

        Mov   SI,RightCol
        Mov   CL,[SI]
        Mov   SI,LeftCol
        Sub   CL,[SI]
        Inc   CL

        Mov   ES,CS:Video_seg
        Lds   SI,ArrayAddress
        Mov   BP,BX
        Mov   BL,CL

R_Next_Row:
        Mov   CL,BL
        Mov   DI,BP

R_Next_Col:
        Or    DL,DL
        Jz    R_No_CGA

Loop3:
        In    AL,DX
        Test  AL,1
        Jnz   Loop3
        Cli
```

Listing A.1 continues

```
Loop4:
    In   AL,DX
    Test AL,1
    Jz   Loop4

R_No_CGA:
    Movsw                         ; move character:byte from
    Sti                           ;     array to screen
    Dec  CL
    Jnz  R_Next_Col

    Mov  AX,160
    Add  BP,AX
    Dec  CH
    Jnz  R_Next_Row

    HRet

; Place storage space for variables here in code segment so
;     code does not require a data segment.

    Video_seg  DW ?
    CGA_port   DW ?

HEndp

End                ; end of SCREENS.ASM
```

****

Using SCREENS

The first step in using the routines in SCREENS.ASM is to assemble it
(a process analogous to compilation) to create the object file SCREENS.OBJ.
SCREENS.ASM was developed using the Microsoft Macro Assembler
Version 5.0. If you are using this assembler, assemble SCREENS.ASM with
the command

```
masm screens;
```

Note that SCREENS.ASM uses the include file MIXED.INC, which contains the definitions for the macros HProc, HRet, and HEndp. MIXED.INC is included with the macro assembler package, and must be present in the current directory during assembly. Assuming that your assembler is set up properly, and that SCREENS.ASM was typed in without mistakes, the program will be assembled and the file SCREENS.OBJ created.

SCREENS can also be assembled using Borland's Turbo Assembler, with the command

```
tasm screens
```

You will get several Arithmetic overflow warning messages, but they can be ignored.

If you have the latest version of the Microsoft Macro Assembler, Version 5.1, you will have to modify the program slightly before assembling it. Here is what to do:

1. Delete the line Include Mixed.Inc (you no longer need the include file).

2. Change the line .Model Medium to read .Model Medium, BASIC.

3. Change the line that begins HProc SaveScreen, <uses DS>, to begin SaveScreen Proc, Uses DS, (the remainder of the line is unchanged).

4. Change the line that begins HProc RestoreScrn, <Uses DS>, to begin RestoreScrn Proc, Uses DS,.

5. At the end of the SaveScreen procedure (about halfway through the listing) change the line HRet to Ret and the line HEndp to SaveScreen Endp.

6. At the end of the RestoreScrn procedure (near the end of the listing) change the line HRet to Ret and the line HEndp to RestoreScrn Endp.

After these changes, the program can be assembled using MASM Version 5.1. For more information on assembly language and assembly language programming, consult your assembler documentation or one of the many books that have been published on the subject.

Now that SCREENS.ASM is assembled into SCREENS.OBJ, you are ready to incorporate it into the program. I show how to do this later in the appendix.

Incorporating *VideoHardware$*

Because the Windows program also uses the `VideoHardware$` function, you also need to incorporate it into the windowing program. You could, of course, just include the `VideoHardware$` source code in the windows program, but this method involves unnecessary work and violates the principles of modular programming discussed in Chapter 2. It is better to create an object file containing the `VideoHardware$` routine. There are two ways to do this:

From within the QB environment:

1. Load the program VIDEO.BAS (listing 10.2), then delete all of the module-level code except the function declaration, the `$INCLUDE` statement, and the `END` statement.

2. Select `Make EXE File` from the Run menu, then select `Stand-Alone EXE File`). QB created both VIDEO.OBJ and VIDEO.EXE; you can delete the latter file, because the .OBJ file is all that you need.

Stand-alone:

1. Load VIDEO.BAS into your program editor, and delete all of the module level code except the `$INCLUDE` statement. Save the modified file to disk, using a different name if you wish to keep the original VIDEO.BAS.

2. Use the BC command-line compiler to create an object file. This is done by entering the command `bc video/o;` at the DOS prompt. If you renamed the source file but want the .OBJ file to have the name VIDEO.OBJ, enter `bc newname, video /o;`.

In either case, the result is a file named VIDEO.OBJ.

Creating the Final Program

Now you have two .OBJ files, SCREENS.OBJ and VIDEO.OBJ, and you are ready to create the final executable file WINDOWS.EXE. Remember that you must also include the `INTERRUPTX` routine, which is used by the video hardware detection routine in VIDEO.OBJ. You can use either stand-alone development to create the final executable program, or work in the QB environment. A necessary ingredient in creating an executable windowing program is, of course, the BASIC source code. If you want to run the demonstration program from Chapter 11, use WINDOWS.BAS in listing 11.1. If you are writing your own windowing program, follow the program development guidelines presented at the end of Chapter 11. For the rest of this section, I assume that you are using WINDOWS.BAS.

Stand-Alone Development

The first step in using stand-alone development is to prepare the source file as described in Chapter 11. If you are using the QB editor, be sure to save the file using Save As..., selecting the Text-Readable by Other Programs option.

The next step is to compile WINDOWS.BAS using the command-line compiler. To do this, enter the following command at the DOS prompt:

bc windows/e/o;

You now have the file WINDOWS.OBJ plus the two other object files, SCREENS.OBJ and VIDEO.OBJ, created as just described. There are two ways to assemble these components into a final program. One method keeps the three object files discrete and links them together with the library to create an .EXE file. The command used is

LINK windows + video + screens,,,qb;

Recall that QB.LIB contains the definition of the INTERRUPTX procedure. The output of the LINK process is the executable file WINDOWS.EXE, that can be run from the DOS command line to demonstrate how the windows procedures work.

The other technique involves putting the secondary .OBJ files, VIDEO.OBJ and SCREENS.OBJ, into a library. They can be put into their own library, or incorporated along with the QB.LIB routines into a single library. In either case, you use the LIB.EXE library utility that is supplied with the QB package.

To create a new library named DISPLAY.LIB that contains the SCREENS and VIDEO routines, enter the command **lib** at the DOS prompt and respond to the prompts as shown here (user responses are shown in bold):

```
C>lib
Microsoft (R) Library Manager  Version 3.14
Copyright (C) Microsoft Corp 1983-1988. All rights reserved.
Library name:display
Library does not exist.  Create? (y/n) y
Operations:+screens+video
List file:
```

The **+screens+video** response to the Operations: prompt tells the librarian to add the specified .OBJ files to the library. Once the new library is created, link Windows with the following command:

link windows,,,qb + display;

The second option is to create a single library that contains the SCREENS and VIDEO routines plus the QB.LIB routines.

To do this, the responses to the LIB prompts are the same as just given, except that in response to the Operations: prompt you should enter

+screens+video+qb.lib

If this approach is taken, the LINK command is

LINK windows,,,display;

Whether you keep your object files separate or combine them in a library depends on your preferences. The final program is functionally the same in either case. If you write a large number of related routines, dealing with screen display, for example, it is convenient to combine them in a library and then link your programs with the library rather than having to keep track of a large number of object files. Final program size does not suffer, because the linker includes in the final .EXE file only those library routines that the program actually uses.

QuickBASIC-Environment Development

To use the routines in SCREENS in a program developed within the QB environment, SCREENS must be incorporated into a quick library. This is done with the program LINK.EXE, using the command

LINK /Q screens,,,bqlb45.lib;

The /Q option tells LINK to create a quick library, and the library BQLB45.LIB contains routines used in quick library creation. The result of this command is a quick library named SCREENS.QLB that can be loaded into QB in the usual manner.

For this windowing application, however, you cannot use this technique. Here is why. Because the routines in SCREENS need to know the type of video hardware installed, WINDOWS.BAS uses the automatic video hardware detection function VideoHardware$ developed in Chapter 10. VideoHardware$ uses the INTERRUPTX function, which is defined in the default quick library QB.QLB.

Here is where the problem arises. It is quite easy to create a new quick library containing routines written in other languages, as shown earlier for SCREENS. It is also easy to add user-written BASIC routines to an existing quick library. It is not possible, however, to directly add non-BASIC routines to an existing quick library. Therefore, to create a quick library that contains both the SCREENS routines and the routines in QB.QLB, an indirect approach is necessary.

The first step in this process is to extract the INTERRUPTX code from the library QB.LIB. This is done using the Microsoft library manager program, LIB.EXE. The command to do this is

lib qb *intrpt

Respond to the List file: prompt by pressing Enter. Intrpt is the name of the section of QB.LIB that contains the code for INTERRUPTX (it also contains INTERRUPT). The asterisk tells LIB.EXE to extract INTRPT.OBJ from QB.LIB. This operation creates the file INTRPT.OBJ; the library QB.QLB is not changed.

To create a quick library that includes SCREENS, VIDEO, and INTERRUPTX, issue the following command:

LINK /Q screens+video+intrpt,,,bqlb45.lib;

The result is SCREENS.QLB, which can be loaded into the QB environment in the usual way. With this quick library loaded, you can compile and run WINDOWS.BAS from within the QB environment.

Other Languages

If you are writing routines in a language other than assembler, such as C, Pascal, or FORTRAN, you would, of course, use the appropriate language compiler to produce the .OBJ files. Once you have the .OBJ file(s), the library and linking procedures outlined here are the same.

B

ASCII Character Codes

The ASCII codes are the numeric codes used internally by the computer to represent letters, punctuation marks, and other characters. The QuickBASIC functions ASC and CHR$ are used to translate between characters and their ASCII codes. For example:

```
ASC("X") = 88
CHR$(88) = "X"
```

and for any single-character string X$, the following is true:

```
CHR$(ASC(X$)) = X$
```

ASCII codes range from 0 through 255. Decimal and hexadecimal notation for the codes and the corresponding characters are shown in the following table. The characters with codes between 32 and 127 are the so-called standard ASCII characters. This range includes all letters, numerals, and punctuation marks. They display on all monitors and print on all printers. The characters with codes above 127 are the extended ASCII set; you can use them in your QB programs, but they may not display/print on all hardware combinations.

Hex	Dec	Screen	Ctrl	Key		Hex	Dec	Screen
00h	0		NUL	^@		2Eh	46	.
01h	1	☺	SOH	^A		2Fh	47	/
02h	2	●	STX	^B		30h	48	0
03h	3	♥	ETX	^C		31h	49	1
04h	4	♦	EOT	^D		32h	50	2
05h	5	♣	ENQ	^E		33h	51	3
06h	6	♠	ACK	^F		34h	52	4
07h	7	•	BEL	^G		35h	53	5
08h	8	◘	BS	^H		36h	54	6
09h	9	○	HT	^I		37h	55	7
0Ah	10	◙	LF	^J		38h	56	8
0Bh	11	♂	VT	^K		39h	57	9
0Ch	12	♀	FF	^L		3Ah	58	:
0Dh	13	♪	CR	^M		3Bh	59	;
0Eh	14	♫	SO	^N		3Ch	60	<
0Fh	15	☼	SI	^O		3Dh	61	=
10h	16	►	DLE	^P		3Eh	62	>
11h	17	◄	DC1	^Q		3Fh	63	?
12h	18	↕	DC2	^R		40h	64	@
13h	19	‼	DC3	^S		41h	65	A
14h	20	¶	DC4	^T		42h	66	B
15h	21	§	NAK	^U		43h	67	C
16h	22	▬	SYN	^V		44h	68	D
17h	23	↨	ETB	^W		45h	69	E
18h	24	↑	CAN	^X		46h	70	F
19h	25	↓	EM	^Y		47h	71	G
1Ah	26	→	SUB	^Z		48h	72	H
1Bh	27	←	ESC	^[		49h	73	I
1Ch	28	∟	FS	^\		4Ah	74	J
1Dh	29	↔	GS	^]		4Bh	75	K
1Eh	30	▲	RS	^^		4Ch	76	L
1Fh	31	▼	US	^_		4Dh	77	M
20h	32					4Eh	78	N
21h	33	!				4Fh	79	O
22h	34	"				50h	80	P
23h	35	#				51h	81	Q
24h	36	$				52h	82	R
25h	37	%				53h	83	S
26h	38	&				54h	84	T
27h	39	'				55h	85	U
28h	40	(				56h	86	V
29h	41	)				57h	87	W
2Ah	42	*				58h	88	X
2Bh	43	+				59h	89	Y
2Ch	44	,				5Ah	90	Z
2Dh	45	-				5Bh	91	[

Hex	Dec	Screen	Hex	Dec	Screen	Hex	Dec	Screen
5Ch	92	\	8Ah	138	è	B8h	184	╕
5Dh	93	]	8Bh	139	ï	B9h	185	╣
5Eh	94	^	8Ch	140	î	BAh	186	║
5Fh	95	_	8Dh	141	ì	BBh	187	╗
60h	96	`	8Eh	142	Ä	BCh	188	╝
61h	97	a	8Fh	143	Å	BDh	189	╜
62h	98	b	90h	144	É	BEh	190	╛
63h	99	c	91h	145	æ	BFh	191	┐
64h	100	d	92h	146	Æ	C0h	192	└
65h	101	e	93h	147	ô	C1h	193	┴
66h	102	f	94h	148	ö	C2h	194	┬
67h	103	g	95h	149	ò	C3h	195	├
68h	104	h	96h	150	û	C4h	196	─
69h	105	i	97h	151	ù	C5h	197	┼
6Ah	106	j	98h	152	ÿ	C6h	198	╞
6Bh	107	k	99h	153	Ö	C7h	199	╟
6Ch	108	l	9Ah	154	Ü	C8h	200	╚
6Dh	109	m	9Bh	155	¢	C9h	201	╔
6Eh	110	n	9Ch	156	£	CAh	202	╩
6Fh	111	o	9Dh	157	¥	CBh	203	╦
70h	112	p	9Eh	158	₧	CCh	204	╠
71h	113	q	9Fh	159	ƒ	CDh	205	═
72h	114	r	A0h	160	á	CEh	206	╬
73h	115	s	A1h	161	í	CFh	207	╧
74h	116	t	A2h	162	ó	D0h	208	╨
75h	117	u	A3h	163	ú	D1h	209	╤
76h	118	v	A4h	164	ñ	D2h	210	╥
77h	119	w	A5h	165	Ñ	D3h	211	╙
78h	120	x	A6h	166	ª	D4h	212	╘
79h	121	y	A7h	167	º	D5h	213	╒
7Ah	122	z	A8h	168	¿	D6h	214	╓
7Bh	123	{	A9h	169	⌐	D7h	215	╫
7Ch	124	|	AAh	170	¬	D8h	216	╪
7Dh	125	}	ABh	171	½	D9h	217	┘
7Eh	126	~	ACh	172	¼	DAh	218	┌
7Fh	127	Δ	ADh	173	¡	DBh	219	█
80h	128	Ç	AEh	174	«	DCh	220	▄
81h	129	ü	AFh	175	»	DDh	221	▌
82h	130	é	B0h	176	░	DEh	222	▐
83h	131	â	B1h	177	▒	DFh	223	▀
84h	132	ä	B2h	178	▓	E0h	224	α
85h	133	à	B3h	179	│	E1h	225	β
86h	134	å	B4h	180	┤	E2h	226	Γ
87h	135	ç	B5h	181	╡	E3h	227	π
88h	136	ê	B6h	182	╢	E4h	228	Σ
89h	137	ë	B7h	183	╖	E5h	229	σ

Hex	Dec	Screen
E6h	230	μ
E7h	231	τ
E8h	232	Φ
E9h	233	θ
EAh	234	Ω
EBh	235	δ
ECh	236	∞
EDh	237	ϕ
EEh	238	$\in$
EFh	239	$\cap$
F0h	240	$\equiv$
F1h	241	$\pm$
F2h	242	$\geq$
F3h	243	$\leq$
F4h	244	$\lceil$
F5h	245	$\rfloor$
F6h	246	$\div$
F7h	247	$\approx$
F8h	248	$\circ$
F9h	249	•
FAh	250	·
FBh	251	$\sqrt{\ }$
FCh	252	n
FDh	253	^{2}
FEh	254	■
FFh	255	

Keyboard Scan Codes

The *keyboard scan codes* are the codes returned when you use the INKEY\$ function. For some (but not all) keys, the scan code is the same as the character's ASCII code. INKEY\$ returns either a one- or two-character code; the two-character codes are called *extended codes*. The first character of an extended code is always NUL (ASCII value 0), and the second character identifies the key. Thus, the identity of a keystroke returned by INKEY\$ is determined by the code's length and its ASCII value. Examine this code fragment:

The identity of any pressed key can be determined by the values of the variables *extended%* and *code%*.

To become familiar with the codes for various key combinations, you can experiment with the program in listing C.1. This program displays the scan code, if any, for key combination pressed. For nonextended codes, the ASCII value is displayed; for extended codes, the ASCII value of the second byte is displayed with a preceding zero. To exit this program, press Ctrl-Break.

```
****************************************************************

CONST YES = 1, NO = 0

DO
     K$ = INKEY$
LOOP UNTIL K$ <> ""

IF LEN(K$) = 2 THEN
     extended% = YES
     code% = ASC(RIGHT$(K$,1))
ELSE
     extended% = NO
     code% = ASC(K$)
END IF

****************************************************************
```

Listing C.1. *SCANCODE.BAS*

```
****************************************************************

DEFINT A-Z
CLS

DO

DO
    k$ = INKEY$
LOOP UNTIL k$ <> ""

IF LEN(k$) = 2 THEN
    PRINT "0"; ASC(RIGHT$(k$, 1))
ELSE
    PRINT " "; ASC(k$)
END IF

LOOP

END

****************************************************************
```

Table C.1 presents the scan codes for all of the keys on the IBM keyboard when they are pressed alone or in combination with the Shift, Alt, or Ctrl key. Nonextended codes are listed as the ASCII value of the single character returned; extended codes are listed as the ASCII code of the second character preceded by 0. If no code is listed for a particular combination, it means that combination does not return a code.

Table C.1. *Keyboard Scan Codes*

Key	Alone	Shift	Ctrl	Alt
Esc	27	27	27	27
1	49	33		0 120
2	50	64	0 3	0 121
3	51	35		0 122
4	52	36		0 123
5	53	37		0 124
6	54	94	30	0 125
7	55	38		0 126
8	56	42		0 127
9	57	40		0 128
0	48	41		0 129
-	45	95	31	0 130
=	61	43		0 131
Backspace	8	8	127	
Tab	9	0 15		
a	97	65	1	0 30
b	98	66	2	0 48
c	99	67	3	0 46
d	100	68	4	0 32
e	101	69	5	0 18
f	102	70	6	0 33
g	103	71	7	0 34
h	104	72	8	0 35
i	105	73	9	0 23
j	106	74	10	0 36
k	107	75	11	0 37
l	108	76	12	0 38
m	109	77	13	0 50
n	110	78	14	0 49
o	111	79	15	0 24

Table C.1 continues

Table C.1 continued

Key	Alone	Shift	Ctrl	Alt
p	112	80	16	0 25
q	113	81	17	0 16
r	114	82	18	0 19
s	115	83	19	0 31
t	116	84	20	0 20
u	117	85	21	0 22
v	118	86	22	0 47
w	119	87	23	0 17
x	120	88	24	0 45
y	121	89	25	0 21
z	122	90	26	0 44
F1	0 59	0 84	0 94	0 104
F2	0 60	0 85	0 95	0 105
F3	0 61	0 86	0 96	0 106
F4	0 62	0 87	0 97	0 107
F5	0 63	0 88	0 98	0 108
F6	0 64	0 89	0 99	0 109
F7	0 65	0 90	0 100	0 110
F8	0 66	0 91	0 101	0 111
F9	0 67	0 92	0 102	0 112
F10	0 68	0 93	0 103	0 113
F11	0 133	0 135	0 137	0 139
F12	0 134	0 136	0 138	0 140
`	96	126		
,	44	60		
.	46	62		
/	47	63		
;	59	58		
'	39	34		
\	92	124	28	
[	91	123	27	
]	93	125	29	
spacebar	32	32	32	32
Enter	13	13	10	
up arrow	0 72	55		
down arrow	0 80	50		
right arrow	0 77	54		

Key	Alone	Shift	Ctrl	Alt
left arrow	0 75	52		
Home	0 71	55	0 119	
End	0 79	49	0 117	
PgUp	0 73	57	0 132	
PgDn	0 81	51	0 118	
Ins	0 82	48		
Del	0 83	46		

D

Internal Data Formats
Used by QuickBASIC

For the most part, you need not be concerned with QuickBASIC's internal data formats. When you use the variable name in your program, QB takes care of the details. Occasionally, however, there is a need to access variables directly. In this situation you need to know how QB stores variables in memory.

Variable-Length Strings

Accessing a variable-length string is a two-step process. QuickBASIC stores the string itself in sequential memory locations in the default data segment. QB also stores information about the string's address and length in a string descriptor. When you use the VARPTR function with a variable-length string variable, it returns the address of the string descriptor. The string descriptor is 4 bytes long and has the format shown in figure D.1.

Fig. D.1. *The format of a string descriptor.*

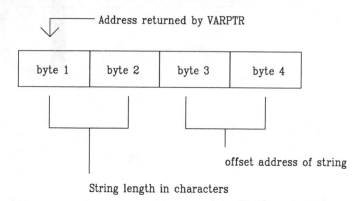

String length in characters

offset address of string

For each element in the string descriptor, the high order byte is the most significant byte. Thus, the length of a variable-length string X$ can be obtained as follows:

```
length% = PEEK(VARPTR(X$)) + 256 * PEEK(VARPTR(X$) + 1)
```

The short program in listing D.1 demonstrates using the information in the string descriptor to access a variable-length string.

Listing D.1. *STRING.BAS*

```
*****************************************************************

DEFINT A-Z

CLS

INPUT "Enter string: ", x$

y = VARPTR(x$)

length% = PEEK(y) + 256 * PEEK(y + 1)
address% = PEEK(y + 2) + 256 * PEEK(y + 3)

PRINT
```

```
FOR i = 0 TO length% - 1
    PRINT CHR$(PEEK(address% + i));
NEXT i

END
```

****

Fixed-Length Strings

String descriptors are not used with fixed-length strings. The `VARPTR` function returns the address of the first byte, or character, of the string. Subsequent characters are located at higher addresses. The following code shows how to access a fixed-length string.

****

```
DIM x AS STRING * 10

CLS

INPUT "Enter string: ", x

y = VARPTR(x)

FOR i = y TO y + LEN(x) - 1
    PRINT CHR$(PEEK(i));
NEXT i

END
```

****

Integers

QB stores integers in binary format, with negative numbers represented in two's complement format. This means that the highest order bit is 0 for positive integers and 1 for negative integers. The least significant byte of an integer is the low order byte, that is, the byte pointed to by the `VARPTR` function.

The following is an example. The integer 12959 is stored in 2 bytes, as shown in figure D.2.

Fig. D.2. *Binary storage format for integers.*

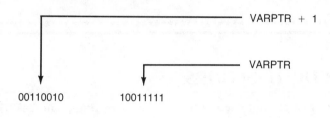

The two's complement of a positive integer is formed by reversing all the bits (0s become 1s and vice versa), then adding 1. For 12959,

0011 0010 1001 1111	+ 12959
1100 1101 0110 0000	reverse all bits
+ 1	add 1
1100 1101 0110 0001	− 12959

Integers and long integers are handled in the same manner, except that integers are stored in 2 bytes, whereas long integers are stored in 4 bytes.

Floating-Point Numbers

Floating-point numbers are stored in a format that breaks them down into a sign bit, a mantissa, and an exponent. QB uses the IEEE format, which allocates 4 bytes for single-precision numbers and 8 bytes for double-precision numbers. The format is shown in figure D.3.

For both single- and double-precision formats, the mantissa is normalized, meaning that there is an implicit binary 1. preceding the binary value actually stored in memory. Also, the exponent is biased, by &H7F for single precision and &H3FF for double precision. This means that the bias value is added to the actual exponent before it is stored.

There is rarely—if ever—a need to manipulate floating-point numbers directly. It is best to let QB handle the details.

Fig. D.3. *Storage format for floating-point numbers.*

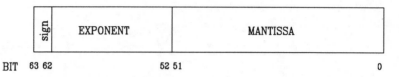

Index

Special Characters

/QUICKLIBRARY option, 37
$INCLUDE metacommand, 69

A

adapters
    Hercules Graphics, 349-352
    video, 343
Add Watch command, 86-88
Add Watch dialog box, 86-87
algorithms, 229, 234
ALIAS keyword, 79
arguments, 50-51
    data type, 58
    passing, 58
    passing by value or reference, 60-61
    type checking, 57
    with CodeView, 114
arrays, 187-188
    passing elements, 59
    passing entire, 60
    row-major order, 30
    transferring index contents to disk, 216
AS clause, 61
ASCII
    character codes, 441-444
    format, saving files in, 11
ASCIIZ string, 160
assembly display mode, CodeView, 114-116
assembly language, 427
asynchronous communications port, 29
attribute byte, 306, 368
automatic, STATIC keyword default, 50

B

background colors, 20
BASIC
    programming language, 1-2
    programs, interfacing with non-BASIC procedure,
        77-80
BAT file extension, 40
batch files, 40-41
BC.EXE file, 25, 28-34
BCOM45.EXE, 19
BCOM45.LIB file, 18-19
BEEP statement, 109
binary format, 453
binary search, 230-233, 264-265
binary trees, 202-214
    deleting records, 204
    displaying records in sorted order, 204
    finding records, 204

457

D

E

F

G

H

I

L

M

N

O

S

W

PROGRAM DISK AVAILABLE

You can save yourself a lot of tedious typing by ordering the **QUICK BASIC ADVANCED TECHNIQUES** program disk. This disk contains the source code for all of the listings in the book, plus object and library files for the windows routines.

Note: This disk offer is made directly by the author, not by Que Corporation.

---ORDER FORM---

Please send me _____ copies of the **QUICK BASIC ADVANCED TECHNIQUES** program disk at $14.95 each   _____

North Carolina residents add 5% sales tax ($0.75 per disk)   _____

Total   _____

Disk size: _____ 5-1/4"   _____ 3-1/2"

Name _____

Address _____

_____

City _____ State _____ Zip _____

Payment: ___ Check   ___ Money Order   ___ Visa   ___ MasterCard

Credit card no. _____ Exp. date: _____

Signature: _____

Send your order with payment or credit card information to:
Peter Aitken, P.O. Box 3214, Durham, NC 27715.
Please allow 2-3 weeks for delivery.

More Computer Knowledge from Que